ARIS & PHILLIPS CLASSICAL TEXTS

LUCRETIUS

De Rerum Natura III

with an Introduction, Translation and Commentary by

P. Michael Brown

Aris & Phillips is an imprint of
Oxbow Books

First published 1997. Reprinted with corrections 2007.

ISBN 0-85668-695-6
ISBN 978-0-85668-695-5

A CIP record for this book is available from the British Library

Printed and bound by CPI Group (UK) Ltd, Croydon, CR0 4YY

Contents

Preface

This edition is designed to make the third book of Lucretius' poem, with its universal message, easily accessible: in it, I have attempted to provide all the help required by the comparative novice in Latin, while at the same time including material which I hope may be of use to the more advanced student and of interest to the Lucretian scholar and specialist. My first aim has been to elucidate the philosophical argument throughout: I hope to have thrown new light on two areas in particular, firstly the poet's use of terminology for the soul and its two parts, which has sometimes confused editors, and secondly the twin aims of his conclusion, where he seeks not only to prove that death is the end of consciousness but also to reconcile the reader to the prospect. My second aim has been to do what justice I could to the poetry (for the full appreciation of which a proper understanding of the philosophical argument is naturally a prerequisite), by analysing some of the book's literary and artistic features. The text (which includes no emendations of my own) is designed to provide as complete and continuously readable a version as possible without resort to extravagant conjecture; the prose translation is as literal as the aim to produce a reasonably idiomatic version allowed. As usual in this series, the notes are keyed to the translation, not to the Latin text.

My debt to the work of previous scholars, in particular of Lambinus, Munro, Bailey, Kenney and M.F.Smith, is immense and will be immediately apparent; many of the parallel passages which I cite are taken over from them, with only occasional acknowledgment, nor have I usually recorded where I have followed or differed from them on a given point.

I am grateful to Adrian Phillips and his colleagues for this opportunity to make a second contribution to their classical series and for all their assistance throughout. Once more, I am especially indebted to Professor Malcolm Willcock, who read drafts firstly of half the work and later of the whole, and whose scrupulous attention and perceptive comments have again proved invaluable and rescued me from many errors; for the defects that remain, I am again solely responsible. Sections I, II, III, and V of the introduction are based partly on the introduction to my edition of book I for the Bristol Classical Press, and I am grateful to John Betts for his agreement over this. My thanks are also due to Professors M.F.Smith and D.A.West, for encouragement and profitable discussion over many years. It is an especial pleasure to acknowledge my debt to my daughter, Lindsay MacLeod, for designing the cover illustration: I must also thank all those who have patiently helped to initiate me, as a complete novice, into the mysteries of the word-processor in order to produce this edition.

Department of Classics
University of Glasgow

August 1997

Introduction

I. THE POEM

Few poems have such a clear-cut purpose, and leave so little doubt as to their 'meaning', as that of Lucretius. The six books provide, in outline, an account of Epicurean physics, seeking thereby to explain the nature of the universe and of everything in it in scientific terms. But this science is not expounded academically, for its own sake, but in order to serve two practical goals, also inherited from Epicurus: as the poet constantly reminds us, he has a twofold object, the removal of the two great religious fears which he thinks plague mankind, the fear that the gods control, or intervene in, the workings of the universe, and the fear of death. As with Epicurus, the first fear is eliminated by the demonstration that the universe and all its processes are governed, not by capricious deities, but by scientific law: the fear of death is eradicated by the demonstration that the soul, the organ of consciousness, is material and dissolved at death, making any form of conscious after-life impossible; in the conclusion to III Lucretius seeks not only to draw this inference but also to reconcile the reader to the prospect of death as the end of consciousness (see introductory notes to 830–1094 and 931–77).

The six books fall naturally into three pairs. The first pair establishes the basics of the physical system: I presents the arguments for the existence of the two ultimate constituents of the universe, atoms and void, attacks rival views of the ultimate nature of reality, and concludes with arguments for the infinity of atoms and of void, and of the universe which they comprise. II deals principally with varieties of atomic motion and of atomic shape, and with the differences which these produce in visible atomic compounds, and ends with the argument that the universe contains an infinite number of finite worlds roughly similar to our own.

I and II prepare first for III and IV, which together cover Lucretian psychology, his account of the soul or *psyche*: in III the exposition of its physical constitution leads on first to the long sequence of arguments for its mortality, which follows inevitably from its atomic nature, and then to the triumphant conclusion aimed not only at fear of any form of after-life but also at fear of ceasing to exist. IV is complementary to III, in its attempt to explain in outline how all forms of perception, emotion and consciousness can be explained on the hypothesis of an atomic, material, destructible soul, thus helping to corroborate the thesis of III that the soul is material and therefore destructible.

I and II are preparatory secondly for V and VI, which together deal with various aspects of our, finite, world and by implication of the infinite number of other, roughly similar, worlds in the universe: V deals first with its ultimate destructibility and conversely with its origin, of which a reconstruction is provided, then with its astronomy (a feature of a given world, not of the universe at large, since each world had its own set of heavenly bodies), and finally with the origin and development of all types of life on earth, culminating in a rather *a priori* account of the development of human civilisation. VI goes on to cover a miscellany of the world's more specialised natural phenomena, including thunder, whirlwinds, earthquakes, volcanoes and plague.

This analysis reveals how closely the whole poem is geared to the elimination of the two great religious fears. V and VI, prepared for by I and II, are designed to banish the fear of divine control or intervention in the workings of nature, by setting out an explanation of all phenomena in terms of scientific law. III and IV, for which I and II have also provided the ground-work, are primarily aimed, as already described, at the eradication of the fear of death, by showing that the soul is material and therefore destructible: at the same time, they have a secondary relevance to the removal of the first fear, in their attempt to show that all aspects of psychology can be explained in natural rather than in divine terms.

The poem follows a tradition of personal appeal in the Epicurean school, taking the form of an attempt to convert Memmius, a Roman politician (see Introduction II below), to the philosophy; similarly, Epicurus' works had sometimes taken the form of letters addressed to specific disciples. Though Memmius is not named in III, IV and VI, the second-person addresses in these books sometimes, as at III 417–24, echo the language associated with him in I, II and V, and it is only through Memmius that the general reader is addressed throughout the poem.

Like Virgil's *Aeneid*, the work never underwent final revision by its author. Though the poet has clearly carried out the bulk of his design (at VI 92–3 the sixth book is announced as the last), the promise to give an extended account of the refined atomic structure of the gods, or of their abodes, or of both (V 155) is nowhere fulfilled, and in the eyes of many readers the poem cannot have been intended to end, as it does, with a grim detail in the account of the Great Plague of Athens. While the repetition of a number of shorter passages within the poem is clearly intentional, the use of I 926–50, from the famous account of the poet's mission, to open Book IV has the appearance of a temporary expedient which would not have survived revision. Though the text is generally better organised than to justify the wholesale transposition of arguments once popular with Lucretian editors (see, e.g., introductory note to 417–829), there are occasional difficulties of transition and, in addition to passages which might have been clarified in revision, a number of loose ends, sometimes apparently arising from the inclusion of alternative versions of an argument or passage (e.g. III 615–23 and 784–99, IV 26–44 and 45–53, IV 722–76 and 777–817) or the addition of afterthoughts unadjusted to their context (e.g. III 806–18 and 1076–94).

II. THE POET

Apart from writing his poem in the first half of the first century B.C., Lucretius, as far as the modern reader is concerned, has satisfied the Epicurean requirement to live one's life unnoticed (λάθε βιώσας), and reliable biographical information is minimal. Cicero, in a letter of February 54, has a famous comment agreeing with his brother's assessment of Lucretius' poetry: *Lucreti poemata, ut scribis, ita sunt, multis luminibus ingeni, multae tamen artis: sed cum ueneris* (*Ad Quintum Fratrem* II 9.3: 'Lucretius' poetry is as you describe, with much inspired brilliance, yet much conscious artistry: but more when you get here'). This shows that the poem (or at least substantial extracts from it: on the sense of *poemata* see F.H.Sandbach, *Classical Review* 54 (1940) 72ff.) was in the brothers' hands by this date, and that the poet, unless he had made the incomplete poem (or some parts of it) available to them for some purpose, was now dead.

According to St. Jerome, augmenting Eusebius' Chronicle in the late fourth century, Lucretius was driven insane by a love-potion, composed his poem in the lucid intervals of insanity and committed suicide at the age of forty-four: the poem was subsequently 'corrected' by Cicero (the activity claimed in *emendauit* most probably amounts to something like proof-reading). This story, even if derived from Suetonius, which is questionable, can safely be discounted: were it true, the absence, in the four and a half centuries after Lucretius' death, of any earlier allusion to such sensational material, especially in writers hostile to the poet and to his philosophy, would be incredible, as is the idea that such a coherently organised and rationally argued work could have been composed by a madman. The account may have originated as a 'pious fiction', designed by religious or philosophical opponents to discredit the poet's views: it may be based on fanciful inference from the poem and from other sources, a procedure for which the ancient biographers of Juvenal provide ample parallels. Thus the story of the love-potion, if it was not inspired by confusion of Lucretius with Lucullus (cf. Pliny, *Natural History* XXV 25), might have been suggested by the denunciation of the passion of love at the end of book IV, making the poet seem a suitable candidate: the abrupt end of the poem, apparently in the middle of a grim account of the Athenian plague, might have suggested suicide brought on by morbid depression: Statius' allusion (*Siluae* II 2.76) to the 'lofty frenzy of the learned Lucretius' (*docti furor arduus Lucreti*, where *furor* alludes to poetic inspiration) might have suggested, or been taken to confirm, the story of insanity, while Cicero's letter to Quintus cited above might have given rise to the idea that he was about to 'correct' the work. Nor can too much reliance be placed on the accuracy of Jerome's dates for the poet (94–50 B.C., though there are manuscript variants suggesting 93–49 or 96–52), or, in turn, on Donatus' claim in his *Life of Virgil* that Lucretius died on Virgil's seventeenth birthday (53 B.C.) which he inconsistently places in the second consulship of Pompey and Crassus (55 B.C.).

The poet's name, his familiarity with Roman scenes, and the tone in which he addresses the aristocratic Memmius, though not affording conclusive evidence, support the generally held view that he was a Roman noble; his allusion to 'our (i.e. Roman) wives' at IV 1277 makes it more likely than not that, despite Epicurus' reservations about conjugal life, he was married. The Memmius to whom the poem is formally addressed (see Introduction I above) is clearly Gaius Memmius, the son-in-law of Sulla and an active politician (cf. I 42–3) who was tribune in 66 B.C. and, as praetor in 58, attacked Caesar's legislation of the previous year: in 54, however, he stood for the consulship as a supporter of Caesar, only to be defeated and to go into exile when charged with electoral corruption; he was dead by 46 B.C. It was doubtless his literary rather than his political interests which first commended him to Lucretius: not only was Memmius an exponent of erotic verse himself, but as propraetor in Bithynia in 57 he included on his staff the poets Cinna and Catullus, although the latter subsequently writes contemptuously of him in poems 10 and 28; his partiality for Greek literature, attested by Cicero, *Brutus* 247, makes him a suitable dedicatee for a poem preaching Epicureanism. His moral standards, however, clearly fell far short of the Epicurean ideal, perhaps recommending him to Lucretius as a suitable subject for conversion: however, his quarrel with the Athenian Epicureans during his exile in 52, when he acquired the remains of Epicurus' house and, though he abandoned his plan to build on the site, refused to surrender it to the school's current head (Cicero, *Ad Familiares* XIII 1), suggests that the dedicatee of the poem had failed to absorb its Epicurean message.

III. EPICUREAN PHILOSOPHY AND LUCRETIUS

The philosophy originally propounded in Athens by Epicurus (341–270 B.C.) was, like Stoicism, ultimately practical, and aimed to provide a code by which men might live in the religious and moral confusion of the Hellenistic age, but the practical conclusions, as also in Stoicism, were based on a comprehensive theoretical account of the universe and of man's place in it. The Epicurean system comprised three branches, the Logic (or Canonic), the rules of procedure by which the conclusions of the rest of the system were arrived at, the Physics, a scientific account of the universe and all its processes, and the Ethics, the practical code for which the Physics provided the indispensable basis and which was not only the most original but also to Epicurus the most important part of the system.

Logic

Epicurus insisted on sensation as the first criterion of factual truth, regarding it as infallible in itself, and attributing error in its interpretation to the mind. Where sensation could not itself provide direct evidence, reasoning on the basis of sense-experience took over, i.e. hypotheses could be formed on the basis of experience and then checked against further experience. Eminently respectable as these principles appear by modern standards, Epicurus lacked the detailed experimental evidence available to the modern scientist and thus could not check his hypotheses with anything like the necessary rigour; he also sometimes pressed his reliance on sensation too far, as in his notorious contention that the sun, moon and stars are not much larger than they appear to the naked eye of the earthly observer, and in his acceptance of plurality of causes, whereby different explanations of a given phenomenon must, if not contradicted by sensation, each be true, at least for the occurrence of that phenomenon in some part of the universe. The Logic also established the criterion of practical truth, which determined not what was the case but what was to be done: see under Ethics below.

Physics

Since the sixth century B.C., Greek philosophers had looked for some permanent reality underlying the visible world of change: in the fifth century, Leucippus and Democritus had taken this reality to lie in atoms and void, and it was their theory, which, after a century's neglect, Epicurus took over and adapted as the basis of his Physics.

The atom ('the uncuttable') was a solid, uniformly hard, homogeneous unit of matter, too small to be individually perceptible, and postulated primarily to provide a limit to the divisibility of objects, without which, it was argued, the visible world would lack stability and disintegrate; its complete solidity (the absence of any void within it which would allow it to be penetrated or crushed) guaranteed its indivisibility and indestructibility. Void, the only other ultimate reality, was postulated to allow for motion, which a totally solid universe would preclude. As they were unchangeable and indestructible, atoms and void, and the universe which they comprised, must always have existed and would always continue to exist. The Epicurean universe contained an infinite number of atoms moving in an infinite expanse of void in accordance with scientific laws; an infinite universe was postulated largely because the alternative, a finite universe without more matter or more space or a combination of the two beyond its boundaries, was inconceivable. The atoms had three properties only, size, shape and weight, and were quite devoid of secondary qualities, such as colour, sound or taste, which only atomic compounds could acquire; void, by contrast, had no properties at all and could not act or be acted upon. The natural movement of the atoms was vertically downwards, as a result of their weight, but mutual collision, from which they rebounded, led to motion in other directions, and they were also liable to a slight and unpredictable swerve, an innovation in atomic theory devised by Epicurus in order to escape from the complete mechanical determinism of Democritus and to leave a loophole for human free will: however, the argument, like the modern invocation of unpredictability at the atomic level, as set out in quantum physics, in the same cause, would appear to prove too much, making free will purely random and arbitrary.

Even in compounds, the atoms remained in constant motion; a compound was formed when a group of suitable atoms was driven together and fell into a pattern of repeated mutual collision. After formation, all compounds underwent a continuous give and take of atoms, which was the basis of their growth and decay; with the sole exception of the gods, they were all ultimately destroyed by resolution into their components. Varieties in different types of compound resulted from varieties in the type, the motions and the arrangement of the component atoms: volatile substances, for example, contained a high proportion of tiny, smooth and round atoms, whereas those of viscous or solid substances tended to be larger, rougher and more jagged (cf. 186–205 and notes); pleasant sensations were generally caused by smooth, round atoms, unpleasant by a more angular, spikier variety. All compounds contained atoms of more than one type: there was a limit to the number of atomic types (though the universe contained an infinite stock of atoms of each type), and a limit also to the possibilities of their combination, in order to explain the limit to the varieties observable in nature.

Epicurus' infinite universe contained an infinite number of finite worlds roughly similar to our own; each world was no more than a complex, large-scale atomic compound, formed as a result of the entirely chance collision of appropriate atoms and subject to eventual dissolution. The cosmology has to be carefully differentiated from modern conceptions: each world was spherical in shape, with a flat, dish-shaped earth located at its centre; this earth was rather mysteriously suspended in the middle of a sphere of air, or atmosphere, beyond which lay a spherical outer shell of fire or ether, comprising the world's heavens; each world had its own heavenly bodies which performed their orbits somewhere between the ether and the atmosphere. Each Epicurean world was thus self-contained, and it was impossible to see physically beyond its boundaries and to look out into the universe at large. The earth contained a stock of atoms of every type, and so gave rise to vegetable and animal life, the latter originating from wombs put forth on its surface. Some species were better equipped than others to survive: though Epicurus believed in fixity of species, he broadly anticipated the Darwinian theory of natural selection. All consciousness and mental and emotional processes depended on the possession of a material soul; an account of its two parts and the terminology for them, vital for the understanding of Lucretius III, is provided separately in Introduction IV below.

Ethics

Epicurean Ethics, for which the Physics provided the indispensable foundation, embraced firstly the two conclusions central to Lucretius' poem, the non-participation of the gods in the workings of the universe and the mortality of the soul: fear of the gods or of an after-life was accordingly groundless. But while denying that the gods could control or intervene in nature's processes, Epicurus categorically asserted their existence, on the grounds of their constant appearance to men, especially in dreams, which must result from atomic emanations from their bodies entering men's souls. The Epicurean gods were anthropomorphic, immortal beings, of a very refined atomic texture; they dwelt in the spaces between worlds in the universe, where they lived perfect lives in exact conformity with Epicurean ethical principles, making them perfect models for human conduct. In allowing the existence of the gods as the sole category of eternal atomic compound in his universe, Epicurus seems to have sacrificed the unity of his system, nor is it clear how he explained their eternity in physical terms; again, his account of other psychological phenomena suggests reasonably obvious alternative ways in which he might have explained the appearance of the gods in mental processes, without conceding their existence. While one might thus be tempted to wonder just how literally his account of the gods is intended, and though his opponents certainly accused him of hypocrisy and of claiming their existence only in order to escape a charge of impiety, the ancient sources attest his reverence for his gods, on whom, in lost works, he wrote copiously: as reflected by Lucretius at VI 68–78, contemplation and imitation of their ideally tranquil life amounted respectively to acts of worship and of piety.

The starting-point for the main body of the Ethics, which laid down a complete code of practical conduct, lay once more in the physical theory, and in the idea that every human action or experience is accompanied by a feeling of pleasure or pain. Just as the Logic made sensation the first criterion of factual knowledge, so it made this feeling the first criterion of practical knowledge: a feeling of pleasure meant that the course of action which gave rise to it was to be pursued, a feeling of pain that it was to be avoided: Epicurus regarded it as self-evident that the end of every action was the pursuit of pleasure and the avoidance of pain. Such a view is only too readily misinterpreted: Epicurus was not advocating the 'let us eat, drink and be merry' hedonism which subsequently became unjustly associated with his name (hence the derivative 'epicure'), and which, significantly, Lucretius attacks at III 912–8; arguing that the true end of pleasure is the removal of pain and that, once this has been achieved, pleasure cannot be increased but only varied, he defined the true goal of life not as continuous sensual gratification but as a more negative, passive state of freedom from bodily pain and from mental disturbance (ἀπονία and ἀταραξία). Since man's real needs were few, pleasure in this sense was relatively easy for almost anyone to achieve. All the body required was enough food, clothing and shelter to ward off the pain of hunger, cold and similar distress: the potential sources of mental pain were rather more numerous. The mind's first requirement was freedom from the two great religious fears, of the gods and an after-life, against which the study of Epicurean philosophy provided the only sure protection. Secondly it needed to be free from harmful desires whose pursuit was likely to bring disproportionate pain: the most dangerous of these were (a) avarice, the desire for superfluous riches, when all that was required was adequate resources to provide essential food, clothing and shelter for the body; (b) ambition, desire for honour and position, which not only made enemies but was usually disappointed, so that the faithful Epicurean obeyed the injunction to live his life unnoticed (λάθε βιώσας, cited in Introduction II above) and contracted out of political life altogether; (c) passionate involvement in love, which undermined self-sufficiency and was one of the greatest potential causes of mental disturbance and pain, so that sexual desire could be satisfied only if emotional independence was maintained, while even marriage and family life were discouraged because of the 'distractions and unpleasantnesses' thought to be involved. The mind's third requirement was freedom from the pangs of guilty conscience, which were attributed entirely to fear of punishment, its fourth a feeling of security from other members of society: to achieve both these ends, conformity with conventional justice was essential. In Epicurus' egoistic system, justice was not valued for its own sake, but rather as a means to the twin ends of clear conscience and security in society, a broad anticipation of the Hobbesian view of justice as a social contract between men not to harm and not to be harmed. As a further guarantee of security, Epicurus recommended the cultivation of friends who would rally round if it was threatened: despite this utilitarian basis, friendship appears to be one of the two highest, most positive pleasures open to the Epicurean, the other lying in the contemplation of the true nature of the universe as revealed by Epicurean philosophy.

Whereas the elimination of the two religious fears follows logically enough from the physics, the practical ethical code, despite Epicurus' claims, does not. Even if one accepted the feeling of pleasure or pain as the ultimate practical criterion, it certainly does not follow that the pleasure to be pursued is the negative, passive type which Epicurus made his ideal. In recommending this type of pleasure Epicurus is simply giving us his value-judgment, which may have validity as a value-judgment, but which certainly cannot be proved true on the basis of any factual, physical theory.

The Lucretian treatment and its targets

While Lucretius concentrates on the Physics and its vital implications about the gods and an after-life, and does not treat the Logic and the main body of the Ethics in the same systematic way, his poem reveals him to be an equally faithful and committed disciple of his master in these areas also, and all their most fundamental points receive emphasis in the course of it; his moral disquisitions in particular, including his attacks on acquisitiveness, political ambition and the passion of love, where he clearly saw the Epicurean message as vitally relevant to the contemporary scene, are animated by the same missionary fervour with which he attacks conventional religion, a fervour so passionate as to be scarcely compatible with the mental tranquillity (ἀταραξία) which was the Epicurean ideal. Though the bulk of

Epicurus' voluminous writings has not survived (see note on line 10) so that knowledge of his philosophy often depends on secondary sources, nothing suggests that Lucretius, who makes no claim to philosophical originality, professing himself an imitator rather than a competitor at III 3–6, introduced any personal innovations into the system, however original his organisation and presentation of the material and however much of the abundant graphic illustration is his own.

Lucretius' concentration on the elimination of the two great religious fears has sometimes been thought anachronistic and more relevant to the climate of opinion in the Greece of Epicurus than in first century Rome, where the educated classes (the sole audience he can have hoped to reach directly with his poem) are sometimes sceptical of the state religion and disavow belief in an after-life; Cicero, indeed, likes to suggest that even the Roman masses scorned the old wives' tales about an underworld which the Epicureans were concerned to disprove, although allowance has to be made for his anti-Epicurean bias, and for his off-guard admission (*Tusculan Disputations* I 46) that it would be terrible if the dead really experienced those ills in which they are popularly imagined. But while considerable prominence is given in the poem to the less sophisticated forms of religious belief (e.g. at I 80–101, where the sacrifice of Iphigeneia serves as an archetypal example of the ills which religion can inspire, I 102–11, where fear of eternal punishment is presented as a trump-card in the hands of the prophets of religion, or III 978–1023, where the fabled torments of Hades exist not in death but in life), much space is also devoted to the refutation of rival philosophical views (e.g. III 94–135 and 670–783: see introductory notes there), and to regard primitive superstition as the poet's only target is clearly mistaken: his first aim, as the whole structure of the argumentation reflects, is positive, to establish correct belief about the gods and the mortality of the soul on the indispensable basis of Epicurean physics, and thus to rule out every category of rival view, however crude or sophisticated, whether superstitious, religious or philosophical. Even the professed but non-Epicurean sceptic needed conversion, since without the sound scientific basis of Epicurean physics his scepticism was likely to crumble in time of stress (III 41–54, providing clear proof that Lucretius is casting his net far wider than is often assumed). The fear of death attacked in III (for which *metus Acheruntis* 37 may be seen as colourful poetic shorthand: see note there) thus embraces not only dread of punishment in a mythical underworld, but apprehensions about any form of after-life, while in the course of his conclusion (cf. Introduction I above) Lucretius goes still further, seeking to eradicate fear of death when viewed as the end of consciousness.

IV. THE EPICUREAN SOUL

For Epicurus, the soul had two primary roles, rendering its possessor capable (a) of all forms of consciousness and sensation, whether mental, emotional or physical, and

(b) of self-determined motion and activity. Each of these capacities suggested a soul comprising two distinct but mutually interdependent parts, which had the same atomic constitution (described by Lucretius at 177–322) but which differed in their function and location. The two components may be seen as rudimentary counterparts of the brain and central nervous system, to which a modern materialist would generally assign their respective roles.

The first part, a concentration of soul atoms situated in the chest, was the seat of (a) the intellect and all mental consciousness, (b) the emotions and (c) the will. The placing of the intellect in the breast rather than the head, which strikes the modern reader as odd, was not peculiar to Epicurus: from Homer onwards, the Greeks had generally associated the intellect with the emotions and placed them together either in the breast (as did Aristotle) or in the head; Plato was one of the few to separate them, placing the intellect in the head and the emotions in the breast. The second part of the soul, distributed and interwoven throughout the whole body, was the organ of physical sensation: it was the basis of the five senses, being present in the eyes, the ears and the organs of taste and smell, and rendering the whole body capable of the sensation of touch, and also of experiencing pain deep within it, even in hard parts like the teeth (cf. 691–4). The twofold soul was thus postulated partly to account for two distinct categories of consciousness, mental and physical, but also to explain how the soul could set the body in motion: the act of will took place in the breast, but the chain of command was then passed on by the second part of the soul, which initiated the appropriate motion in the parts of the body concerned.

Epicurus' novel concept of the soul (ψυχή) results in terminological problems in the absence in Greek, Latin and English of ready-made vocabulary for the two parts. Epicurus distinguished 'the rational part' (τὸ λογικὸν μέρος) located in the chest from 'the non-rational part' (τὸ ἄλογον μέρος) dispersed throughout the body, though this terminology obscures the fact that the former was the seat not only of reason but also of the emotions. For the 'rational' part Lucretius' standard term is *animus*, for the 'non-rational' part *anima*; the words are given far more specialised, technical senses than they bear outside Lucretius, where *animus* approximates to 'mind', 'heart' or 'soul' according to context, and *anima* (retaining more of the root connection with Greek ἄνεμος or wind than does *animus*) to 'breath' and so to 'life-breath' or 'spirit'. But however specialised their senses, the use of similar, related words for the two parts has the advantage of reflecting their similarity of constitution and their close union and interdependence. The main terminological problem in this area, which illustrates the poverty of the Latin tongue (*patrii sermonis egestas*) of which the poet complains at 260, is that the specialised application of *animus* and *anima* leaves no available term for the sum of the two parts, for the soul as a whole (Epicurean ψυχή). The obvious, but potentially tedious, solution of coupling the terms is frequently adopted (e.g. 161, 167, 212); the other expedient, announced in the introduction to the arguments for the soul's mortality at 421–4 (see notes there), is to use either term inclusively, non-technically, as a sort of shorthand to embrace both parts. Though this practice has often confused editors, and though the sometimes technical, sometimes inclusive usage of the terms might be expected to result in great ambiguity, the context in practice normally makes their application abundantly clear: what is potentially more confusing is that their inclusive use, announced at 421–4, is anticipated at several earlier points (e.g. with *anima* at 143, 150, 275 and 280–1, with *animus* at 169, 175, 177 and 237). In the translation, I have resorted to 'mind' and 'spirit' respectively for *animus* and *anima* in their technical senses (even though there is little of the spiritual about the Lucretian *anima*), and employed 'soul' where either term is used inclusively: it is obviously of vital importance to remember that 'mind' usually and 'spirit' always bears a highly specialised sense.

V. LUCRETIUS' POETIC MEDIUM AND ACHIEVEMENT

The tradition of didactic poetry, which ancient critics did not formally differentiate from epic, went back to Hesiod, whose combination of moral with agricultural instruction in the *Works and Days* shows some of the same earnest commitment which is conspicuous in Lucretius. In the sixth and fifth centuries three Greek thinkers, Xenophanes, Parmenides and Empedocles, had expounded their philosophical ideas in hexameter verse, continuing the Hesiodic tradition and partly rivalling, or seeking to replace, the subject-matter of his *Theogony*; of this trio, Empedocles alone seems to have risen to any great poetic heights, and he was Lucretius' principal model in Greek poetry, as the rapturous eulogy of I 716–33, preceding the demolition of his pluralist theory, reflects. The great proliferation of the genre with the Alexandrian Greek poets of the third and second centuries, whose subjects range from astronomy to gastronomy and from geography to medicine, reflects their preoccupation with learning and with literary form as an end in itself; Lucretius, for whom the message is paramount, is at the opposite pole. These poets were nevertheless generally popular with the Romans and strongly influenced Roman didactic: Cicero's *Aratea*, a youthful version of the astronomical and meteorological poetry of Aratus, had appeared fairly soon before Lucretius embarked on his poem, which occasionally echoes Cicero's language but differs totally in spirit.

Against this background, in which the only precedents for a full-scale philosophical poem dated back some four centuries, the decision to convey the Epicurean message in poetry is, on the surface, surprising. One apparent obstacle lay in Epicurus' general antipathy to the arts; but though he regarded Epicurean philosophy as the only essential study and treated other forms of culture, which he doubtless saw as a rival moral influence, with hostility, he can scarcely have seriously objected to a poem preaching the Epicurean gospel. A rule of Epicurean Logic, according to which words were to be used in their basic, most obvious senses, was a second apparent deterrent, since strict adherence would preclude the figurative language essential in poetry and so widely utilised by Lucretius; but despite inevitable violations (from which Epicurus is scarcely free himself), the need for lucidity in philosophical exposition is a prime concern throughout, as I 136–45 and I 933–4 reflect, and one type of poetic licence is explicitly justified at II 655–60 (see on 221). The technical difficulties of expounding the philosophy in poetry were a much more serious problem. Epicurean physics, in its details if not in its overall scheme, is a vastly complicated subject, difficult enough sometimes to express clearly in prose, let alone to accommodate in Latin hexameter verse and to invest with poetic power. The sheer metrical problems should not be underestimated (an aspect of the poverty of Lucretius' native tongue of which he complains at III 260: cf. Introduction IV above): words awkward or inadmissible in the hexameter might include crucial technical or semi-technical terms; thus *primordia*, one of the poet's words for the primary particles or atoms, had to be replaced in the genitive, dative and ablative by *principia*, and *magnitudo* ('size') by the approximations *figura* and *filum* ('shape' and 'outline') and once by the coined by-form *maximitas*.

From Lucretius' own account of his mission at I 921–50, it emerges that he sees his philosophical message as primary, and his poetry as secondary, serving as a means to further his philosophical end. The point is expressed in the famous image in which his poetry corresponds to the honey smeared round the edge of a cup of bitter-tasting philosophical medicine, with the object of luring the young patient to drink and so to profit from its healing properties; on Lucretius' own admission, the poetry is designed to sugar the philosophical pill, to make the philosophical subject-matter more attractive and more readily assimilable. While the main idea is clearly that the poetry will help to sustain the interest of the reader who has already embarked on the poem, Lucretius no doubt also has in mind that his medium is likely to attract a wider audience in the first place: prose treatises on the philosophy were already available, and literarily-minded Romans, like Memmius, were likely to find a poetic exposition of far greater interest and to be lured to the philosophy by the poetic bait. But even though Lucretius sees his poetry as utilitarian, it certainly does not follow that he set his poetic sights low. The same passage on his mission refers not only to his delight in poetic composition but to his lofty poetic ambition (though ambition was strictly un-Epicurean, poetic ambition in the service of the Epicurean cause seems a venial enough offence): he hopes to win a crown from the Muses as the first poet to expound his subject. Behind this allusion to poetic ambition lies a recognition by Lucretius that the inspiration afforded him by Epicurean philosophy was poetic, and it is this which ultimately dictated his medium. To regard him, with J.D.Duff, as a poet 'unfortunate in his choice of subject-matter', as if some other subject could have given him the same inspiration, is to miss the point. To Lucretius, no subject was more worthy to be enshrined in poetry; indeed, at V 1–2 he asks who can compose a poem worthy of the majesty of the subject-matter and of Epicurus' discoveries.

Given the formidable difficulties which confronted him, the level of Lucretius' poetic achievement is remarkable. Because of the range of its subject-matter, the poem, like Virgil's *Georgics*, is obviously not always on the same poetic plane; equally obviously, the poet never intended that it should be. A broad distinction may be drawn between the passages of scientific exposition, which make up the bulk of the poem and are represented in III by 94–829, and the non-expository passages, comprising the introductions to the various books and other passages which dilate on the poet's central philosophical aims and conclusions or preach moral lessons, represented in III by 1–93 and 830–1094. Despite considerable overlapping, the expository passages tend broadly to be written in a plainer style, appropriate to their purpose of instruction, and aim primarily at clarity, while the non-expository passages tend broadly to be pitched in a grander style and make a stronger and more consistent appeal to the emotions. The poetic quality of the non-expository passages is universally acknowledged; it is here that the emotional content expected in poetry is most in evidence, in Lucretius' passionate commitment to his Epicurean themes and message and in the apostolic fervour with which he seeks converts to the religion of scepticism. In the passages of scientific exposition, however, hostile critics sometimes find the poetic honey, with the exception of certain purple passages, thinly spread, and regard the poem as a patchwork, consisting mainly of versified prose, with a few passages of high poetic relief. Such a view, which would mean that Lucretius had failed in his declared objective of touching *everything* (i.e. the whole poem, not just parts of it) with the charm of the Muses (I 934), greatly exaggerates the unevenness of the poem and seriously underestimates the poetic qualities of the exposition and the poetic unity of the whole, as the following considerations reflect.

Firstly, the poetic honey imparted throughout the work by the metre should not be overlooked or underestimated. Lucretius handles the hexameter with remarkable skill. As his main literary model in Latin, he chose the epic style of Ennius, who had introduced the measure into Latin (cf. the literary tribute paid him at I 117–9), perhaps in part to suggest a rivalry between his own, philosophical, work and traditional epic. But while sometimes echoing a characteristic Ennian cadence, Lucretius naturally refines considerably on his predecessor's pioneering versification, without showing the sophistication and subtle delicacy of Virgil: he is more prepared than Virgil, for example, to include lines which lack a normal main caesura (see on 83, 258 and 612), or to allow clash between ictus (the metrical emphasis falling in the hexameter on the first syllable of each foot) and stress (the accentuation of syllables in normal prose pronunciation) in the last two feet of the line by admitting polysyllabic or monosyllabic words in the final position, even though the clash in some cases is appropriate to the sense, and in many others, where a monosyllabic or quadrisyllabic word is 'protected' by a preceding monosyllable, is minimised. But while the Lucretian hexameter is, in general, a rather more rugged, less polished, measure than the Virgilian, this makes it an ideal instrument for the poem, reflecting the poet's didactic enthusiasm and his relentless pursuit, whatever the obstacles, of his philosophical goal, and helping to carry on the emotional drive of the poem over the passages of sustained exposition. Further, the imitative and expressive effects of rhythm are frequently exploited (see, e.g., 136–7, 159, 174, 190–1, 196–202, 249, 253, 300–1, 527, 545, 652–3, 793, 907, 1000–2 and 1065, and notes) to match or underline the sense and so to enhance the graphic quality of the description; such effects, again, may often be more straightforward, less subtle than Virgil's, but this is entirely appropriate to their illustrative didactic purpose. Again, alliteration and assonance, which Lucretius exploits to a far greater extent than any other fully extant Roman poet and which had been popular with Ennius, his foremost Latin model, and with the older Latin poets in general, make a fundamental contribution to the music of his verse, sometimes imparting unity and impressiveness to a phrase (e.g. *moenia mundi* 16), sometimes, in their context, acquiring an expressive effect (see, e.g. 18–24, 152, 297–8, 493–4, 751, 993 and 1002, and notes) or even taking on an air of mockery (e.g. 623, 696, 871–4, 888, 985–6, 990–1), sometimes contributing not only pleasing sound but continuity to the lines, helping, like the relentless hexameter itself, to speed the reader through the argument to the philosophical conclusion. Given the difficulties of treating the subject in verse, the Lucretian hexameter is, all in all, a remarkably melodious and expressive measure, which imparts a degree of honey to all parts of the poem.

Secondly, the vocabulary and diction remains relatively consistent throughout the work. The whole poem has a strong flavour of archaism, as a result of the liberal, but intermittent, incorporation of archaic vocabulary and grammatical forms and the occasional use of archaic syntax. These features evoke the style of Ennius and reflect Lucretius' admiration for his principal Latin model. While many of the archaic words and forms are of metrical advantage, this is by no means always the case, and the archaising tendency is no mere metrical expedient but has an artistic basis, in that it lends added dignity, solemnity and grandeur to the poem, an effect of archaism attested by Cicero, *De Oratore* III 153; the extremely rare archaic forms in Virgil, like the disyllabic first declension genitive singular in *-ai* for the normal *-ae* (see on 83) or the passive or deponent infinitive in *-ier* for the usual *-i* (see on 67), seem designed to produce a similar effect much more occasionally and to pay tribute to a tradition. Again, the language of the scientific passages is considerably less prosaic than the technicalities of the subject-matter might lead one to expect. Certainly Lucretian exposition exhibits features of style which are untypical of Roman poetry: for example, the sentences are sometimes unusually long and involve unusual degrees of subordination, though the dexterity and technique with which they are handled should not be overlooked; unlike the Augustans, the poet is not afraid to use demonstrative pronouns in prominent positions or to place the verb 'to be', even when unemphatic, at the beginning or end of a line; again, his signposting of arguments with recurrent introductory formulae like *primum*, *principio*, *praeterea*, *denique*, *quin etiam* and *huc accedit uti* is uncompromisingly functional, even if it may, like the repetition of key lines and phrases (see, e.g., on 87–93) and the use of periphrases like *uis* and *natura* with a genitive (see on 8 and 130–1), be a conscious replacement for the repeated formulae of epic, so suggesting a rivalry between the epic of action and his own more serious, more important epic of thought. But despite such inevitable concessions to his subject-matter, the poet's deliberate avoidance of the prosaic is illustrated by his approach to scientific, technical vocabulary, where, as he himself complains (see on 260), Latin often had no ready-made terms available, most conspicuously so in the case of the atoms. While the simplest solution would have been to transliterate the Greek ἄτομοι, as Cicero does in his philosophical prose, Lucretius prefers less prosaic, less technical-sounding terms, which involve a degree of metaphor, like *semina* (seeds) and *primordia* (first-beginnings), denoting the source of all compounds, and corresponding respectively to σπέρματα and ἀρχαί which were similarly applied by the Greek physicists (cf. on 31 and 236). Again, his terms for atomic combination and dissolution, *concilium* (see on 805) and *discidium* (see on 342), suggest personification of the atoms and carry political and legal overtones. Such personification of the inanimate is widespread in the poem, and is especially common in the case of the atoms, which much of the time take on the role of the heroes in the philosophical epic.

Thirdly, imagery, which the use of essentially metaphorical technical vocabulary itself exemplifies, and to which commentators have not always been sufficiently sensitive, makes an enormous contribution to the poetic quality of the whole work. In the non-expository passages, the same image sometimes recurs and provides a thematic link between them; for example, the image of light, as a symbol of Epicurean philosophy which dispels the darkness of ignorance and superstition, is carefully sustained, and varied, throughout the poem (cf. 1–2 and 1042–4, and notes). But imagery plays an equally prominent role in the passages of scientific argumentation, where it falls into two categories: not only is there an abundance of straight metaphor, exemplified in the use of political and legal metaphor for the relationships of the atoms and for scientific law, or in memorable personifications of death (cf. 530 and note), but the imagery is often functional, and not only enriches the poem but serves to further the poet's scientific purpose; hypotheses about the unobservable are constantly illustrated, and corroborated, by imaginative similes drawn from the visible world, as when light, smooth poppy-seeds provide a model for the invisible atoms of water, a fluid compound, and heavy stones and spiky corn-ears for those of the more viscous honey (see on 196–9), or when the dissipation of a liquid once its vessel is shattered is used to show how quickly the soul will be dissipated once its own vessel, the body, is shattered at death (see on 434–9). The importance of analogy in Epicurean reasoning, which presupposed a degree of uniformity in nature and a parallelism in its processes at different levels on the scale of size, afforded Lucretius with abundant opportunities to incorporate functional imagery of this kind, which not only adorns the poem but is an integral part of the scientific argument.

Fourthly, conspicuous amongst Lucretius' literary qualities are his visual mind and his powers of conveying his vision precisely and graphically. He and Juvenal, in their very different fields, are perhaps the two most visual of Roman poets and the two who can conjure up a scene with the most accuracy, as opposed to more evocative description in the style of a poet like Virgil. These gifts are ideally suited to the requirements of Lucretius' subject-matter, which embraces all the processes of nature from the tiny, invisible world of the atoms to the vast scale of the infinite universe. Throughout the whole exposition his prime stylistic aim is lucidity, as is reflected in his claim (I 933–4) to be writing light-filled verses (*lucida carmina*) on a dark subject (even though the light-image also evokes the deliverance afforded by Epicurean philosophy), and his graphic powers, and the precision with which he constantly summons up visual diagrams by the functional use of imagery described above, generally enable him to achieve it. The graphic quality of his descriptions is often reinforced, not only by the expressive use of rhythm and of alliteration and assonance mentioned earlier, but also by the use of a word-pattern that matches the pattern in nature which is being traced (a habit which West (1969) 119 has called 'syntactical onomatopoea': see, e.g., 70–1, 262, 283, 331–2, 663 and 860, and notes), while similarities between words are sometimes exploited to highlight correspondences in the world (see, e.g., on 96–7 and 144). As well as extending over an immense range, his descriptions evoke a range of contrasting emotions, sometimes conjuring up scenes of great natural beauty, like the rising of morning mist at V 460–6 (where the image is again functional), sometimes gruesome and horrific scenes, exemplified by the mutilated warriors and the severed snake at III 642–63: the feature common to all these descriptions is their vividness and immediacy. While Lucretius' graphic powers are not exclusively a poetic gift, they enhance his poem, and simultaneously enable him to achieve the lucidity in exposition which was his stylistic priority.

Fifthly, despite the obvious difficulties in treating the subject-matter in poetry, its poetic potential is no less obvious. However technical the details of the exposition may sometimes be, as in the account of the soul's constitution in III, especially at 258–322 where the relationship and effects of its four elements are described, the central concept of the physics, of an infinite, eternal universe with two eternal constituents, atoms and void, is awe-inspiring in its simplicity and in its breadth, as is the recurrent theme of the impermanence and comparative insignificance of the whole of the visible world, including man, which by contrast is subject to change and decay in nature's continuous cycle of creation and destruction. At the same time, the subject-matter provides ample scope for Lucretius' notable bent for satirical poetry, when he ridicules rival theories, as at III 713–83 where he attacks the idea of the transmigration of souls, concluding with a characteristic *reductio ad absurdum*, or when he mocks human folly, as at various points in the conclusion of III (830–

1094), including Nature's harangue to mortals reluctant to accept their mortality (931–62). Again, if Epicurean physics was a factual subject, it evoked an emotional response in its true adherents. Even if the expository passages in the poem are aimed primarily at the intellect, Lucretius' emotional involvement and missionary fervour are evident in the urgency, liveliness and directness of the argumentation, to which the use of formulae like *nunc age* (417), rhetorical questions and *reductiones ad absurdum* contribute. Again, for the Epicurean, contemplation of the true nature of the universe was not only the source of the highest form of pleasure, but did not exclude a feeling of wonder and awe that it should be so constituted: at III 28–30, Lucretius refers to the combined emotions of godlike pleasure and trembling awe (*diuina uoluptas atque horror*) inspired by Epicurus' revelation of nature's secrets.

As a result of these factors the poem, while obviously not rising consistently to the same poetic heights, has a greater poetic unity, and a more liberal coating of poetic honey, than is always allowed: it has, moreover, an emotional unity, which depends not only on the deep satisfaction and awe inspired in the poet by the contemplation of the manifold facets of nature, but also on his passionate conviction of the validity of every aspect of Epicurean philosophy and on his fervent desire to communicate it and so to achieve his readers' salvation.

VI. THE MANUSCRIPTS

The two most important surviving manuscripts of the poem, housed in the library of the University of Leiden, are *Oblongus* (O) and *Quadratus* (Q), which are so called from their shape. Both are in Carolingian minuscules and were written in the ninth century; they derive ultimately from a single archetype written in capitals probably in the fourth or fifth century. Fragments of two ninth or tenth century manuscripts closely related to Q, G–V and U, of which V includes lines 1–621 of Book III, are also preserved, G (*Schedae Gottorpienses*) in Copenhagen, V and U (*Schedae Vindobonenses priores et posteriores*) in Vienna. All the other extant Lucretian manuscripts, written in Italy in the fifteenth century and later and known collectively as *Itali*, derive from a manuscript discovered in 1418 by the humanist scholar Poggio Bracciolini but subsequently lost: Poggio's copy has also perished, but a copy of it made by his friend Niccoli is preserved in the Laurentian Library in Florence (L, *Codex Laurentianus* 35.30) and is the most important of the *Itali*; other valuable Italian manuscripts include A (*Codex Vaticanus* 3276), B (*Codex Vaticanus Barberinus lat.* 154), C (*Codex Cantabrigiensis*), F (*Codex Laurentianus* 35.31, a copy made by an often discerning scholar) and M (*Codex Monacensis*). As argued by Müller, *Museum Helueticum* 30 (1973) 166–78, the manuscript discovered by Poggio may have been copied from O, which would mean that the *Itali* have no independent value for the reconstruction of the archetype.

TITI LVCRETI CARI
DE RERVM NATVRA
LIBER TERTIVS

TITUS LUCRETIUS CARUS
ON THE NATURE OF THINGS
BOOK THREE

O tenebris tantis tam clarum extollere lumen
qui primus potuisti inlustrans commoda uitae,
te sequor, o Graiae gentis decus, inque tuis nunc
ficta pedum pono pressis uestigia signis,
non ita certandi cupidus quam propter amorem 5
quod te imitari aueo; quid enim contendat hirundo
cycnis, aut quidnam tremulis facere artubus haedi
consimile in cursu possint et fortis equi uis?
tu pater es, rerum inuentor, tu patria nobis
suppeditas praecepta, tuisque ex, inclute, chartis, 10
floriferis ut apes in saltibus omnia libant,
omnia nos itidem depascimur aurea dicta,
aurea, perpetua semper dignissima uita.
nam simul ac ratio tua coepit uociferari
naturam rerum, diuina mente coorta, 15
diffugiunt animi terrores, moenia mundi
discedunt, totum uideo per inane geri res.
apparet diuum numen sedesque quietae,
quas neque concutiunt uenti nec nubila nimbis
aspergunt neque nix acri concreta pruina 20
cana cadens uiolat, semperque innubilus aether
integit et large diffuso lumine ridet.
omnia suppeditat porro natura, neque ulla
res animi pacem delibat tempore in ullo.
at contra nusquam apparent Acherusia templa 25
nec tellus obstat quin omnia dispiciantur,
sub pedibus quaecumque infra per inane geruntur.
his ibi me rebus quaedam diuina uoluptas
percipit atque horror, quod sic natura tua ui
tam manifesta patens ex omni parte retecta est. 30

Et quoniam docui cunctarum exordia rerum
qualia sint et quam uariis distantia formis
sponte sua uolitent aeterno percita motu
quoue modo possint res ex his quaeque creari,

---

1 O *OVA* : E *BM*: *omisit Q*
11 libant *Auancius*: limant *OQV*
15 coorta *Orelli*: coortam *O*: coartam *QV*

O thou, who in such deep darkness wert the first to be able to hold up so bright a light, illuminating life's blessings, 'tis thee I follow, o glory of the Grecian race, and 'tis in the tracks planted by thee that I now
5 firmly set my own footsteps, not so much in eagerness to compete as because, out of love, I long to imitate thee; for why should the swallow contend with the swan, and what could kids with their wavering limbs achieve in a race to match the might of the powerful horse? Thou art a
10 father to us, the discoverer of truth, thou suppliest us with a father's precepts, and from thy illustrious pages, just as bees in flower-filled glades savour all the blooms, even so do we feast upon all thy golden words, golden indeed, most worthy forever of everlasting life. For as
15 soon as thy philosophy, sprung from thy godlike intellect, begins to proclaim the nature of the universe, the terrors of the mind flee away, the walls of the world part, and I behold the processes at work throughout the whole void. There stands revealed the divine presence of the gods, and their tranquil abodes which are neither buffeted by
20 winds nor spattered by clouds with rains nor sullied by the white fall of snow, congealed by biting frost; an ever cloudless ether covers them, and beams in the bounteous flood of light. Nature, further, supplies all their needs, and nothing impairs their peace of mind at any time. But
25 nowhere, on the other hand, stand revealed the realms of Acheron, and yet the earth presents no obstacle to perception of all the manifold processes taking place beneath our feet, through the void below. Hereupon, at these prospects, a sort of godlike pleasure and trembling awe seize me, that through thy power nature has thus been uncovered
30 and stands so manifestly exposed on every side.

And since I have shown the nature of the ultimate components of all things and their manifold varieties of shape, as they fly about spontaneously, stimulated by ceaseless motion, and how different

hasce secundum res animi natura uidetur 35
atque animae claranda meis iam uersibus esse
et metus ille foras praeceps Acheruntis agendus,
funditus humanam qui uitam turbat ab imo
omnia suffundens mortis nigrore neque ullam
esse uoluptatem liquidam puramque relinquit. 40
nam quod saepe homines morbos magis esse timendos
infamemque ferunt uitam quam Tartara leti
et se scire animi naturam sanguinis esse
aut etiam uenti, si fert ita forte uoluntas, [46]
nec prorsum quicquam nostrae rationis egere, 45[44]
hinc licet aduertas animum magis omnia laudis [45]
iactari causa quam quod res ipsa probetur.
extorres idem patria longeque fugati
conspectu ex hominum, foedati crimine turpi,
omnibus aerumnis adfecti denique, uiuunt 50
et quocumque tamen miseri uenere parentant
et nigras mactant pecudes et manibu' diuis
inferias mittunt multoque in rebus acerbis
acrius aduertunt animos ad religionem.
quo magis in dubiis hominem spectare periclis 55
conuenit aduersisque in rebus noscere qui sit;
nam uerae uoces tum demum pectore ab imo
eliciuntur et eripitur persona, manet res.
denique auarities et honorum caeca cupido,
quae miseros homines cogunt transcendere finis 60
iuris et interdum socios scelerum atque ministros
noctes atque dies niti praestante labore
ad summas emergere opes, haec uulnera uitae
non minimam partem mortis formidine aluntur.
turpis enim ferme contemptus et acris egestas 65
semota ab dulci uita stabilique uidetur
et quasi iam leti portas cunctarier ante;
unde homines dum se falso terrore coacti
effugisse uolunt longe longeque remosse,

---

43 animi *O*: anime *QV*: animae *Lachmann*
44[46] *hic locauit Bentley*
58 manet res *CF*: manare *OQV*

35 things can be created from them, it is clear that following these topics I must now illumine in my verses the nature of mind and spirit, and must drive out headlong that fear of Acheron which utterly clouds human life from its very depths, suffusing everything with the 40 blackness of death, and leaves no pleasure pure and unsullied. Certainly men often assert that disease and a life of dishonour are more to be feared than the Tartarus of death, and that they know that the soul is composed of blood or again of wind, if the whim happens so to take 45 them, and that they have no need whatsoever of our philosophy; but all their boasts are designed to create an impression rather than based on conviction of the actual facts, as you can tell from this: these same people, in exile from their native land and banished far from the sight of their fellow-men, disgraced by a shameful charge, the victims in 50 short of every distress, continue to live, and wherever the wretches find themselves they still offer sacrifices to their ancestors, slaughter black victims and send offerings to the spirits of the dead; in their painful plight, they pay far keener attention to religious ritual. This 55 makes it more appropriate to examine a man in time of doubt and trial, and to discover his character in adversity, because this is the time when truthful words are elicited from the depths of his heart and the mask is snatched away; the reality remains. Again, avarice and blind 60 desire for office, which compel men in their wretchedness to overstep the bounds of what is right, and sometimes as allies and instruments in crime to strive night and day with surpassing effort to reach the pinnacle of wealth - these sores of life are nurtured in no small degree 65 by the dread of death. This is because ignominious contempt and biting poverty generally seem divorced from a life of pleasure and security, and to be lingering already, so to speak, in front of the doors of death; while men, under the compulsion of groundless terror, long to have escaped thence and to have removed

sanguine ciuili rem conflant diuitiasque 70
conduplicant auidi, caedem caede accumulantes;
crudeles gaudent in tristi funere fratris
et consanguineum mensas odere timentque.
consimili ratione ab eodem saepe timore
macerat inuidia ante oculos illum esse potentem, 75
illum aspectari, claro qui incedit honore;
ipsi se in tenebris uolui caenoque queruntur.
intereunt partim statuarum et nominis ergo;
et saepe usque adeo mortis formidine uitae
percipit humanos odium lucisque uidendae 80
ut sibi consciscant maerenti pectore letum
obliti fontem curarum hunc esse timorem.
....
hunc uexare pudorem, hunc uincula amicitiai
rumpere et in summa pietatem euertere suadet.
nam iam saepe homines patriam carosque parentis 85
prodiderunt, uitare Acherusia templa petentes.
nam ueluti pueri trepidant atque omnia caecis
in tenebris metuunt, sic nos in luce timemus
interdum nilo quae sunt metuenda magis quam
quae pueri in tenebris pauitant finguntque futura. 90
hunc igitur terrorem animi tenebrasque necessest
non radii solis neque lucida tela diei
discutiant, sed naturae species ratioque.

Primum animum dico, mentem quam saepe uocamus,
in quo consilium uitae regimenque locatum est, 95
esse hominis partem nilo minus ac manus et pes

---

72 fratris *Macrobius*: fratres *OQV*
78 statuarum *F*: statum *OQV*
post 82 *uersum (e.g.* qui miseros homines cogens scelus omne patrare) *intercidisse putauit Munro*
83 hunc...hunc *MSS*: hic...hic *Bergson*
84 pietatem *F*: pietate *OV*: piaetate *Q*
suadet *OQV*: fundo *Lambinus*: fraude *Lachmann*: clade *Bernays*: suesse *Merrill*: suauem *Everett*: sorde *Diels*: suasu *Ernout*: *alii alia*
94 quam *Charisius*: quem *OQV*

70 themselves far, far away, they amass a fortune by spilling the blood of fellow-citizens and greedily multiply their riches, heaping slaughter on slaughter; they take callous delight in the tragedy of a brother's death, and spurn in fear the tables of their kith and kin. Similarly often, as a 75 result of this same fear, they are racked with envy that they behold this man powerful, that this man, stepping out with the distinctions of office, is the object of attention; they themselves, they complain, wallow in the mire of obscurity. Some of them lose their lives in quest of statues and a name; and often, because of their dread of death, 80 hatred for life and for the sight of the light of day so far takes hold of humankind, that with sorrowful hearts they inflict death on themselves, forgetting that this fear is the source of their cares . . . it persuades one man to betray his sense of honour, another to break the bonds of 85 friendship and in short to overturn the ties of duty; why, often before now men have betrayed their country and their dear parents, whilst seeking to avoid the realms of Acheron. For just as children are alarmed and afraid of everything in blinding darkness, so we in 90 daylight sometimes fear things no more formidable than what children tremble at in the dark and imagine about to happen. Therefore this terror and darkness of the mind must be dispelled not by the rays of the sun and the bright shafts of day, but by nature's outward appearance and its explanation.

95 First I say that the mind, which we often call the intellect, in which the rational and controlling power of life is situated, is a part of a man, no

atque oculi partes animantis totius exstant.

....

sensum animi certa non esse in parte locatum,
uerum habitum quendam uitalem corporis esse,
harmoniam Grai quam dicunt, quod faciat nos 100
uiuere cum sensu, nulla cum in parte siet mens,
ut bona saepe ualetudo cum dicitur esse
corporis, et non est tamen haec pars ulla ualentis.
sic animi sensum non certa parte reponunt,
magno opere in quo mi diuersi errare uidentur. 105
saepe itaque in promptu corpus quod cernitur aegret,
cum tamen ex alia laetamur parte latenti,
et retro fit uti contra sit saepe uicissim,
cum miser ex animo laetatur corpore toto,
non alio pacto quam si, pes cum dolet aegri, 110
in nullo caput interea sit forte dolore.
praeterea molli cum somno dedita membra
effusumque iacet sine sensu corpus onustum,
est aliud tamen in nobis quod tempore in illo
multimodis agitatur et omnis accipit in se 115
laetitiae motus et curas cordis inanis.
nunc animam quoque ut in membris cognoscere possis
esse neque harmonia corpus sentire solere,
principio fit uti detracto corpore multo
saepe tamen nobis in membris uita moretur; 120
atque eadem rursum, cum corpora pauca caloris
diffugere forasque per os est editus aer,
deserit extemplo uenas atque ossa relinquit,
noscere ut hinc possis non aequas omnia partis
corpora habere neque ex aequo fulcire salutem, 125
sed magis haec, uenti quae sunt calidique uaporis
semina, curare in membris ut uita moretur.
est igitur calor ac uentus uitalis in ipso
corpore qui nobis moribundos deserit artus.

---

post 97 *uersum uel uersus intercidisse indicauerunt Itali (e.g.* at quidam contra haec falsa ratione putarunt *Bailey)*

106 aegret *Macrobius*: aegrum *OQV*

less than a hand or foot or the eyes constitute parts of the complete
living being. <Some, on the contrary, have falsely supposed> that the
mind's consciousness is not situated in a specific part, but that it is a
100 sort of life-giving state of the body, which the Greeks call a
'harmony', a thing which causes us to have conscious life, without the
intellect residing in any bodily part; similarly, good health is often
attributed to the body, yet without this being any part of the healthy
person. Thus, they do not place the mind's consciousness in a specific
105 part, in which they seem to me to wander very far astray. So it is that
the body, which is plainly seen, often ails when, nevertheless, we feel
pleasure in another part, which is hidden, and in turn the exact
converse often comes about, when someone wretched in mind feels
110 pleasure throughout his body, in exactly the same way as if, when an
invalid's foot is painful, his head chanced to be free of any pain.
Again, when our limbs have surrendered to the relaxation of sleep and
the burdened body lies spread-eagled and insensate, there is
115 nevertheless something else in us which is simultaneously stirred by
manifold impulses and takes in all the emotions of joy and the
anxieties of the heart, empty as they are. Now, so that you may be able
to discover that the spirit also exists, situated in the limbs, and that the
body is not in the habit of experiencing sensation as a result of a
'harmony', in the first place it often happens that, when much of the
120 body has been taken away, life nevertheless remains in our limbs, and
again, conversely, when a few particles of heat have escaped and air is
given out through the mouth, it suddenly deserts the veins and leaves
125 the bones - so that you can learn from this that not all particles play an
equal role or act as equal props to our well-being, but rather that it is
those which are the seeds of wind and warming heat that ensure that
life remains in our limbs. Thus, there exist in our body itself life-giving heat and wind, which desert our frame at the time of death.

quapropter quoniam est animi natura reperta 130
atque animae quasi pars hominis, redde harmoniai
nomen, ad organicos alto delatum Heliconi,
siue aliunde ipsi porro traxere et in illam
transtulerunt, proprio quae tum res nomine egebat.
quidquid id est, habeant; tu cetera percipe dicta. 135

Nunc animum atque animam dico coniuncta teneri
inter se atque unam naturam conficere ex se,
sed caput esse quasi et dominari in corpore toto
consilium quod nos animum mentemque uocamus.
idque situm media regione in pectoris haeret; 140
hic exsultat enim pauor ac metus, haec loca circum
laetitiae mulcent, hic ergo mens animusquest.
cetera pars animae per totum dissita corpus
paret et ad numen mentis momenque mouetur.
idque sibi solum per se sapit, id sibi gaudet, 145
cum neque res animam neque corpus commouet una.
et quasi, cum caput aut oculus temptante dolore
laeditur in nobis, non omni concruciamur
corpore, sic animus nonnumquam laeditur ipse
laetitiaque uiget, cum cetera pars animai 150
per membra atque artus nulla nouitate cietur.
uerum ubi uementi magis est commota metu mens,
consentire animam totam per membra uidemus
sudoresque ita palloremque exsistere toto
corpore et infringi linguam uocemque aboriri, 155
caligare oculos, sonere auris, succidere artus,
denique concidere ex animi terrore uidemus
saepe homines, facile ut quiuis hinc noscere possit
esse animam cum animo coniunctam, quae cum animi ui
percussast, exim corpus propellit et icit. 160

Haec eadem ratio naturam animi atque animai
corpoream docet esse; ubi enim propellere membra,
corripere ex somno corpus mutareque uultum
atque hominem totum regere ac uersare uidetur,
quorum nil fieri sine tactu posse uidemus 165

---

146 una *OQV*: ulla *F teste Büchnero, editio Iuntina, Naugerius*

130 Therefore, since the mind and spirit have been found to be, as it were, a part of a man, give back the name 'harmony', which was borne down to the musicians from the heights of Helicon - or perhaps they themselves drew it from another source in their turn and applied it to 135 something which as yet had no name of its own. Whatever it is, let them keep it; do you listen to the rest of my words.

I now say that the mind and spirit are bound together in mutual union and between them make up a single nature, but that it is the rational power, which we call the mind and the intellect, that is, so to speak, 140 the head and that holds sway in the body as a whole. And this has its fixed place in the central area of the breast, because this is where fear and dread surge up, this is the vicinity in which joys caress us; here therefore is the mind and the intellect. The rest of the soul, distributed throughout the whole body, obeys, and moves at the mind's impulse 145 and behest. And the mind possesses understanding independently by itself, it feels joy by itself, when neither spirit nor body is simultaneously stirred by the process. And just as, when our head or eye hurts at the onset of pain, we are not racked simultaneously 150 throughout all the body, so the mind sometimes feels pain or is buoyed up by joy on its own, when the rest of the soul is stirred by no new impulse throughout the limbs and frame. But when the mind is disturbed by more violent fear, we witness the whole spirit throughout the limbs suffering with it and sweatings and pallor thus arising all 155 over the body, the tongue stumbling and the voice fading, the eyes darkening, the ears ringing, the knees buckling - in short we often see men collapse as a result of the mind's terror, so that anyone can easily realise from this that the spirit is linked together with the mind; when 160 stricken by the impulse of the mind, it then strikes and propels the body.

This same reasoning teaches us that the mind and spirit are bodily in nature; for when they can be seen to propel the limbs, to arouse the body from sleep, to change the expression and to guide and steer the 165 whole individual, none of which we see can happen without touch, nor

nec tactum porro sine corpore, nonne fatendumst
corporea natura animum constare animamque?
praeterea pariter fungi cum corpore et una
consentire animum nobis in corpore cernis.
si minus offendit uitam uis horrida teli 170
ossibus ac neruis disclusis intus adacta,
at tamen insequitur languor terraeque petitus
suauis et in terra mentis qui gignitur aestus,
interdumque quasi exsurgendi incerta uoluntas.
ergo corpoream naturam animi esse necessest, 175
corporeis quoniam telis ictuque laborat.

Is tibi nunc animus quali sit corpore et unde
constiterit pergam rationem reddere dictis.
principio esse aio persubtilem atque minutis
perquam corporibus factum constare. id ita esse 180
hinc licet aduertas animum ut pernoscere possis.
nil adeo fieri celeri ratione uidetur
quam sibi mens fieri proponit et incohat ipsa.
ocius ergo animus quam res se perciet ulla,
ante oculos quorum in promptu natura uidetur. 185
at quod mobile tanto operest, constare rutundis
perquam seminibus debet perquamque minutis,
momine uti paruo possint impulsa moueri.
namque mouetur aqua et tantillo momine flutat
quippe uolubilibus paruisque creata figuris. 190
at contra mellis constantior est natura
et pigri latices magis et cunctantior actus;
haeret enim inter se magis omnis materiai
copia, nimirum quia non tam leuibus exstat
corporibus neque tam subtilibus atque rutundis. 195
namque papaueris aura potest suspensa leuisque
cogere ut ab summo tibi diffluat altus aceruus:
at contra lapidum conlectum spicarumque

---

183 sibi *Wakefield*: si *OQV*
194 leuibus exstat *MSS*: leuibu' constat *Heinze*
198 conlectum *Muretus*: coniectum *OQV*

touch in turn without body, must it not be admitted that mind and spirit have a bodily nature? What's more, you discern that our soul is affected equally with the body and suffers together with it in the body. 170 If the shuddering impact of a weapon, driven inside its victim and exposing the bones and sinews, fails to deal death, yet nevertheless there ensue faintness, the pleasant sensation of seeking the ground, the mental tide generated on the ground, and sometimes a sort of vague 175 desire to arise. Therefore the soul must be corporeal in nature, since it is afflicted by corporeal weapons and blows.

I shall now proceed to explain to you in my discourse what sort of matter this soul comprises and how it is made up. In the first place I 180 assert that it is exceptionally refined and stands composed of exceedingly minute bodies. That this is the case your mind may grasp from what follows, to enable you to appreciate it fully. We can see that nothing happens as quickly as what the mind presents to itself as happening and itself initiates. Therefore the mind stirs itself into 185 motion more swiftly than any of the things which can be plainly seen before our eyes. But something so mobile has to consist of exceedingly round and exceedingly minute seeds, so that they can move when impelled by a slight impulse. Water, for example, is set in motion and 190 flows under the tiniest momentum, seeing that it is made of small shapes which roll easily: but honey, on the other hand, is naturally thicker, its liquid more sluggish and its motion more hesitant; for the whole mass of its matter coheres more, undoubtedly because it does 195 not consist of such smooth, such refined and such round bodies. Again, with poppy-seed, you will find that a slight, checked breath can cause a high heap of it to stream down from the top, but on the other hand, with a collection of stones or corn-ears, it

noenu potest. igitur paruissima corpora proquam
et leuissima sunt, ita mobilitate fruuntur: 200
at contra quaecumque magis cum pondere magno
asperaque inueniuntur, eo stabilita magis sunt.
nunc igitur quoniam est animi natura reperta
mobilis egregie, perquam constare necessest
corporibus paruis et leuibus atque rutundis. 205
quae tibi cognita res in multis, o bone, rebus
utilis inuenietur et opportuna cluebit.
haec quoque res etiam naturam dedicat eius,
quam tenui constet textura quamque loco se
contineat paruo, si possit conglomerari, 210
quod simul atque hominem leti secura quies est
indepta atque animi natura animaeque recessit,
nil ibi libatum de toto corpore cernas
ad speciem, nil ad pondus: mors omnia praestat
uitalem praeter sensum calidumque uaporem. 215
ergo animam totam perparuis esse necessest
seminibus, nexam per uenas uiscera neruos,
quatenus, omnis ubi e toto iam corpore cessit,
extima membrorum circumcaesura tamen se
incolumem praestat nec defit ponderis hilum. 220
quod genus est Bacchi cum flos euanuit aut cum
spiritus unguenti suauis diffugit in auras
aut aliquo cum iam sucus de corpore cessit;
nil oculis tamen esse minor res ipsa uidetur
propterea neque detractum de pondere quicquam, 225
nimirum quia multa minutaque semina sucos
efficiunt et odorem in toto corpore rerum.
quare etiam atque etiam mentis naturam animaeque
scire licet perquam pauxillis esse creatam
seminibus, quoniam fugiens nil ponderis aufert. 230

Nec tamen haec simplex nobis natura putanda est.
tenuis enim quaedam moribundos deserit aura
mixta uapore, uapor porro trahit aera secum.
nec calor est quisquam, cui non sit mixtus et aer;

---

224 nil *Itali*: nihil *OQV*: nilo *Heinsius*

200 can in no way achieve this. Therefore, bodies enjoy mobility in proportion to their smallness and smoothness, but on the other hand the greater their weight and roughness prove, the greater is their stability. Now therefore, since the mind has been found to be by nature 205 exceptionally mobile, it must consist of exceedingly small, smooth and round bodies. Knowledge of this fact, good sir, will be found useful and prove advantageous in many contexts. Again, this fact also proclaims its nature, how tenuous is its texture and in how small a 210 space it would be contained, if it could be gathered together, that as soon as the carefree peace of death has taken possession of a man and the substance of his mind and spirit has departed, autopsy reveals nothing taken away from the body as a whole judging by the appearance, nothing judging by the weight; death safeguards 215 everything except the consciousness of life and the warmth of heat. Therefore the spirit as a whole must consist of exceptionally small seeds, woven as it is throughout the veins, the flesh and the sinews, in so far as, once it has completely departed from the whole body, the 220 outer contour of the limbs is nevertheless preserved intact and no tittle of weight is lost. It is like this when the bouquet of wine has passed away or when the sweet breath of an unguent has been dissipated to the breezes or when the flavour has now departed from some 225 substance; the object itself, however, seems no smaller to the eyes on that account and nothing seems to have been removed from its weight, undoubtedly for this reason, that it is many minute seeds in the total mass of the objects that make up flavour and scent. Therefore one can see again and again that the substance of mind and spirit is made up of 230 exceptionally tiny seeds, since as it flees it takes away no weight.

This substance, however, should not be thought to be single. For a sort of tenuous breath deserts us at the time of death, combined with heat, and heat in turn draws air with it. Indeed, there is no heat in which air

rara quod eius enim constat natura, necessest 235
aeris inter eum primordia multa moueri.
iam triplex animi est igitur natura reperta,
nec tamen haec sat sunt ad sensum cuncta creandum,
nil horum quoniam recipit mens posse creare
sensiferos motus et mens quaecumque uolutat. 240
quarta quoque his igitur quaedam natura necessest
attribuatur. east omnino nominis expers,
qua neque mobilius quicquam neque tenuius exstat
nec magis e paruis et leuibus ex elementis,
sensiferos motus quae didit prima per artus. 245
prima cietur enim, paruis perfecta figuris;
inde calor motus et uenti caeca potestas
accipit, inde aer; inde omnia mobilitantur,
concutitur sanguis, tum uiscera persentiscunt
omnia, postremis datur ossibus atque medullis 250
siue uoluptas est siue est contrarius ardor.
nec temere huc dolor usque potest penetrare neque acre
permanare malum, quin omnia perturbentur
usque adeo ut uitae desit locus atque animai
diffugiant partes per caulas corporis omnis. 255
sed plerumque fit in summo quasi corpore finis
motibus; hanc ob rem uitam retinere ualemus.

Nunc ea quo pacto inter sese mixta quibusque
compta modis uigeant rationem reddere auentem
abstrahit inuitum patrii sermonis egestas; 260
sed tamen, ut potero summatim attingere, tangam.
inter enim cursant primordia principiorum
motibus inter se, nil ut secernier unum

---

239 mens *MSS*: res *Bernays*
240 et mens quaecumque *Frerichs*: quaedam quae (*uel* quedamque) mente *OQV*: et quaecumque ipsa *Saunders, Mnemosyne iv.28 (1975) 296-8*: *alii alia*
244 e *OQV*: est *Itali* ex *OQV*: est *Wakefield*

235 is not also mixed, for because it is rarefied in nature, many primary particles of air must be in motion within it. The nature of the soul has therefore been found to be threefold; yet all these components are not enough to create consciousness, since the mind does not admit that any 240 of these can create the motions that carry sensation and the manifold reflections of the mind. Therefore, some sort of fourth substance must also be added to these. It is altogether nameless, and nothing exists which is more mobile or more tenuous than this, or composed of 245 smaller, smoother basic components; it is this which is first to distribute the motions that carry sensation throughout our members, because it is first to be stirred, being made up of small shapes; next heat and wind, with its unseen power, take up the movements, then air; then everything is set in motion, the blood feels the shock, then all the 250 flesh begins to feel the sensation everywhere, finally it is communicated to the bones and marrow, whether it is pleasure or its searing opposite. And pain cannot lightly penetrate as far as this, or its keen torment seep through, without everything being so completely 255 disturbed that there remains no place for life and the parts of the spirit escape through all the body's apertures. But usually the motions end as it were on the surface of the body; because of this, we have the strength to retain life.

Now, eager as I am to give an account of the manner in which those elements are mingled with one another and the ways in which they are 260 combined and have their effect, I am unwillingly held back by the poverty of my native tongue; but still, I will touch on the theme as best I can in outline. The primary particles rush to and fro among one another, with the motions proper to them, in such a way that no single

possit nec spatio fieri diuisa potestas,
sed quasi multae uis unius corporis exstant. 265
quod genus in quouis animantum uiscere uulgo
est odor et quidam color et sapor et tamen ex his
omnibus est unum perfectum corporis augmen,
sic calor atque aer et uenti caeca potestas
mixta creant unam naturam et mobilis illa 270
uis, initum motus ab se quae diuidit ollis,
sensifer unde oritur primum per uiscera motus.
nam penitus prorsum latet haec natura subestque,
nec magis hac infra quicquam est in corpore nostro
atque anima est animae proporro totius ipsa. 275
quod genus in nostris membris et corpore toto
mixta latens animi uis est animaeque potestas,
corporibus quia de paruis paucisque creatast,
sic tibi nominis haec expers uis facta minutis
corporibus latet atque animae quasi totius ipsa 280
proporrost anima et dominatur corpore toto.
consimili ratione necessest uentus et aer
et calor inter se uigeant commixta per artus
atque aliis aliud subsit magis emineatque
ut quiddam fieri uideatur ab omnibus unum, 285
ni calor ac uentus sorsum sorsumque potestas
aeris interimant sensum diductaque soluant.
est etenim calor ille animo, quem sumit in ira
cum feruescit et ex oculis micat acribus ardor.
est et frigida multa comes formidinis aura, 290
quae ciet horrorem membris et concitat artus.
est etiam quoque pacati status aeris ille,
pectore tranquillo qui fit uultuque sereno.

---

267 color *Lambinus*: calor *OQV*
280 animae quasi *MSS*: animai *Lachmann*
284 aliis *MSS*: alias *Brieger*
288 etenim *Faber*: etiam *OQV*
289 acribus *Lambinus*: acrius *OQV*

265 element can be isolated nor its powers spatially divided, but they form, so to speak, many forces of a single body. Just as in the flesh from any living creature there is regularly smell, taste, and a particular colour,
270 and yet all these go to make up a single bodily bulk, so a single entity is formed by the combination of heat, air and the unseen power of wind, along with that volatile force, which distributes from itself to them the beginning of the motion which is the initial source of sense-bearing motion throughout the flesh. This substance, you see, lies most deeply hidden and buried, and there is nothing more unobtrusive than
275 this in our body; it is itself in its turn the soul of the complete soul. Just as in our limbs and our whole body the force of the mind and the power of the spirit are latently mingled, because they are formed from a few small bodies, so, I can assure you, this nameless substance lies
280 latent, being made of minute bodies, and is, as it were, the soul of the complete soul and holds sway in the body as a whole. Similarly, wind, air and heat must be intermingled with one another throughout the members as they produce their effects, with one more unobtrusive or
285 more prominent than the others, yet in such a way that they all clearly go to make up a single entity; otherwise heat, wind, and air along with its powers would each be isolated and by their separation would disrupt and destroy sensation. The mind, you see, possesses that heat which it takes on when it seethes in anger and fire flashes from the
290 fierce eyes. There is also the abundance of chilling breeze, the companion of terror, which makes the flesh creep and the limbs tremble. Again, there is also that tranquil state of air which comes about when the heart is at peace and the expression serene. But

sed calidi plus est illis quibus acria corda
iracundaque mens facile efferuescit in ira. 295
quo genere in primis uis est uiolenta leonum,
pectora qui fremitu rumpunt plerumque gementes
nec capere irarum fluctus in pectore possunt.
at uentosa magis ceruorum frigida mens est
et gelidas citius per uiscera concitat auras, 300
quae tremulum faciunt membris exsistere motum.
at natura boum placido magis aere uiuit,
nec nimis irai fax umquam subdita percit
fumida, suffundens caecae caliginis umbra,
nec gelidis torpet telis perfixa pauoris: 305
interutrasque sitast, ceruos saeuosque leones.
sic hominum genus est. quamuis doctrina politos
constituat pariter quosdam, tamen illa relinquit
naturae cuiusque animi uestigia prima,
nec radicitus euelli mala posse putandumst, 310
quin procliuius hic iras decurrat ad acris,
ille metu citius paulo temptetur, at ille
tertius accipiat quaedam clementius aequo.
inque aliis rebus multis differre necessest
naturas hominum uarias moresque sequaces, 315
quorum ego nunc nequeo caecas exponere causas
nec reperire figurarum tot nomina quot sunt
principiis, unde haec oritur uariantia rerum.
illud in his rebus uideo firmare potesse,
usque adeo naturarum uestigia linqui 320
paruula quae nequeat ratio depellere nobis,
ut nil impediat dignam dis degere uitam.

Haec igitur natura tenetur corpore ab omni
ipsaque corporis est custos et causa salutis;
nam communibus inter se radicibus haerent 325
nec sine pernicie diuelli posse uidentur.
quod genus e turis glaebis euellere odorem
haud facile est quin intereat natura quoque eius,

---

295 ira *OQV*: iram *Bentley*
304 umbra *Q*: umbram *OV*
306 interutrasque *MSS*: inter utrosque *Auancius*

295 those whose blazing hearts and irascible temperament readily boil over in anger possess a greater quantity of heat. A prime example of this is the violent breed of lions, who frequently growl so as to burst their breasts with their roaring and are unable to contain the waves of their passions in their breasts. But the chilly hearts of deer possess more 300 wind, and more swiftly arouse cold breezes in their flesh, causing a trembling motion to manifest itself in their limbs. But cattle are better endowed by nature with calm air, and they are never unduly stirred by the application of the smoky torch of anger, enveloping them in a pall 305 of blinding darkness, nor are they numbed by being transfixed with the cold shafts of fear: they form an intermediate between deer and savage lions. So it is with the human race. Although education gives certain of them an equal polish, it nevertheless leaves behind the original traces 310 of the natural temperament of each, and it must not be supposed that their faults can be plucked out by the roots so as to stop one man hastening too precipitately into fits of fierce anger, another being assailed a little too quickly by fear, and a third accepting certain things with more than reasonable forbearance. It must also be that the various 315 temperaments of men, and their consequent behaviour, differ in many other details, but I cannot now reveal the hidden causes of these differences, or find names for all the shapes of the primary particles, which are the source of this variety in character. This much I see I can 320 assert in this area, that the traces of temperament which are left and are such that they cannot be driven from us by philosophy are so very slight, that nothing prevents our living a life worthy of the gods.

This then is the substance which is housed by the whole body, and is itself the guardian of the body and the cause of its well-being; this is 325 because they cohere with one another, having common roots, and obviously cannot be plucked apart without their destruction. Just as it is not easy to pluck the scent from lumps of frankincense without its

sic animi atque animae naturam corpore toto
extrahere haud facile est quin omnia dissoluantur. 330
implexis ita principiis ab origine prima
inter se fiunt consorti praedita uita.
nec sibi quaeque sine alterius ui posse uidetur
corporis atque animi sorsum sentire potestas,
sed communibus inter eas conflatur utrimque 335
motibus accensus nobis per uiscera sensus.
praeterea corpus per se nec gignitur umquam
nec crescit neque post mortem durare uidetur.
non enim, ut umor aquae dimittit saepe uaporem
qui datus est, neque ea causa conuellitur ipse, 340
sed manet incolumis, non inquam, sic animai
discidium possunt artus perferre relicti,
sed penitus pereunt conuulsi conque putrescunt.
ex ineunte aeuo sic corporis atque animai
mutua uitalis discunt contagia motus 345
maternis etiam membris aluoque reposta,
discidium ut nequeat fieri sine peste maloque,
ut uideas, quoniam coniunctast causa salutis,
coniunctam quoque naturam consistere eorum.

Quod superest, si quis corpus sentire refutat 350
atque animam credit permixtam corpore toto
suscipere hunc motum quem sensum nominitamus,
uel manifestas res contra uerasque repugnat.
quid sit enim corpus sentire quis adferet umquam,
si non ipsa palam quod res dedit ac docuit nos? 355
at dimissa anima corpus caret undique sensu:
perdit enim quod non proprium fuit eius in aeuo,
multaque praeterea perdit cum expellitur aeuo.
dicere porro oculos nullam rem cernere posse,
sed per eos animum ut foribus spectare reclusis, 360
difficilest, contra cum sensus ducat eorum;

---

350 refutat *OQV*: renutat *Lambinus*

358 perdit cum expellitur aeuo *ABF*: perditum expellitur aeuo quam *OQV*

330 whole nature also being destroyed, so it is not easy to extract the substance of mind and spirit from the complete body without the whole fabric being dissolved. They are created with their primary particles so intertwined with one another from their earliest origin, and are endowed with a life which they share as co-heirs. And it is clear that neither body nor soul has the capacity to feel independently for 335 itself without the aid of the other, but our sensation is kindled and fanned throughout the flesh by the motions shared between them on each side. Further, the body is never born and never grows by itself, and obviously never endures by itself after death. It is not, you see, 340 like liquid water, which often loses heat which has been imparted to it yet is not for that reason itself wrenched apart but remains intact; unlike that, I contend, the abandoned limbs cannot survive divorce from the spirit but are wrenched apart and perish utterly, rotting completely away. In such a way, from the beginning of their span, do 345 body and spirit by their mutual contacts learn the motions responsible for life, while still contained in their mother's frame and womb, that their divorce cannot take place without doom and disaster, so that you can see that, since the cause of their well-being is linked, their natures are linked also.

350 To continue, if anyone disputes that the body feels, and thinks that it is the spirit, intermingled throughout the whole body, that takes on this motion which we refer to as sensation, he is rebelling against the quite 355 manifest truth. Why, who will ever explain what bodily sensation is, if it is not what the facts themselves have plainly presented and taught us? You may claim that when the spirit has dispersed the body is totally devoid of sensation; but this is because it loses something that was not its permanent property in its lifetime, like many other features which it loses when it is banished from life. Further, to say that the 360 eyes cannot discern any object, but that the mind looks through them, as we do through open doors, is not easy, because the sensation in

sensus enim trahit atque acies detrudit ad ipsas,
fulgida praesertim cum cernere saepe nequimus,
lumina luminibus quia nobis praepediuntur.
quod foribus non fit; neque enim, qua cernimus ipsi, 365
ostia suscipiunt ullum reclusa laborem.
praeterea si pro foribus sunt lumina nostra,
iam magis exemptis oculis debere uidetur
cernere res animus sublatis postibus ipsis.

Illud in his rebus nequaquam sumere possis, 370
Democriti quod sancta uiri sententia ponit,
corporis atque animi primordia singula priuis
apposita alternis uariare ac nectere membra.
nam cum multo sunt animae elementa minora
quam quibus e corpus nobis et uiscera constant, 375
tum numero quoque concedunt et rara per artus
dissita sunt, dumtaxat ut hoc promittere possis,
quantula prima queant nobis iniecta ciere
corpora sensiferos motus in corpore, tanta
interualla tenere exordia prima animai. 380
nam neque pulueris interdum sentimus adhaesum
corpore nec membris incussam sidere cretam,
nec nebulam noctu neque aranei tenuia fila
obuia sentimus, quando obretimur euntes,
nec supera caput eiusdem cecidisse uietam 385
uestem nec plumas auium papposque uolantis,
qui nimia leuitate cadunt plerumque grauatim,
nec repentis itum cuiusuiscumque animantis
sentimus nec priua pedum uestigia quaeque,
corpore quae in nostro culices et cetera ponunt. 390
usque adeo prius est in nobis multa ciendum
quam primordia sentiscant concussa animai
semina, corporibus nostris immixta per artus,

---

372 priuis *Bentley*: primis *OQV*
393 *ante* 392 *transposuit Marullus*

them leads in the opposite direction; why, sensation drags and forces us to the very pupils, especially as we are often unable to discern shining objects, because the brightness of our vision is dimmed by the 365 brightness of the light. This does not happen to doors; the open doorways through which we ourselves see do not undergo any pain. Further, if our eyes act as doors, then the mind obviously ought to have a better view after their removal, with the doorposts and all taken away.

370 In this connection one can by no means accept the view posited by the revered sage Democritus, that the primary particles of body and soul are juxtaposed one next to another, and make up the fabric of our limbs by alternate variation. For not only are the basic components of 375 the soul much smaller than those which make up our body and flesh, but they are also fewer in number, and dispersed only thinly 380 throughout our limbs, so that this much at least one can guarantee, that the ultimate bodies which comprise the soul are at intervals which match the size of the smallest bodies which can, on contact with us, arouse the motions which carry sensation in our body. Sometimes, you see, we do not feel either dust clinging to our body or sprinkled chalk settling on our limbs, or feel mist at night, or the spider's slender 385 threads in our path, when we are enmeshed as we proceed, or that the same creature's shrivelled coat has fallen on our head, or again feathers from birds or floating thistle-down, which generally, because of their excessive lightness, find falling a heavy task, and we do not feel the progress of every single creeping creature or each individual 390 footstep which gnats and the other insects set on our bodies. So true is it that many things have to be stirred in us before the seeds of the soul, commingled in our bodies throughout our frame, begin to feel the

et tantis interuallis tuditantia possint
concursare coire et dissultare uicissim. 395

Et magis est animus uitai claustra coercens
et dominantior ad uitam quam uis animai.
nam sine mente animoque nequit residere per artus
temporis exiguam partem pars ulla animai,
sed comes insequitur facile et discedit in auras 400
et gelidos artus in leti frigore linquit.
at manet in uita cui mens animusque remansit;
quamuis est circum caesis lacer undique membris
truncus, adempta anima circum membrisque remota,
uiuit et aetherias uitalis suscipit auras. 405
si non omnimodis, at magna parte animai
priuatus, tamen in uita cunctatur et haeret,
ut, lacerato oculo circum si pupula mansit
incolumis, stat cernundi uiuata potestas,
dummodo ne totum corrumpas luminis orbem 410
et circum caedas aciem solamque relinquas;
id quoque enim sine pernicie non fiet eorum.
at si tantula pars oculi media illa peresa est,
occidit extemplo lumen tenebraeque sequuntur,
incolumis quamuis alioqui splendidus orbis. 415
hoc anima atque animus uincti sunt foedere semper.

Nunc age, natiuos animantibus et mortalis
esse animos animasque leuis ut noscere possis,
conquisita diu dulcique reperta labore
digna tua pergam disponere carmina uita. 420

---

394 tantis *Wakefield*: quantis *OQV*: quam in his *Lachmann*: quam illis *M.F.Smith*
404 remota Q^1: remot *Q*: remotus *OV*: remotis *Itali*
405 aetherias *OQV*: aerias *Lachmann*
415 alioqui *MSS*: alioquist *Kannengiesser*
420 uita *MSS*: cura *Lachmann*

shaking of the primary particles and before they can exchange repeated
395 blows over such large intervals, as they rush together, meet and leap
apart in turn.

Also, the mind has a much firmer hold on the bolts of life and is a
more dominant influence as regards life than is the spirit. Indeed
without the mind and intellect no part of the spirit is able to abide in
400 the limbs for any short spell of time; instead it readily follows as its
companion and is scattered to the breezes, leaving the limbs cold in the
chill of death. But anyone whose mind and intellect has remained with
him remains alive; however lacerated is the trunk, with the
surrounding limbs everywhere mutilated and the surrounding spirit lost
405 and released from the limbs, he lives and draws the heavenly breaths
that give him life. Though deprived, if not totally, at least of a large
part of his spirit, he nevertheless lingers in life and clings to it.
Similarly, if the surrounding eye has been lacerated but the pupil has
410 remained undamaged, the lively power of sight survives, provided only
that you do not impair the whole eye-ball and cut round the pupil and
leave it isolated, since that too will not take place without their
destruction. But if that middle part of the eye, tiny as it is, is eaten
415 away, the light of the eye suddenly fades and darkness falls, however
unimpaired in other respects is the gleaming ball. By this compact
have spirit and mind ever been bound.

Come now, so that you may be able to appreciate that the insubstantial
420 minds and spirits of living creatures are subject to birth and to death, I
shall proceed to set out poetry, the product of long research and

tu fac utrumque uno sub iungas nomine eorum,
atque animam uerbi causa cum dicere pergam,
mortalem esse docens, animum quoque dicere credas,
quatenus est unum inter se coniunctaque res est.

Principio, quoniam tenuem constare minutis 425
corporibus docui multoque minoribus esse
principiis factam quam liquidus umor aquai
aut nebula aut fumus (nam longe mobilitate
praestat et a tenui causa magis icta mouetur,
quippe ubi imaginibus fumi nebulaeque mouetur, 430
quod genus in somnis sopiti ubi cernimus alte
exhalare uaporem altaria ferreque fumum;
nam procul haec dubio nobis simulacra feruntur),
nunc igitur, quoniam quassatis undique uasis
diffluere umorem et laticem discedere cernis 435
et nebula ac fumus quoniam discedit in auras,
crede animam quoque diffundi multoque perire
ocius et citius dissolui in corpora prima,
cum semel ex hominis membris ablata recessit.
quippe etenim corpus, quod uas quasi constitit eius, 440
cum cohibere nequit conquassatum ex aliqua re
ac rarefactum detracto sanguine uenis,
aere qui credas posse hanc cohiberier ullo,
corpore qui nostro rarus magis incohibensquest?

Praeterea gigni pariter cum corpore et una 445
crescere sentimus pariterque senescere mentem.
nam uelut infirmo pueri teneroque uagantur
corpore, sic animi sequitur sententia tenuis.
inde ubi robustis adoleuit uiribus aetas,

---

431 alte *Lachmann*: alta *OQV*

433 haec *MSS*: hinc *Bentley*
feruntur *Creech*: geruntur *OQV*: genuntur *Lachmann*

444 incohibensquest *Bergk*: incohibescit *OQV*: is cohibessit? *Lachmann*: *alii alia*

pleasurable toil, which is worthy of your career. You are to make sure that you link each of them under a single name and that when I proceed to speak, say, of the spirit, teaching that it is mortal, you assume that I am referring also to the mind, since between them they make up a single thing and are a united object.

425 In the first place, I have shown that it is refined, consists of minute bodies and comprises much smaller primary particles than water's liquid moisture or mist or smoke, since it far excels them in mobility 430 and is set in motion by the impact of a more refined impulse, seeing that it is moved by images of smoke and mist, as when we are lulled in slumber and see altars breathing out their hot smoke and carrying it aloft; for that these images are carried to us is beyond doubt. As a 435 consequence, since you see that liquid, once its vessels are shattered, is dissipated and its moisture dispersed in all directions, and since mist and smoke disperse into the breezes, you must believe that the soul in turn drains away, perishes much more swiftly and dissolves more quickly into its original particles, once it has escaped and departed 440 from a man's frame. To be sure, when the body, which comprises its vessel, so to speak, cannot hold it together once it has itself been shattered as a result of some event or has become less dense through the loss of blood from the veins, how are you to suppose that the soul could ever be held together by air, which is more rarefied and less capable of holding it together than our body?

445 Moreover, we perceive that the mind is born simultaneously with the body, grows together with it and ages simultaneously. Indeed, just as children of undeveloped and immature physique have an unsteady gait, so their mental judgment is correspondingly slender. Then, when

consilium quoque maius et auctior est animi uis. 450
post ubi iam ualidis quassatum est uiribus aeui
corpus et obtusis ceciderunt uiribus artus,
claudicat ingenium, delirat lingua, labat mens;
omnia deficiunt atque uno tempore desunt.
ergo dissolui quoque conuenit omnem animai 455
naturam, ceu fumus, in altas aeris auras,
quandoquidem gigni pariter pariterque uidemus
crescere et, ut docui, simul aeuo fessa fatisci.

Huc accedit uti uideamus, corpus ut ipsum
suscipere immanis morbos durumque dolorem, 460
sic animum curas acris luctumque metumque;
quare participem leti quoque conuenit esse.
quin etiam morbis in corporis auius errat
saepe animus; dementit enim deliraque fatur
interdumque graui lethargo fertur in altum 465
aeternumque soporem oculis nutuque cadenti,
unde neque exaudit uoces nec noscere uultus
illorum potis est, ad uitam qui reuocantes
circumstant lacrimis rorantes ora genasque.
quare animum quoque dissolui fateare necessest, 470
quandoquidem penetrant in eum contagia morbi.
nam dolor ac morbus leti fabricator uterquest,
multorum exitio perdocti quod sumus ante. 473

Denique cur, hominem cum uini uis penetrauit 476
acris et in uenas discessit diditus ardor,
consequitur grauitas membrorum, praepediuntur
crura uacillanti, tardescit lingua, madet mens,
nant oculi, clamor singultus iurgia gliscunt, 480
et iam cetera de genere hoc quaecumque sequuntur
cur ea sunt, nisi quod uemens uiolentia uini
conturbare animam consueuit corpore in ipso?
at quaecumque queunt conturbari inque pediri

---

453 labat *Lachmann*: *omiserunt OQV*

474 (= 510) *et* 475 (et pariter mentem sanari corpus inani) *secluserunt Naugerius, Lambinus*

450 they reach maturity and full physical strength, their rational faculty too is greater and their mental powers more developed. Later, once the body has been shattered by the pressing power of time and the limbs have drooped with their powers blunted, the intellect limps, the tongue strays, the mind totters; everything breaks down and fails at the same 455 time. Therefore it is natural that the whole substance of the soul in turn dissolves, like smoke, into the lofty breezes of the air, since we see that they are born together, grow together and, as I have shown, gape wearily with the chinks of age at the same time.

There is the additional point that, just as we see the body for its part 460 undergo intense illness and cruel pain, so we see the mind undergo keen anxieties, grief and fear; therefore it is natural that it too participates in death. What's more, in bodily diseases the mind often loses its path and strays; reason deserts it, its utterances are delirious, 465 and sometimes it is carried by overpowering drowsiness, as the head nods and the eyes droop, into a deep and endless sleep, from which it neither hears the voices nor is able to recognise the countenances of those who stand round recalling the victim to life and bedewing their 470 faces and cheeks with tears. Therefore you must confess that the mind too is dissolved, since the contagion of the disease penetrates to it. For pain and disease are twin artificers of death, as we well know from the deaths of many in the past.

476 Again, why is it, when the keen potency of wine has penetrated a man and its heat has spread and been distributed into the veins, that there ensues heaviness of the limbs, his legs are impeded and he staggers, 480 his speech grows slurred, his mind is saturated, his eyes swim, and shouting, sobbing and quarrelling proliferate, and why are there all those other accompanying symptoms of this sort, if it is not because the fierce ferocity of the wine is accustomed to wreak disorder on the soul while it is actually in the body? But anything that can suffer

significant, paulo si durior insinuarit 485
causa, fore ut pereant aeuo priuata futuro.

Quin etiam subito ui morbi saepe coactus
ante oculos aliquis nostros, ut fulminis ictu,
concidit et spumas agit, ingemit et tremit artus,
desipit, extentat neruos, torquetur, anhelat 490
inconstanter, et in iactando membra fatigat,
nimirum quia ui morbi distracta per artus
turbat agens anima spumas, ut in aequore salso
uentorum ualidis feruescunt uiribus undae.
exprimitur porro gemitus, quia membra dolore 495
adficiuntur et omnino quod semina uocis
eiciuntur et ore foras glomerata feruntur
qua quasi consuerunt et sunt munita uiai.
desipientia fit, quia uis animi atque animai
conturbatur et, ut docui, diuisa seorsum 500
disiectatur eodem illo distracta ueneno.
inde ubi iam morbi reflexit causa reditque
in latebras acer corrupti corporis umor,
tum quasi uaccillans primum consurgit et omnis
paulatim redit in sensus animamque receptat. 505
haec igitur tantis ubi morbis corpore in ipso
iactentur miserisque modis distracta laborent,
cur eadem credis sine corpore in aere aperto
cum ualidis uentis aetatem degere posse?

Et quoniam mentem sanari, corpus ut aegrum, 510
cernimus et flecti medicina posse uidemus,
id quoque praesagit mortalem uiuere mentem.
addere enim partis aut ordine traiecere aequumst
aut aliquid prorsum de summa detrahere hilum,

---

492 ui *Brieger*: uis *OQV*
post 492 *lacunam indicauit Brieger*
493 anima spumas *Tohte*: animam spumans *OQV*
ut *Itali*: *omiserunt OQV*
497 eiciuntur *Lambinus*: eliciuntur *OQV*

485 disorder and impediment demonstrates that, if infiltrated by a slightly harsher influence, it will perish, deprived of future life.

What's more, often before our very eyes an individual is suddenly overcome by the violence of his disease, as by the impact of a thunderbolt, and collapses, foams at the mouth and groans; his limbs 490 shake, his senses desert him, his muscles grow rigid; he writhes, gasps irregularly, and tosses his limbs to the point of exhaustion. This is undoubtedly because his *spirit* has been torn asunder throughout his frame by the violence of the disease and is in turmoil, driving foam before it just as the waves on the salt sea seethe under the powerful 495 impact of the winds. Groaning, in turn, is wrung from him because his limbs are affected by pain, and because the seeds of his voice are all expelled together and carried out from the mouth *en masse*, where their habitual route lies, so to speak, and there is a paved path. Loss of his 500 senses occurs, because the functions of mind and spirit are thrown into confusion, and, as I have shown, they are divided and separated, thrown apart and torn asunder by that same poison. Next, once the cause of the malady has turned back and the venomous secretion of the diseased body has returned to its lair, the victim then for the first time 505 gets unsteadily to his feet, gradually regains full consciousness and recovers his soul. Therefore, when mind and spirit are buffeted by such great maladies and racked and torn asunder in wretched wise while actually in the body, why do you suppose that, without the body, in the open air, they can nonetheless prolong their existence in company with the buffeting breezes?

510 And the fact that we see that the mind can be cured, like the ailing body, and witness that it can be swayed by medicine, also foretells that its life is mortal. For it is fair to assume that one is adding parts, or transposing them, or subtracting something, however minuscule,

commutare animum quicumque adoritur et infit 515
aut aliam quamuis naturam flectere quaerit.
at neque transferri sibi partis nec tribui uult
immortale quod est quicquam neque defluere hilum.
nam quodcumque suis mutatum finibus exit,
continuo hoc mors est illius quod fuit ante. 520
ergo animus siue aegrescit, mortalia signa
mittit, uti docui, seu flectitur a medicina:
usque adeo falsae rationi uera uidetur
res occurrere et effugium praecludere eunti
ancipitique refutatu conuincere falsum. 525

Denique saepe hominem paulatim cernimus ire
et membratim uitalem deperdere sensum,
in pedibus primum digitos liuescere et unguis,
inde pedes et crura mori, post inde per artus
ire alios tractim gelidi uestigia leti. 530
scinditur atque animae quoniam natura nec uno
tempore sincera exsistit, mortalis habendast.
quod si forte putas ipsam se posse per artus
introrsum trahere et partis conducere in unum
atque ideo cunctis sensum deducere membris, 535
at locus ille tamen, quo copia tanta animai
cogitur, in sensu debet maiore uideri:
qui quoniam nusquamst, nimirum, ut diximus ante,
dilaniata foras dispargitur, interit ergo.
quin etiam si iam libeat concedere falsum 540
et dare posse animam glomerari in corpore eorum
lumina qui linquunt moribundi particulatim,
mortalem tamen esse animam fateare necesse,
nec refert utrum pereat dispersa per auras

---

531 atque *MSS*: itque *Munro*: ergo *Heinze*: atqui *Lambinus*: aeque *Bernays* animae *Lambinus*: animo haec *MSS*: animae hoc *Munro*: animae haec *Bailey*

544 auras *MSS*: artus *J.D.Duff*

515 from the sum, if one is entering on an attempt to alter the mind or seeking to sway the nature of anything else whatever. But an immortal object allows neither rearrangement of its parts nor any addition to them nor the ebbing away of a single jot. For whenever an object is 520 changed and quits its natural bounds, this automatically involves the death of what existed before. Therefore the mind displays the signs of mortality whether, as I have shown, it falls ill, or whether it is swayed by medicine: to such an extent can truth be seen to confront false 525 reasoning, to shut off its escape as it flees, and to triumph over falsehood with double-edged refutation.

Again, we often see a man pass away gradually, and lose the sensation of life limb by limb; first we see the toes and nails on his feet take on a 530 livid hue, then the feet and legs die, next the other members in turn subjected to the slow advance of the chill footsteps of death. And since the spirit's substance is *severed* and does not depart as a whole at the same instant, it must be considered mortal. But if you happen to suppose that it can draw itself inside through the limbs and can 535 contract its parts into one and that this is why it withdraws sensation from all the members, yet nevertheless the spot where such a large proportion of spirit is being concentrated ought to be manifestly more sensitive: but since there is no such spot, it is indubitably rent asunder, as we have already said, and scattered outside; therefore it perishes. 540 What's more, even if we chose to allow a false assumption and to grant that the spirit can be condensed in the bodies of those who leave the light of life by a piecemeal death, you must nevertheless concede that the spirit is mortal, nor does it make any difference whether it

an contracta suis e partibus obbrutescat, 545
quando hominem totum magis ac magis undique sensus
deficit et uitae minus et minus undique restat.

Et quoniam mens est hominis pars una, loco quae
fixa manet certo, uelut aures atque oculi sunt
atque alii sensus qui uitam cumque gubernant, 550
et ueluti manus atque oculus naresue seorsum
secreta ab nobis nequeunt sentire neque esse
sed tamen in paruo liquuntur tempore tabe,
sic animus per se non quit sine corpore et ipso
esse homine, illius quasi quod uas esse uidetur 555
siue aliud quid uis potius coniunctius ei
fingere, quandoquidem conexu corpus adhaeret.

Denique corporis atque animi uiuata potestas
inter se coniuncta ualent uitaque fruuntur:
nec sine corpore enim uitalis edere motus 560
sola potest animi per se natura nec autem
cassum anima corpus durare et sensibus uti.
scilicet auulsus radicibus ut nequit ullam
dispicere ipse oculus rem sorsum corpore toto,
sic anima atque animus per se nil posse uidetur. 565
nimirum quia per uenas et uiscera mixtim
per neruos atque ossa, tenentur corpore ab omni
nec magnis interuallis primordia possunt
libera dissultare, ideo conclusa mouentur
sensiferos motus, quos extra corpus in auras 570
aeris haud possunt post mortem eiecta moueri
propterea quia non simili ratione tenentur.
corpus enim atque animans erit aer, si cohibere
in se animam atque in eos poterit concludere motus

---

553 liquuntur *Vossius*: linguntur *OQV*
tabe *Creech*: tali *OQ*: tale *V*: tabi *Vossius*

566 mixtim *L*: mixti *OV*: mixta *Q*

574 in se animam *Wakefield*: sese anima *O*: esse anima *Q*:
esse animam *V* eos *OQV*: eo *Faber*

545 perishes by being scattered to the breezes or grows numb after contracting its parts, since the victim as a whole loses more and more of his sensitivity on every side, and on every side less and less of life remains.

Also, the mind is a specific part of a man, which remains fixed in a set 550 place, as are the ears and eyes and all the other sense-organs that guide our lives; it follows that, just as a hand or an eye or the nostrils cannot either feel or exist separately, when removed from us, but on the 555 contrary in a short time decompose in decay, so the mind cannot exist on its own without the body and the actual person, as the body is clearly, so to speak, the mind's vessel, or whatever else you care to picture instead which is more closely linked to it, since the body clings to it with intimate bonds.

Again, body and soul, with their lively powers, thrive and enjoy life by 560 virtue of their mutual ties: without the body, the soul on its own cannot independently generate the motions of life, nor in turn can the body, devoid of the soul, endure and avail itself of the senses. It is clear that, just as an eye torn away from its roots cannot discern anything by 565 itself, in isolation from the body as a whole, so the mind and the spirit can plainly do nothing independently. It is undoubtedly because their primary particles, mingled throughout the veins and the flesh, throughout the sinews and the bones, are held in by the whole body and cannot leap apart freely over great intervals, that they are confined 570 and move with the motions conveying sensation, with which they cannot move outside the body, when they have been cast out into the breezes of the air after death, precisely because they are not similarly held in. Why, the air will be a body and indeed an animate creature, if it is going to be able to enclose the soul within itself and to

quos ante in neruis et in ipso corpore agebat. 575
quare etiam atque etiam resoluto corporis omni
tegmine et eiectis extra uitalibus auris
dissolui sensus animi fateare necessest
atque animam, quoniam coniunctast causa duobus.

Denique cum corpus nequeat perferre animai 580
discidium quin in taetro tabescat odore,
quid dubitas quin ex imo penitusque coorta
emanarit uti fumus diffusa animae uis,
atque ideo tanta mutatum putre ruina
conciderit corpus, penitus quia mota loco sunt 585
fundamenta, foras anima emanante per artus
perque uiarum omnis flexus in corpore qui sunt
atque foramina? multimodis ut noscere possis
dispertitam animae naturam exisse per artus
et prius esse sibi distractam corpore in ipso 590
quam prolapsa foras enaret in aeris auras.

Quin etiam finis dum uitae uertitur intra,
saepe aliqua tamen e causa labefacta uidetur
ire anima ac toto solui de corpore uelle
et quasi supremo languescere tempore uultus 595
molliaque exsangui cadere omnia corpore membra.
quod genus est, animo male factum cum perhibetur
aut animam liquisse, ubi iam trepidatur et omnes
extremum cupiunt uitae reprehendere uinclum.
conquassatur enim tum mens animaeque potestas 600
omnis et haec ipso cum corpore collabefiunt,
ut grauior paulo possit dissoluere causa.
quid dubitas tandem quin extra prodita corpus
imbecilla foras, in aperto, tegmine dempto,

---

586 anima emanante *Wakefield*: manant animaeque *OQV*
592-606 *post* 614 *locauit Giussani, post* 575 *Munro*
594 uelle *Lachmann*: omnia membra *OQV (ex* 596*)*
596 cadere omnia corpore membra *F*: cadere omnia membra *OQV*: trunco cadere omnia membra *Lachmann*

575 confine it to allow those motions which it previously performed in the sinews and the actual body. Therefore again and again you must confess that, once all the body's shelter has been dissolved and the vital breaths cast outside, the consciousness of mind and spirit is dissolved, since the well-being of the partners is linked.

580 Again, since the body cannot endure the sundering of the soul without decomposing amidst an appalling stench, why do you doubt that the soul has arisen and seeped out from deep down in its depths, scattered 585 like smoke, and that the reason why the crumbling body has been transformed and collapsed in such ruins is that its foundations have been shifted from their position deep down, as the soul seeped outside through the limbs and through all the winding ways and apertures which the body contains? This provides you with multiple evidence that the soul's substance has undergone division before its departure 590 through the members and that its parts have been disrupted while actually in the body before it could glide outside and swim into the breezes of the air.

What's more, even while it remains within the boundaries of life, it is often observed that the soul, undermined by some agency, is nevertheless ready to depart and to be released completely from the 595 body, and that the expression grows glazed as if at the hour of death and all the limbs fall limp on the bloodless body. This sort of thing occurs when the mind is said to have had a black-out, or the spirit to have suffered a turn, when consternation reigns and everyone is 600 desperate to hold on to the last link with life. The reason is that the powers of mind and spirit are at that moment entirely shattered and they are reduced to collapse with the body itself, so that a slightly severer shock could dissolve them. Why, I ask, do you doubt that the soul, thrust forth in its weakness outside the body, out of doors, in the

non modo non omnem possit durare per aeuum 605
sed minimum quoduis nequeat consistere tempus?

Nec sibi enim quisquam moriens sentire uidetur
ire foras animam incolumem de corpore toto,
nec prius ad iugulum et supera succedere fauces,
uerum deficere in certa regione locatam, 610
ut sensus alios in parti quemque sua scit
dissolui: quod si immortalis nostra foret mens,
non tam se moriens dissolui conquereretur,
sed magis ire foras uestemque relinquere, ut anguis.

Denique cur animi numquam mens consiliumque 615
gignitur in capite aut pedibus manibusue, sed unis
sedibus et certis regionibus omnibus haeret,
si non certa loca ad nascendum reddita cuique
sunt et ubi quicquid possit durare creatum
atque ita multimodis perfectis artubus esse, 620
membrorum ut numquam exsistat praeposterus ordo?
usque adeo sequitur res rem, neque flamma creari
fluminibus solitast neque in igni gignier algor.

Praeterea si immortalis natura animaist
et sentire potest secreta a corpore nostro, 625
quinque, ut opinor, eam faciundum est sensibus auctam.
nec ratione alia nosmet proponere nobis
possumus infernas animas Acherunte uagari;
pictores itaque et scriptorum saecla priora
sic animas introduxerunt sensibus auctas. 630
at neque sorsum oculi neque nares nec manus ipsa
esse potest animae neque sorsum lingua neque aures:
haud igitur per se possunt sentire neque esse.

---

post 619 *lacunam indicauit Munro*

620 perfectis *Lachmann*: pertotis *OQV*: partitis *Bernays*

628 uagari *Gifanius*: uacare *OQ*: uagare *Q'*

633 haud igitur *Lachmann*: auditum *OQ*

605 open, with its shelter taken away, so far from being able to endure through the whole of time, could not hold together for the briefest spell you care to nominate?

Indeed, it is clear that no one, as he dies, feels that his soul is going outside intact from the whole of his body, or that it is first making its 610 way up to the throat and gullet above, but rather that it is failing in the specific area where it is stationed, just as he knows that each of his senses is being dissolved in its own area: yet if our soul was immortal, it would not complain, as it died, that it was being dissolved, but would rather sense that it was proceeding outside and shedding its garb, like a snake.

615 Again, why is it that the intellect and rational power of the mind is never born in the head or the feet or the hands, but rather clings in all men to a single abode and a specific location, if it is not that specific places are allotted to each type of thing for its birth and where each can 620 endure after its creation and comprise members made up in manifold ways, but without a reversal in the order of its limbs ever coming about? So surely does one thing go closely with another, and flame is not in the habit of being created in rivers or cold of being born in fire.

Besides, if the spirit is immortal and capable of sensation after 625 separation from our body, we must, I suggest, imagine it to be equipped with the organs of the five senses. This is the only way in which we can picture to ourselves the underworld spirits wandering in Acheron; this is why the painters and writers of earlier generations have portrayed spirits equipped with sense-organs in this way. But in 630 isolation from the body neither eyes nor nose nor, by itself, can a hand exist for the benefit of the spirit, nor, in isolation, can a tongue or ears; spirits therefore are incapable of sensation or existence on their own.

Et quoniam toto sentimus corpore inesse
uitalem sensum et totum esse animale uidemus, 635
si subito medium celeri praeciderit ictu
uis aliqua ut sorsum partem secernat utramque,
dispertita procul dubio quoque uis animai
et discissa simul cum corpore dissicietur.
at quod scinditur et partis discedit in ullas, 640
scilicet aeternam sibi naturam abnuit esse.
falciferos memorant currus abscidere membra
saepe ita de subito permixta caede calentis,
ut tremere in terra uideatur ab artubus id quod
decidit abscisum, cum mens tamen atque hominis uis 645
mobilitate mali non quit sentire dolorem
et simul in pugnae studio quod dedita mens est;
corpore relicuo pugnam caedesque petessit,
nec tenet amissam laeuam cum tegmine saepe
inter equos abstraxe rotas falcesque rapaces, 650
nec cecidisse alius dextram, cum scandit et instat;
inde alius conatur adempto surgere crure,
cum digitos agitat propter moribundus humi pes,
et caput abscisum calido uiuenteque trunco
seruat humi uultum uitalem oculosque patentis, 655
donec reliquias animai reddidit omnis.
quin etiam tibi, si lingua uibrante, minanti
serpentem cauda, procero corpore utrimque
sit libitum in multas partis discidere ferro,
omnia iam sorsum cernes ancisa recenti 660
uulnere tortari et terram conspargere tabo,
ipsam seque retro partem petere ore priorem
uulneris ardenti, ut morsu premat, icta dolore.
omnibus esse igitur totas dicemus in illis

---

657 minanti *O*: *omisit Q*: micanti *Lachmann*
658 serpentem *Marullus*: serpentis *OQ*
cauda *O'*: caude *OQ*: cauda e *Lachmann*
utrimque *Marullus*: utrumque *OQ*: truncum *Giussani*

635 Also, since we feel that the sensation of life is present throughout the whole body and can see that the whole of it is animate, if some force suddenly cuts it in two with a lightning blow, so as to sever and isolate each part, the spirit also will beyond doubt be divided, sundered and
640 forced apart simultaneously with the body. But anything that is split asunder and separates into any parts obviously renounces any claim to eternal status. They record how scythed chariots, in the heat of indiscriminate slaughter, often hew off limbs so suddenly, that the part
645 which has been hewn off and fallen from the frame is seen to quiver on the ground, while the warrior's mind is nevertheless unable to sense the pain because of the suddenness of the disaster and at the same time because his mind is preoccupied with lust for battle; with the remainder of his body he keeps trying to fight and to deal death, and often he does not grasp that his left arm, along with his shield, has
650 been lost and carried away amongst the horses by the wheels and their greedy scythes, or another that his right arm has gone, as he climbs up and attacks; another in turn tries to stand up on a leg which has been amputated, while nearby, on the ground, the dying foot twitches its
655 toes, and a head hewn from a warm, living trunk retains, on the ground, its expression of life and its wide-open eyes, until it has surrendered all the remnants of the spirit. What's more, imagine a snake with a darting tongue, a threatening tail and an extensive body and suppose you had a whim to cut it apart with a hatchet, at each end,
660 into many segments: you will then, while the wound is fresh, observe each portion which has been hewn writhing separately and spattering the ground with gore, and the front part making for its own hind part with its mouth, in order to bite it, stricken as it is by the searing pain of the wound. Are we therefore going to say that there are complete

particulis animas? at ea ratione sequetur 665
unam animantem animas habuisse in corpore multas.
ergo diuisast ea quae fuit una simul cum
corpore: quapropter mortale utrumque putandumst,
in multas quoniam partis disciditur aeque.

Praeterea si immortalis natura animai 670
constat et in corpus nascentibus insinuatur,
cur super anteactam aetatem meminisse nequimus
nec uestigia gestarum rerum ulla tenemus?
nam si tanto operest animi mutata potestas
omnis ut actarum exciderit retinentia rerum, 675
non, ut opinor, id ab leto iam longius errat:
quapropter fateare necessest quae fuit ante
interiisse et quae nunc est nunc esse creatam.

Praeterea si iam perfecto corpore nobis
inferri solitast animi uiuata potestas 680
tum cum gignimur et uitae cum limen inimus,
haud ita conueniebat uti cum corpore et una
cum membris uideatur in ipso sanguine cresse,
sed uelut in cauea per se sibi uiuere solam
conuenit, ut sensu corpus tamen affluat omne. 685
quod fieri totum contra manifesta docet res: 690
namque ita conexa est per uenas uiscera neruos
ossaque, uti dentes quoque sensu participentur,
morbus ut indicat et gelidai stringor aquai
et lapis oppressus subiit si e frugibus asper. 694
quare etiam atque etiam neque originis esse putandumst 686
expertis animas nec leti lege solutas.
nam neque tanto opere adnecti potuisse putandumst

---

685 *seclusit Lambinus*
affluat *O*: afluat *Q*: arceat *uel* afuat *Lachmann*
690-4 *post* 685 *collocauit Lachmann*
694 subiit si e *Bernays*: subitis e *OQ*: subsit si *A.C.Clark*: subito de *Lambinus*: subito sub *L.A.MacKay*

665 spirits in all those tiny parts? But with that reasoning it will follow that a single animate creature had many spirits in its body. Therefore the single spirit it had has been divided simultaneously with its body; accordingly, each of the two must be considered mortal, since each alike is cut apart into many segments.

670 Besides, if the soul is immortal and winds its way into our body at birth, why are we unable to remember a previous existence as well, and why do we retain no inklings of earlier events? Because if the 675 powers of the mind have been so greatly changed that all recollection of past events has been let slip, then that, it seems to me, is not very far removed from death; you must accordingly admit that the soul which existed before has perished, and that the soul which now exists has only now been created.

680 Moreover, if the soul's lively power is in the habit of being imported into us when our body is already complete, at the moment when we are born and setting foot on the threshold of life, it would not then be appropriate that it should manifestly have grown with the body and 685 together with the limbs in the very blood, but it would be appropriate that it should live in isolation on its own, in its own cage, so to speak, yet in such a way that the whole body was flooded with sensation. 690 Plain fact teaches us that the complete opposite of this is the case, because it is so interlaced through the veins, the flesh, the sinews and the bones, that even the teeth are granted a share in sensation, as is 694 shown by toothache, by the shock of cold water, and by biting on a 686 rough stone encountered in the bread. Therefore again and again it must not be supposed that our souls are either devoid of an origin or exempt from the law of death. For it must not be supposed that they

corporibus nostris extrinsecus insinuatas, 689
nec, tam contextae cum sint, exire uidentur 695
incolumes posse et saluas exsoluere sese
omnibus e neruis atque ossibus articulisque.
quod si forte putas extrinsecus insinuatam
permanare animam nobis per membra solere,
tanto quique magis cum corpore fusa peribit: 700
quod permanat enim dissoluitur, interit ergo.
dispertitus enim per caulas corporis omnis
ut cibus, in membra atque artus cum diditur omnis,
disperit atque aliam naturam sufficit ex se,
sic anima atque animus quamuis integra recens in 705
corpus eunt, tamen in manando dissoluuntur,
dum quasi per caulas omnis diduntur in artus
particulae quibus haec animi natura creatur,
quae nunc in nostro dominatur corpore nata
ex illa quae tunc periit partita per artus. 710
quapropter neque natali priuata uidetur
esse die natura animae nec funeris expers.

Semina praeterea linquuntur necne animai
corpore in exanimo? quod si linquuntur et insunt,
haud erit ut merito immortalis possit haberi, 715
partibus amissis quoniam libata recessit.
sin ita sinceris membris ablata profugit
ut nullas partis in corpore liquerit ex se,
unde cadauera rancenti iam uiscere uermis
exspirant atque unde animantum copia tanta 720
exos et exsanguis tumidos perfluctuat artus?
quod si forte animas extrinsecus insinuari
uermibus et priuas in corpora posse uenire
credis nec reputas cur milia multa animarum

---

702 dispertitus *Lachmann*: dispertitur *OQ*: dispertita *F*
enim *AB*: ergo *OQF*
717 sinceris *OQ*; sincera ex *Faber*

689 could have been laced so closely onto our bodies had they found their
695 way in from outside, and equally, since they are so interwoven, it is clear that they cannot make their way out undamaged and safely extricate themselves from all the sinews, bones and joints. But if you happen to suppose that the soul finds its way into us from outside and
700 is in the habit of permeating our limbs, it will perish all the more, through fusion with the body, because what permeates is dissolved and is therefore destroyed. Why, just as food, by being dispersed through all the apertures of the body when it is distributed to all the limbs and members, perishes in division and makes up another substance out of
705 its own, so the mind and spirit, however whole they enter a fresh body, are nevertheless dissolved in the process of permeation, while there are distributed to the limbs through all the apertures, so to speak, the particles from which this soul of ours is created, which now holds
710 sway in our body, after being born from the one which previously perished by dispersal through the limbs. Therefore the soul can be seen neither to lack a birthday nor to be immune from death.

Besides, are seeds of the soul left behind or not in the deceased body? If they are left and are present in it, it will be quite impossible for it to
715 be justifiably considered immortal, since it was depleted by the loss of parts when it withdrew. But if it is carried off and flees headlong with its members intact, without leaving any parts of itself in the body, how is it that corpses, when the flesh is now putrefying, breathe out worms,
720 and how is it that such a boneless, bloodless host of animate creatures undulates over the swelling limbs? But if you happen to believe that souls can find their way into the worms from outside and can each enter a separate body, and do not pause to reflect why many thousands

conueniant unde una recesserit, hoc tamen est ut 725
quaerendum uideatur et in discrimen agendum,
utrum tandem animae uenentur semina quaeque
uermiculorum ipsaeque sibi fabricentur ubi sint,
an quasi corporibus perfectis insinuentur.
at neque cur faciant ipsae quareue laborent 730
dicere suppeditat. neque enim, sine corpore cum sunt,
sollicitae uolitant morbis alguque fameque.
corpus enim magis his uitiis adfine laborat
et mala multa animus contage fungitur eius.
sed tamen his esto quamuis facere utile corpus 735
cui subeant: at qua possint uia nulla uidetur.
haud igitur faciunt animae sibi corpora et artus.
nec tamen est utqui perfectis insinuentur
corporibus: neque enim poterunt subtiliter esse
conexae neque consensus contagia fient. 740

Denique cur acris uiolentia triste leonum
seminium sequitur, uulpes dolus, et fuga ceruis
a patribus datur et patrius pauor incitat artus,
et iam cetera de genere hoc cur omnia membris
ex ineunte aeuo generascunt ingenioque, 745
si non certa suo quia semine seminioque
uis animi pariter crescit cum corpore quoque?
quod si immortalis foret et mutare soleret
corpora, permixtis animantes moribus essent,
effugeret canis Hyrcano de semine saepe 750
cornigeri incursum cerui tremeretque per auras
aeris accipiter fugiens ueniente columba,
desiperent homines, saperent fera saecla ferarum.
illud enim falsa fertur ratione, quod aiunt
immortalem animam mutato corpore flecti: 755
quod mutatur enim dissoluitur, interit ergo;
traiciuntur enim partes atque ordine migrant;
quare dissolui quoque debent posse per artus,

---

740 consensus *Lachmann*: consensu *OQ*
747 quoque *O*: toto *Q*

725 of souls should assemble at the spot from which one has withdrawn, we must still obviously raise and resolve this question, whether, pray, the souls hunt out the various seeds of the tiny worms and personally construct for themselves somewhere to dwell, or whether they find 730 their way into ready-made bodies, so to speak. But why they should fashion them themselves or go to such pains it is impossible to explain, because, when they are without a body, they float about untroubled by disease, cold and hunger: for the body is more prone to suffer from these afflictions, and the soul goes through many ills because of its 735 intimate contact with it. But still, suppose it as beneficial for them as you like to fashion a body in which to take refuge: there is obviously no way in which they could. Therefore souls do not fashion bodies and members for themselves. Nor in turn is it the case that they find their way into ready-made bodies, because they will not then be able to be 740 subtly interlaced, and the mutual contacts by which they share in sensation will not take place.

Again, why is cruel violence an invariable feature of the truculent breed of lions, or cunning of foxes, and why is the tendency to flight passed on to deer by their sires so that hereditary fear spurs on their 745 limbs, and why do all the other characteristics of this sort originate from the beginning of life in the frame and the temperament, if it is not because the capacities of the mind are fixed and develop equally with each body according to its seed and breed? Yet if it were immortal and in the habit of switching bodies, animate creatures would have 750 interchangeable characters: a hound of Hyrcanian pedigree would often take to flight before the charge of an antlered stag, a hawk would flee in terror through the airy breezes at the approach of a dove, man would be devoid of reason, the wild tribes of beasts rational. Their claim, you see, is based on false reasoning, when they say that an 755 immortal soul alters when it switches bodies, because what changes is dissolved and therefore perishes; for parts are transposed and quit their arrangement; therefore, they must also be

denique ut intereant una cum corpore cunctae.
sin animas hominum dicent in corpora semper 760
ire humana, tamen quaeram cur e sapienti
stulta queat fieri, nec prudens sit puer ullus 762
nec tam doctus equae pullus quam fortis equi uis. 764
scilicet in tenero tenerascere corpore mentem 765
confugient; quod si iam fit, fateare necessest
mortalem esse animam, quoniam mutata per artus
tanto opere amittit uitam sensumque priorem.
quoue modo poterit pariter cum corpore quoque
confirmata cupitum aetatis tangere florem 770
uis animi, nisi erit consors in origine prima?
quidue foras sibi uult membris exire senectis?
an metuit conclusa manere in corpore putri
et domus aetatis spatio ne fessa uetusto
obruat? at non sunt immortali ulla pericla. 775

Denique conubia ad Veneris partusque ferarum
esse animas praesto deridiculum esse uidetur,
exspectare immortalis mortalia membra
innumero numero certareque praeproperanter
inter se quae prima potissimaque insinuetur, 780
si non forte ita sunt animarum foedera pacta
ut quae prima uolans aduenerit insinuetur
prima neque inter se contendant uiribus hilum.

Denique in aethere non arbor, non aequore in alto
nubes esse queunt nec pisces uiuere in aruis 785
nec cruor in lignis neque saxis sucus inesse:
certum ac dispositumst ubi quicquid crescat et insit.
sic animi natura nequit sine corpore oriri
sola neque a neruis et sanguine longius esse.
quod si posset enim, multo prius ipsa animi uis 790
in capite aut umeris aut imis calcibus esse
posset et innasci quauis in parte soleret,
tandem in eodem homine atque in eodem uase manere.

---

763 (=746) *deleuit Lachmann*

able to be dissolved throughout the frame, so that they all finally die
760 together with the body. But if they say that it is always the souls of men that enter human bodies, I shall still ask why a mature soul can turn into a witless one, why no child has discretion and why a foal is
765 not as well trained as a horse at the height of its powers. Of course they will resort to the plea that in a young body the mind becomes young; even if it does, you have to confess that the soul is mortal, since by being so radically changed throughout the frame it loses the
770 life and consciousness it had before. And how will the capacities of the mind be able to grow strong and to reach the coveted flower of their span simultaneously with each body, if it is not going to be its co-heir at the moment of origin? And why does it wish to depart from the aged limbs and to go outside? Is it afraid to stay behind, imprisoned in the crumbling body, in case its house, wearied by the protracted span of its
775 years, collapses on it in ruins? But an immortal entity knows no dangers.

Again, it is manifestly absurd that souls should be on hand at the unions inspired by Venus and at the births of the beasts, and, for all their immortality, should await mortal frames in countless numbers and should compete in precipitate haste with one another to see which
780 one should receive preference and be first to worm its way in - unless the souls happen to have entered into agreements whereby the first one to come flitting to the spot gets in first, and there is no hint of a trial of strength between them.

Again, a tree cannot exist in the heavens nor clouds in the depths of the
785 ocean, nor can fish live in fields nor blood reside in wood nor sap in stones: it is fixed and determined where each thing may reside and grow. Similarly the substance of the mind cannot originate on its own, without the body, or exist too far from the sinews and the blood.
790 Indeed, if it could, the mind and its functions would much more readily be able to exist in the head or the shoulders or right down in the heels, and would be accustomed to be born in any part you like, but at least to remain in the same person and the same vessel. But

quod quoniam nostro quoque constat corpore certum
dispositumque uidetur ubi esse et crescere possit 795
sorsum anima atque animus, tanto magis infitiandum
totum posse extra corpus durare genique.
quare, corpus ubi interiit, periisse necessest
confiteare animam distractam in corpore toto.

Quippe etenim mortale aeterno iungere et una 800
consentire putare et fungi mutua posse
desiperest. quid enim diuersius esse putandumst
aut magis inter se disiunctum discrepitansque,
quam mortale quod est immortali atque perenni
iunctum in concilio saeuas tolerare procellas? 805

Praeterea quaecumque manent aeterna necessest
aut quia sunt solido cum corpore respuere ictus
nec penetrare pati sibi quicquam quod queat artas
dissociare intus partis, ut materiai
corpora sunt quorum naturam ostendimus ante, 810
aut ideo durare aetatem posse per omnem,
plagarum quia sunt expertia, sicut inanest
quod manet intactum neque ab ictu fungitur hilum,
aut etiam quia nulla loci sit copia circum
quo quasi res possint discedere dissoluique, 815
sicut summarum summast aeterna, neque extra
quis locus est quo diffugiant neque corpora sunt quae
possint incidere et ualida dissoluere plaga.
quod si forte ideo magis immortalis habendast,
quod uitalibus ab rebus munita tenetur, 820
aut quia non ueniunt omnino aliena salutis

---

814 (*cf.* V 359) sit *OQ*: fit *Lachmann*
post 818 *lacunam indicauit Marullus*
820 uitalibus *OQ*: letalibus *Lambinus*

795 since in our body too there is a fixed arrangement and it is obviously determined where the spirit and mind can each exist and grow, so much the more must it be denied that they can be born or can endure right outside the body. Therefore, when the body has passed away, you have to confess that the soul has perished and been disrupted throughout the whole body.

800 Indeed, to couple mortal with eternal and to suppose that they can share their feelings with one another and mutually interact is totally irrational. Why, what can be imagined more incompatible or more 805 incongruous and inconsistent than that a mortal object should be coupled in union with something immortal and undying, and thus weather the fury of the storms?

Besides, whatever things last eternally must either comprise solid matter, and therefore reject blows and refuse to allow anything which 810 could disunite their close-set parts within to penetrate them, like the bodies of matter, whose nature I have disclosed earlier; or they must be able to endure throughout the whole of time for this reason, that they are not subject to blows, like void which remains intangible and is not acted upon by impact in the tiniest degree, or again because there was 815 no surrounding supply of space into which things could, so to speak, disperse and be dissolved, which is the secret of the eternity of the all-embracing universe, outside which there is neither any space into which things could scatter nor are there bodies which could assail it and dissolve it with their powerful impact. But in case the soul is to be 820 considered immortal rather for this reason, that it is shielded and protected by life-giving forces, either because influences alien to its well-being do not approach it at all or because those which do

aut quia quae ueniunt aliqua ratione recedunt
pulsa prius quam quid noceant sentire queamus,
....
praeter enim quam quod morbis cum corporis aegret,
aduenit id quod eam de rebus saepe futuris 825
macerat inque metu male habet curisque fatigat,
praeteritisque male admissis peccata remordent.
adde furorem animi proprium atque obliuia rerum,
adde quod in nigras lethargi mergitur undas.

Nil igitur mors est ad nos neque pertinet hilum, 830
quandoquidem natura animi mortalis habetur,
et, uelut anteacto nil tempore sensimus aegri
ad confligendum uenientibus undique Poenis,
omnia cum belli trepido concussa tumultu
horrida contremuere sub altis aetheris oris 835
in dubioque fuere utrorum ad regna cadendum
omnibus humanis esset terraque marique,
sic, ubi non erimus, cum corporis atque animai
discidium fuerit quibus e sumus uniter apti,
scilicet haud nobis quicquam, qui non erimus tum, 840
accidere omnino poterit sensumque mouere,
non si terra mari miscebitur et mare caelo.
et si iam nostro sentit de corpore postquam
distractast animi natura animaeque potestas,
nil tamen est ad nos, qui comptu coniugioque 845
corporis atque animae consistimus uniter apti.
nec, si materiem nostram collegerit aetas
post obitum rursumque redegerit ut sita nunc est
atque iterum nobis fuerint data lumina uitae,
pertineat quicquam tamen ad nos id quoque factum, 850
interrupta semel cum sit repetentia nostri.
et nunc nil ad nos de nobis attinet, ante
qui fuimus, nec iam de illis nos adficit angor.

---

835 oris *Gifanius*: auris *O*: auras *Q*
853 nec *Marullus*: neque *Lachmann*: nil *Merrill*: *omiserunt OQ*
post 823 *lacunam indicauit Lambinus* (*e.g.* hoc fieri totum contra manifesta docet res *Munro, Bailey: cf.* 690)

approach are for some reason repulsed and retreat before we can sense what harm they do, <plain fact teaches us that the complete opposite of this is the case>. For apart from the fact that it falls ill during the 825 body's diseases, it is visited by thoughts about the future which often rack it, reduce it to a sorry state of fear and exhaust it with anxieties, while after past misdeeds its sins torment it with remorse. Consider too the madness peculiar to the mind and forgetfulness of things; consider how it is plunged into the black, oblivious waters of coma.

830 Death therefore is nothing to us and does not concern us in the slightest, since the soul's mortal nature is established. Just as in time past we experienced nothing amiss when the Carthaginians were 835 approaching for conflict from all quarters, and everything beneath the lofty shores of heaven, shaken by the terrifying tumult of war, shuddered and trembled and was uncertain under which nation's dominion on land and sea all mankind must fall, even so when we do not exist, when the divorce of body and soul, whose union gives us our 840 single identity, has taken place, it is clear that nothing at all will be able to befall us or move our senses (at that time we shall not exist), not if the earth is mingled with the sea and the sea with the sky. And even if the mind and spirit do feel after they have been sundered from 845 our body, it is still nothing to us, whose single identity results from the union and marriage of body and soul. Nor, even if time were to collect our matter after our demise and to restore it once more to its present arrangement, and the light of life were bestowed on us a second time, 850 would even that eventuality at all concern us, when our self-remembrance had once been interrupted. At the present time, too, we have no concern about the selves we previously were and are not now

nam cum respicias immensi temporis omne
praeteritum spatium, tum motus materiai 855
multimodis quam sint, facile hoc adcredere possis,
semina saepe in eodem, ut nunc sunt, ordine posta
haec eadem, quibus e nunc nos sumus, ante fuisse. [865]
nec memori tamen id quimus reprehendere mente: [858]
inter enim iectast uitai pausa uageque 860[859]
deerrarunt passim motus ab sensibus omnes. [860]
debet enim, misere si forte aegreque futurumst, [861]
ipse quoque esse in eo tum tempore, cui male possit [862]
accidere. id quoniam mors eximit esseque probet [863]
illum cui possint incommoda conciliari, 865[864]
scire licet nobis nil esse in morte timendum
nec miserum fieri qui non est posse neque hilum
differre an nullo fuerit iam tempore natus,
mortalem uitam mors cum immortalis ademit.

Proinde ubi se uideas hominem indignarier ipsum, 870
post mortem fore ut aut putescat corpore posto
aut flammis interfiat malisue ferarum,
scire licet non sincerum sonere atque subesse
caecum aliquem cordi stimulum, quamuis neget ipse
credere se quemquam sibi sensum in morte futurum. 875
non, ut opinor, enim dat quod promittit et unde,
nec radicitus e uita se tollit et eicit,
sed facit esse sui quiddam super inscius ipse.
uiuus enim sibi cum proponit quisque futurum,
corpus uti uolucres lacerent in morte feraeque, 880
ipse sui miseret: neque enim se diuidit illim
nec remouet satis a proiecto corpore et illum
se fingit sensuque suo contaminat adstans.
hinc indignatur se mortalem esse creatum
nec uidet in uera nullum fore morte alium se 885
qui possit uiuus sibi se lugere peremptum
stansque iacentem se lacerari uriue dolere.

---

856 multimodis *B*: multimodi *OQACFL*

858 [865] *hic locauit Lachmann*

868 an nullo *Pontanus*: annullo anullo *O*: anullo anullo *Q*

855 affected by anguish about them. For when you look back at all the past expanse of measureless time and in turn at the manifold variety of the motions of matter, you could easily come to believe that these same seeds of which we are now composed have often been placed in the same arrangement as they are now. Our minds, however, are unable to 860 retain any memory of this: a severance of life has, you see, been interposed, and all the motions have strayed and wandered in all directions away from the senses. Why, if it chances that misery and distress lie in store, the person must himself exist at that actual point in time for the suffering to be able to overtake him. Since death removes 865 this possibility and rules out the existence of the person on whom misfortunes can be conferred, it is plain to see that we need fear nothing in death, that a non-existent person cannot suffer misery, and that it makes not a jot of difference whether or not he has ever been born in the first place, once his mortal life has been carried off by immortal death.

870 Accordingly, when you see a man complaining of his own future, how after death he will either rot away once buried or be destroyed by flames or the jaws of wild beasts, it is plain to see that he does not ring true and that some subconscious impulse is goading his heart, however 875 much he himself claims not to believe that he will have any consciousness in death. He fails, as I see it, to concede what he professes, and the basis for it, and he does not completely uproot and expel himself from life, but unconsciously imagines that some part of his own self survives. Indeed, when in life each individual pictures to 880 himself that birds and beasts will mangle his body in death, he feels sorry for himself, because he does not divorce himself from it or distance himself adequately from the exposed corpse: he fancies that person to be himself, and infects him with his own consciousness as he 885 stands by. This is why he complains of his mortal birth and fails to see that in actual death there will be no other self which can live to bewail its death and can stand by grieving that the prostrate self is

nam si in morte malumst malis morsuque ferarum
tractari, non inuenio qui non sit acerbum
ignibus impositum calidis torrescere flammis, 890
aut in melle situm suffocari atque rigere
frigore, cum summo gelidi cubat aequore saxi,
urgeriue superne obtritum pondere terrae.

'Iam iam non domus accipiet te laeta neque uxor
optima, nec dulces occurrent oscula nati 895
praeripere et tacita pectus dulcedine tangent.
non poteris factis florentibus esse tuisque
praesidium. misero misere' aiunt 'omnia ademit
una dies infesta tibi tot praemia uitae.'
illud in his rebus non addunt 'nec tibi earum 900
iam desiderium rerum super insidet una.'
quod bene si uideant animo dictisque sequantur,
dissoluant animi magno se angore metuque.
'tu quidem ut es leto sopitus, sic eris aeui
quod superest cunctis priuatu' doloribus aegris: 905
at nos horrifico cinefactum te prope busto
insatiabiliter defleuimus, aeternumque
nulla dies nobis maerorem e pectore demet.'
illud ab hoc igitur quaerendumst, quid sit amari
tanto opere, ad somnum si res redit atque quietem, 910
cur quisquam aeterno possit tabescere luctu.

Hoc etiam faciunt ubi discubuere tenentque
pocula saepe homines et inumbrant ora coronis,
ex animo ut dicant 'breuis hic est fructus homullis;
iam fuerit neque post umquam reuocare licebit.' 915
tamquam in morte mali cum primis hoc sit eorum,
quod sitis exurat miseros atque arida torrat
aut aliae cuius desiderium insideat rei.

---

907 defleuimus *MSS*: deflebimus *editor Brixiensis*
917 torrat O^1 *Q*: torret *O*: torreat *Gifanius*

being mangled or cremated. Indeed, if it is an evil in death to be mauled by the gnawing jaws of wild beasts, I do not see how it is not a
890 cruel fate to be placed on a pyre and scorched by burning flames, or to be stifled by being set in honey and to be stiff with cold while reclining on the smooth surface of a chill slab, or to be crushed by a weight of earth pressing down from above.

'No more now will your household welcome you in joy, or your
895 peerless wife, nor will your darling children run to snatch the first kiss and touch your heart with silent delight. You will not be able to flourish in your achievements or to protect your family. Unhappy man,' they cry 'unhappily has one cruel day stripped you of all the
900 many prizes of life.' In the course of these remarks, what they fail to add is this: 'and at the same time, you now retain no longing for those things either.' Were they to grasp this properly in their minds and to match their words to it, they would release themselves from great mental anguish and fear. 'For your part, you will be lulled in death's
905 sleep, as you are now, for the rest of time, delivered from all pain and distress: but we, when the horrific pyre had reduced you to ashes, stood by and bewept you insatiably, and no day will remove the everlasting sorrow from our hearts.' So the question that must be asked
910 of this individual is what is so enormously bitter, if there is a return to sleep and rest, as to enable anyone to waste away in everlasting sorrow.

Again, when they have reclined at table and are holding their cups and shading their brows with garlands, men often have the habit of saying,
915 in all sincerity, 'Shortlived is this enjoyment for poor mortals; soon it will be over, and it will be impossible ever to recall it later.' As if in death this is to be amongst their foremost tribulations, that parching thirst should burn and scorch the poor wretches or that they should

nec sibi enim quisquam tum se uitamque requirit,
cum pariter mens et corpus sopita quiescunt; 920
nam licet aeternum per nos sic esse soporem,
nec desiderium nostri nos adficit ullum.
et tamen haudquaquam nostros tunc illa per artus
longe ab sensiferis primordia motibus errant,
cum correptus homo ex somno se colligit ipse. 925
multo igitur mortem minus ad nos esse putandumst,
si minus esse potest quam quod nil esse uidemus;
maior enim turba et disiectus materiai
consequitur leto, nec quisquam expergitus exstat,
frigida quem semel est uitai pausa secuta. 930

Denique si uocem rerum natura repente
mittat et hoc alicui nostrum sic increpet ipsa
'quid tibi tanto operest, mortalis, quod nimis aegris
luctibus indulges? quid mortem congemis ac fles?
nam si grata fuit tibi uita anteacta priorque 935
et non omnia pertusum congesta quasi in uas
commoda perfluxere atque ingrata interiere,
cur non ut plenus uitae conuiua recedis
aequo animoque capis securam, stulte, quietem?
sin ea quae fructus cumque es periere profusa 940
uitaque in offensast, cur amplius addere quaeris,
rursum quod pereat male et ingratum occidat omne,
non potius uitae finem facis atque laboris?
nam tibi praeterea quod machiner inueniamque,
quod placeat, nil est: eadem sunt omnia semper. 945
si tibi non annis corpus iam marcet et artus
confecti languent, eadem tamen omnia restant,
omnia si perges uiuendo uincere saecla,

---

928 turba et *Goebel*: turbae *OQ*
941 offensast *Codex Musaei Britannici*: offensost *O'Q*: offensust *Lambinus*

920 have an inner longing for some other thing! Why, at the times when mind and body alike are lulled and at rest, no one misses himself and his waking life: indeed, in this state the sleep might for all it matters to us be everlasting, and no longing for our waking selves affects us. And 925 yet in that case, where a man starts up from sleep and gathers himself together, those primary particles throughout the frame are by no means straying far from the paths of motion that carry sensation. Death is therefore to be regarded as something much less, if there can be anything less than what we can see to be nothing, because a greater disturbance and dispersal of matter ensues at death, nor does anyone 930 wake and rise once the chill severance of life has overtaken him.

Again, suppose Nature were suddenly to take voice and personally to direct this reproach at one of us as follows: 'What ails you, mortal, so desperately, that you indulge to excess in unwholesome grief? Why do 935 you bemoan and bewail death? Think; if your earlier life that is now spent was pleasing to you and all its blessings have not, as if consigned to a punctured vessel, drained away and been ungratefully dissipated, why do you not withdraw like a sated guest at life's banquet and, fool that you are, embrace carefree rest with equanimity? But if whatever 940 things have been placed at your disposal have been poured away and wasted and life is objectionable to you, why do you seek to add anything more, for it all in its turn to be uselessly wasted and to pass unappreciated away, and not rather make an end of life and of 945 tribulation? Why, there is nothing further that I can devise or invent to please you: all things are always the same. If your body is not already withering through its years and your limbs are not languishing in exhaustion, all things nevertheless remain the same, even if you are going to surpass all generations in survival and, what

atque etiam potius, si numquam sis moriturus',
quid respondemus, nisi iustam intendere litem 950
naturam et ueram uerbis exponere causam?
grandior hic uero si iam seniorque queratur [955]
atque obitum lamentetur miser amplius aequo, [952]
non merito inclamet magis et uoce increpet acri? [953]
'aufer abhinc lacrimas, baratro, et compesce querellas. 955[954]
omnia perfunctus uitai praemia marces;
sed quia semper aues quod abest, praesentia temnis,
imperfecta tibi elapsast ingrataque uita
et nec opinanti mors ad caput adstitit ante
quam satur ac plenus possis discedere rerum. 960
nunc aliena tua tamen aetate omnia mitte
aequo animoque agedum iam aliis concede: necessest.'
iure, ut opinor, agat, iure increpet inciletque.
cedit enim rerum nouitate extrusa uetustas
semper, et ex aliis aliud reparare necessest. 965
nec quisquam in barathrum nec Tartara deditur atra;
materies opus est ut crescant postera saecla,
quae tamen omnia te uita perfuncta sequentur;
nec minus ergo ante haec quam tu cecidere cadentque.
sic alid ex alio numquam desistet oriri, 970
uitaque mancipio nulli datur, omnibus usu.
respice item quam nil ad nos anteacta uetustas
temporis aeterni fuerit quam nascimur ante.
hoc igitur speculum nobis natura futuri
temporis exponit post mortem denique nostram. 975
numquid ibi horribile apparet, num triste uidetur
quicquam, non omni somno securius exstat?

Atque ea nimirum, quaecumque Acherunte profundo
prodita sunt esse, in uita sunt omnia nobis.
nec miser impendens magnum timet aere saxum 980
Tantalus, ut famast, cassa formidine torpens,

952[955] *hic locauit Lachmann*
955[954] baratro *Bailey*: baratre *OQ*: balatro *Heinsius*: blatero *Merrill*
962 iam aliis *Marullus*: magnis *OQ*: iam annis *Krokiewicz*: gnatis *Bernays*: humanis *Munro*: *alii alia*
969 ante haec *OQ*: antehac *Heinze*

950 is more, even if you were never going to die.' What do we reply, except that Nature is bringing a just action and presenting a valid case in her plea? But now suppose that someone of maturer, more advanced years made himself wretched by deploring and bewailing his demise beyond reason; would she not justifiably reproach him more sternly 955 and berate him in more aggressive tones? 'Away with your tears, you insatiable glutton, and hush your complaints. You've had your full share of all life's prizes and are withering away, but, because you always long for what is not to hand and despise what is, your life has slipped by incomplete and unenjoyed, and you have unexpectedly 960 found death standing at your head before you can depart filled and sated with good things. Still, forget all behaviour inappropriate to your years: come on, now make way for others with equanimity; it is inevitable.' Justifiably, in my view, would she plead her case, 965 justifiably would she rail and scold. Why, the old order constantly gives way, ousted by the new, and one thing is inevitably made up afresh from others. Nor is anyone surrendered into the darkness of Tartarus and its pit: matter is required so that subsequent generations may grow, all of which, however, will follow you when they have completed their lives; accordingly, they have perished before this no 970 less than will you, and will continue to perish. Thus one thing will never cease to arise from another, and life is given to no one freehold, but to everyone on lease. Look back in turn and see how the eternity of time that elapsed of old before our birth was absolutely nothing to us; 975 this, then, is a mirror-image revealed to us by Nature of the time to come once we finally die. Is anything terrible to be seen there? Is there anything forbidding in the prospect? Is it not more carefree than any slumber?

Indubitably, too, all those things which are recorded as existing in the 980 depths of Acheron exist for us in life. No wretched Tantalus fears a great rock, as the story goes, hanging over him from the air, paralysed

sed magis in uita diuum metus urget inanis
mortalis, casumque timent quem cuique ferat fors.
nec Tityon uolucres ineunt Acherunte iacentem
nec quod sub magno scrutentur pectore quicquam 985
perpetuam aetatem possunt reperire profecto:
quamlibet immani proiectu corporis exstet,
qui non sola nouem dispessis iugera membris
obtineat, sed qui terrai totius orbem,
non tamen aeternum poterit perferre dolorem 990
nec praebere cibum proprio de corpore semper.
sed Tityos nobis hic est, in amore iacentem
quem uolucres lacerant atque exest anxius angor
aut alia quauis scindunt cuppedine curae.
Sisyphus in uita quoque nobis ante oculos est 995
qui petere a populo fascis saeuasque securis
imbibit et semper uictus tristisque recedit.
nam petere imperium quod inanest nec datur umquam
atque in eo semper durum sufferre laborem,
hoc est aduerso nixantem trudere monte 1000
saxum quod tamen e summo iam uertice rursum
uoluitur et plani raptim petit aequora campi.
deinde animi ingratam naturam pascere semper
atque explere bonis rebus satiareque numquam,
quod faciunt nobis annorum tempora, circum 1005
cum redeunt fetusque ferunt uariosque lepores,
nec tamen explemur uitai fructibus umquam,
hoc, ut opinor, id est, aeuo florente puellas
quod memorant laticem pertusum congerere in uas,
quod tamen expleri nulla ratione potestur. 1010
Cerberus et Furiae iam vero et lucis egestas,
Tartarus horriferos eructans faucibus aestus -
haec neque sunt usquam nec possunt esse profecto,

---

993 uolucres *MSS*: aerumnae *Watt, Museum Helueticum 47 (1990) 122*
post 1010 *lacunam indicauerunt editores nonnulli, post* 1011 *Munro*
1013 haec *Marullus*: qui *MSS*

by empty dread, but rather vain fear of the gods oppresses mortals in life and they each fear the fate which may fall by chance to their lot.
985 No winged birds penetrate any prostrate Tityos in Acheron, nor to be sure could they find anything deep in his giant breast to pry into for an eternity of time: however vast you suppose the extent of his spread-eagled body, so that his sprawling limbs cover not merely nine acres
990 but the circle of the whole earth, he will still not be able to keep on suffering everlasting pain or to furnish food from his own body for ever. But Tityos is here amongst us, the man who, prostrated by love, is rent by winged Cupids and devoured by gnawing anguish or torn by
995 cares inspired by any other form of Desire. Sisyphus also exists in life before our eyes, the man who thirsts to seek the rods and cruel axes from the people and always withdraws, beaten and dismayed; because to seek power which is empty and never conferred and always to
1000 undergo harsh tribulation in the process is to labour to thrust a rock up a mountain, only for it to roll back again once it has reached the topmost peak and rapidly revert to the flat surface of the plain. In turn, constantly to feed an ungrateful disposition yet never fill it full or
1005 satisfy it with good things, as the seasons of the year do for us when they come round again bringing their produce and their varied delights without our ever being satisfied by life's fruits, this, as I see it, is the story of the girls in the bloom of their years gathering liquid in a leaky
1010 vessel which despite their efforts can in no way be filled full. As for Cerberus, the Furies, the denial of light, and Tartarus belching horrific hot blasts from its jaws, these things assuredly do not and cannot exist

sed metus in uita poenarum pro male factis
est insignibus insignis scelerisque luella, 1015
carcer et horribilis de saxo iactu' deorsum,
uerbera carnifices robur pix lammina taedae;
quae tamen etsi absunt, at mens sibi conscia factis
praemetuens adhibet stimulos torretque flagellis
nec uidet interea qui terminus esse malorum 1020
possit nec quae sit poenarum denique finis
atque eadem metuit magis haec ne in morte grauescant.
hic Acherusia fit stultorum denique uita.

Hoc etiam tibi tute interdum dicere possis:
'lumina sis oculis etiam bonus Ancu' reliquit 1025
qui melior multis quam tu fuit, improbe, rebus.
inde alii multi reges rerumque potentes
occiderunt, magnis qui gentibus imperitarunt.
ille quoque ipse, uiam qui quondam per mare magnum
strauit iterque dedit legionibus ire per altum 1030
ac pedibus salsas docuit superare lacunas
et contempsit equis insultans murmura ponti,
lumine adempto animam moribundo corpore fudit.
Scipiadas, belli fulmen, Carthaginis horror,
ossa dedit terrae proinde ac famul infimus esset. 1035
adde repertores doctrinarum atque leporum,
adde Heliconiadum comites, quorum unus Homerus
sceptra potitus eadem aliis sopitu' quietest.
denique Democritum, postquam matura uetustas
admonuit memores motus languescere mentis, 1040
sponte sua leto caput obuius obtulit ipse.
ipse Epicurus obit decurso lumine uitae,
qui genus humanum ingenio superauit et omnis
restinxit stellas exortus ut aetherius sol.
tu uero dubitabis et indignabere obire, 1045

1016 iactu' deorsum *Lambinus*: iactus eorum *OQ*: iactu' reorum *Heinsius*

1018 factis *OQ*: facti *Auancius*

1031 superare *L*: super ire *OQ*

1015 anywhere; but there does exist in life signal fear of retribution for signal misdeeds and there exists atonement for crime, incarceration, the horror of precipitation from the rock, the lash, the executioner, the dungeon, the pitch, the metal plate, the torch: even in their absence, the conscience-stricken mind still, in fearful anticipation, applies the goad 1020 and the searing scourge; it fails in the process to see what limit there can be to its ills and what end there finally is to its punishment, and is afraid in case these very evils grow worse in death. In short, it is here on earth that the life of fools becomes a Hell.

This is a further argument you could sometimes address to yourself: 1025 'Even the good Ancus closed his eyes on the light of day, a man in many ways better than you, shameless creature that you are. Since then, many other kings and potentates, who have held sway over great 1030 nations, have passed away. Even the very king who once paved a path over the mighty ocean and enabled his armies to tread their route over the high seas, teaching them to overcome the salty pools on foot and despising the murmurs of the deep as his horses pranced over it - even he forfeited the light of life and breathed out the soul from his dying body. The sturdy scion of the Scipios, that thunderbolt in war, the bane 1035 of Carthage, consigned his bones to the earth as if he were the most abject menial. Consider too the founders of the sciences and the arts, consider the attendants of Helicon's maidens, from whose number Homer, while unique in gaining the sceptre, is lulled in the same rest 1040 as the others. Again, when ripe old age warned Democritus that the motions of memory in his mind were failing, he voluntarily confronted death and himself sacrificed his life to it. Epicurus himself departed, when the daylight of his life had run its course - he who outstripped the human race with his genius and outshone all the stars like the risen 1045 sun in the heavens. And are *you* going to be hesitant and indignant

mortua cui uita est prope iam uiuo atque uidenti,
qui somno partem maiorem conteris aeui
et uigilans stertis nec somnia cernere cessas
sollicitamque geris cassa formidine mentem
nec reperire potes tibi quid sit saepe mali, cum 1050
ebrius urgeris multis miser undique curis
atque animi incerto fluitans errore uagaris?'

Si possent homines, proinde ac sentire uidentur
pondus inesse animo quod se grauitate fatiget,
e quibus id fiat causis quoque noscere et unde 1055
tanta mali tamquam moles in pectore constet,
haud ita uitam agerent ut nunc plerumque uidemus
quid sibi quisque uelit nescire et quaerere semper
commutare locum quasi onus deponere possit.
exit saepe foras magnis ex aedibus ille, 1060
esse domi quem pertaesumst, subitoque reuertit
quippe foris nilo melius qui sentiat esse.
currit agens mannos ad uillam praecipitanter,
auxilium tectis quasi ferre ardentibus instans;
oscitat extemplo, tetigit cum limina uillae, 1065
aut abit in somnum grauis atque obliuia quaerit
aut etiam properans urbem petit atque reuisit.
hoc se quisque modo fugit, at quem scilicet, ut fit,
effugere haud potis est, ingratis haeret et odit
propterea, morbi quia causam non tenet aeger; 1070
quam bene si uideat, iam rebus quisque relictis
naturam primum studeat cognoscere rerum,
temporis aeterni quoniam, non unius horae,
ambigitur status, in quo sit mortalibus omnis
aetas, post mortem quae restat cumque, manenda. 1075

Denique tanto opere in dubiis trepidare periclis
quae mala nos subigit uitai tanta cupido?
certa quidem finis uitae mortalibus adstat,
nec deuitari letum pote quin obeamus.

1052 animi *Lambinus*: animo *OQ*
1061 reuertit *addidit Politianus*: *omiserunt OQ*
1075 manenda *Lambinus*: manendo *OQ*

about departing, you whose life is practically defunct already while you still live and breathe? You waste the greater part of your span in slumber, you snore whilst awake and never rest from daydreaming; 1050 you are saddled with a mind agitated by baseless dread; you are often unable to discover what is the matter with you, when the host of cares besetting you on all sides reduces you to a pathetic stupor and you drift erratically, borne on by the unsteady fluctuation of your mind.'

Men obviously feel that there is a weight on their minds, so heavy that 1055 it wears them out. If they could also discover the causes for this, and the source of this huge mass of woe, as it were, which is constantly in their breasts, they would not lead their lives in the way in which, as it is, we generally see them, with no one knowing what he really wants and always seeking a change of scene as if he could thus lay down his 1060 burden. Often, a man sallies forth from his huge mansion, thoroughly bored with being at home, and suddenly returns, because he finds it no better out of doors. He rushes to his country villa, driving his Gallic 1065 ponies headlong, as if hurrying to bring help to a burning building: he suddenly yawns, once he reaches the villa's threshold, or escapes drowsily into slumber, seeking oblivion, or even makes hastily back to revisit the city. In this way each man flees from himself, but is bound against his will to the self which he obviously cannot actually escape 1070 and loathes it for this reason, that, ill as he is, he knows not the cause of his disease; if each man were to see this clearly, he would then forget everything else and make it his first concern to learn the nature of the universe, since the question at issue is his state not for a single 1075 hour but for eternity - the state in which mortals must await every morsel of the time remaining after their death.

Again, what dire passion for life compels us to suffer such great anxieties amidst uncertainties and perils? An appointed end for life is at hand for mortals, and our encounter with death cannot possibly be

praeterea uersamur ibidem atque insumus usque 1080
nec noua uiuendo procuditur ulla uoluptas.
sed dum abest quod auemus, id exsuperare uidetur
cetera; post aliud, cum contigit illud, auemus,
et sitis aequa tenet uitai semper hiantis.
posteraque in dubiost fortunam quam uehat aetas, 1085
quidue ferat nobis casus quiue exitus instet.
nec prorsum uitam ducendo demimus hilum
tempore de mortis nec delibare ualemus
quo minus esse diu possimus forte perempti.
proinde licet quot uis uiuendo condere saecla: 1090
mors aeterna tamen nilo minus illa manebit,
nec minus ille diu iam non erit, ex hodierno
lumine qui finem uitai fecit, et ille
mensibus atque annis qui multis occidit ante.

1080 avoided. Besides, we dwell and ever have our being in the same place, and no new pleasure is forged by living on; but while what we crave is not to hand, it seems to outstrip everything else; afterwards, once it has come our way, we crave something different, and an undiminished 1085 thirst for life keeps us ever open-mouthed. It is also uncertain what fortune future time may bring, what chance may send our way, or what outcome lies in store. Nor by prolonging life do we take away a single instant from the time-span of our death, nor have we the power to whittle anything away so as somehow to reduce the period of our 1090 extinction; accordingly, you can live to lay to rest as many generations as you like, yet that eternity of death will none the less await you, and the man who has concluded his life by departing today's light will now be non-existent for no shorter a time than the man who passed away many months and years earlier.

Commentary

1-93 INTRODUCTION

1-30 *Praise of Epicurus*

Eulogies of the master are included in the introductions to four of the six books (cf. I 62-79, V 1-54 and VI 1-42); this one alone takes the form of a second person address rather than third person description. All four, however, convey an attitude of quasi-religious awe for Epicurus and his achievements (see on 1-3, 15 and 28-30 below); in III, V and VI, where they open the book, they recall and simultaneously replace the opening invocation of a deity traditional in epic. All four have as their central theme Epicurus' deliverance of mankind; in I and III he has rescued them primarily from the two great religious fears (*animi terrores* 16), of the gods and of death, which are the main targets of the poem, while in V and VI he has provided salvation not only from these but also from the misery resulting from the misguided values condemned by his ethical code (see Introduction III).

1-3 **O thou, who . . . o glory of the Grecian race:** the invocation is hymnic; Epicurus is identified by his achievements (on which 9ff. are to expand) and by his nationality (cf. *Graius homo* I 66), just as a conventional hymn or prayer detailed the deity's powers and favourite haunts. Epicurus' name is excluded from all four eulogies, as if by religious taboo, and appears in the poem only once, in an entirely different context, at III 1042. The rhetorical repetition of the second person in *te . . . tuis* 3 (cf. *tu . . . tu . . . tuisque* 9-10) contributes to the hymnic effect of the long opening apostrophe, and the repetition of *O*, rightly reinstated in 1 by Timpanaro, *Philologus* 104 (1960) 147-9 (though Kenney *ad loc.* and West (1969) 80 exaggerate the inferiority of *E*, 'out of <such great darkness>', the reading generally accepted previously), heightens the emotional impact (cf. Horace, *Odes* I 32.13f.). The alliteration, immediately conspicuous in the successive predominance of *t*, *l* and *p* in the first one and a half lines, further enhances the address.

darkness . . . light, illuminating: a key image, which recurs, with several variations, throughout the poem. Here, in its primary application, the light of philosophy dispels the darkness of ignorance, unhappiness and superstitious fear (cf., e.g., V 11-12). The image dominates the whole eulogy, where the central theme is of revelation (*uideo* 17, *apparet* 18, *nusquam apparent* 25, *omnia dispiciantur* 26, *manifesta, patens* and *retecta est* 30); it reappears in the second part of the introduction (see on 35-6 and 87-93 below) and is taken up again near the end of the book, where it is again applied, in a striking variation, to Epicurus (see on 1042-4).

the first: as at I 66-7 and 9 below (*rerum inuentor*), Lucretius stresses Epicurus' originality, which is here contrasted with his own dependence (*te sequor* 3): he makes no mention of Epicurus' debt to the earlier atomists Leucippus and Democritus, which the master himself had been reluctant to acknowledge. But a more objective analysis is not to be expected in an impassioned eulogy, and in

Lucretius' eyes it was only in the complete Epicurean system that the whole truth, and so salvation, was to be found.

life's blessings: i.e. the things in life pronounced good for men by Epicurean ethical theory (unlike, e.g., power and excessive wealth); though 14-27 go on to concentrate on the elimination of the religious fears, this phrase suggests deliverance from the moral causes of unhappiness.

4 **firmly set my own footsteps:** the firmness of the steps (*ficta* is not here from *fingo*, but the older form of *fixa*, from *figo*), the parallelism between *pedum pono uestigia* and *pressis signis*, and the *p* alliteration all fit the dogged fidelity with which the poet is following his master.

5 **not so much . . . as:** *ita . . . quam* replaces the more usual *tam . . . quam*, affording an extra dactyl.

6-8 **the swallow . . . the swan:** for the twittering of the former, which the Greeks equated with the speech of barbarians, cf. Aristophanes, *Frogs* 93 and 680; for the beauty of the swan's imaginary song, cf. II 505 and Theocritus 5.136-7, where swans are contrasted with hoopoes. Lucretius gives a more generous self-appraisal at IV 180-2, repeated at IV 909-11, where to spur the reader on to the next argument he promises a honeyed exposition rather than a long one, comparing the superiority of the swan's brief song to the raucousness of the crane. Kenney also compares Pindar, *Olympians* 2.87-8, where rival poets resemble ravens screeching at an eagle. The juxtaposition of *hirundo* and *cycnis*, each emphatically placed in its line, heightens the contrast.

kids . . . horse: the contrasted *haedi* and *fortis equi uis* again receive emphasis from their position. The wavering limbs of the former recall the unsteady gambolling of the new-born farm-animals at I 259-61. *fortis equi uis* is a poetic periphrasis modelled on the Homeric use of βίη + a genitive (e.g. 'the might of Heracles' for 'the mighty Heracles'); in such periphrases, *uis* and βίη sometimes lose something of their original sense, which is here reinforced by *fortis*. Such periphrases are a feature of Lucretius' style, and in III are exemplified most frequently in the use of *natura,* or sometimes *uis* or *potestas,* with the genitives *animi* and *animae* to denote the two parts of the soul; see on 130-1 and 277 below.

to match: *consimile et* = the more usual *consimile ac* (sc. *facere possit*).

9-13 Though the lines further develop the subject of 3-8, Lucretius' relationship to his master, the plurals *nobis* 9 and *nos* 12 are probably not merely editorial; they are equally applicable to fellow-devotees of the school, with whom it is natural for him to associate himself.

9-10 **father . . . discoverer . . . suppliest us with a father's precepts:** Epicurus' beneficence is developed rhetorically, in a tricolon climax; for the hymnic anaphora with *tu*, taken further with *tuisque* 10, see on 1-3 above. *pater* and *patria* are doubly appropriate, fitting both a Roman god and a Roman *paterfamilias. rerum inuentor* begins the explanation of the light image in 1-2, and also takes up the theme of Epicurus' originality (*primus* 2).

10-13 **thy illustrious pages:** the vocative *inclute* suggests superhuman status; the poet applies it also to his symbolic Venus at I 40 and to Memmius, the dedicatee of the poem (Introduction I and II), in the context of the assertion of Epicurus' own status as *deus*, at V 8. Epicurus' writings were voluminous, amounting to some three hundred rolls (Diogenes Laertius X 26), and were the counterpart of sacred books to his disciples (cf. *aurea dicta, aurea* 12-13). From them only three letters to disciples (one perhaps the work of a pupil rather than the master) and two collections of maxims survive; the rest, including his *magnum opus*, the 37 books *On Nature*, have perished but for occasional fragments.

just as bees . . . savour . . . even so do we feast upon: an adaptation of the comparison, commonplace in antiquity, between the bee and the poet, who derives honey from the gardens of the Muses (cf., e.g., Plato, *Ion* 534a); Lucretius and his fellow-disciples here derive philosophical honey from the extensive study of Epicurus' works (one of the highest pleasures possible in the system), though in Lucretius' case the inspiration afforded is not only philosophical but also, as in the stock bee-image, poetic. *libant* (literally 'take a little of' and so 'taste' or 'sip'), which is applied to bees also by Virgil, *Georgics* IV 54, best matches *depascimur* if *depascimur dicta = pascimur de dictis.*

flower-filled: compounds like *florifer* (literally 'flower-bearing'), common in Greek and the early Roman poets, are frequent in Lucretius, and are sometimes of his own coinage; they contribute to the archaic flavour of the poem. They are used more sparingly by later writers, and condemned by Quintilian I 5.70 as unsuited to the language.

all the blooms . . . all thy . . . words: the repetition of *omnia* reinforces the comparison and stresses the exhaustiveness of the researches of the poet and his fellow-disciples.

golden . . . golden: the impact of this purely rhetorical repetition (epanalepsis), used very sparingly by the poet, is heightened, as in most of his instances, by the initial position of the repeated word; cf. II 955-6, IV 789-90, V 950-1, VI 528-9 and 1168-9.

14-27 The lines explain (*nam* 14) not only why the *dicta* deserve immortality, but also the terms *pater* and *rerum inuentor* in 9, and the application of the light image in 1-2. 14-27 allude to the elimination of the two great religious fears by the philosophy (*ratio tua* 14), in particular by the physics; 18-24 explain how it dispels fear of the gods, 25-7 how it banishes fear of death, the specific target of book III.

14-15 **sprung from thy godlike intellect:** Epicurean philosophy is here boldly personified, but Kenney's claim of an implicit reference to the birth of Athena from the head of Zeus (an idea pressed still further by West, *Journal of Roman Studies* 62 (1972) 212) is weakened by the fact that the Epicurean intellect was situated not in the head but in the breast (cf. 140 below). *diuina* reflects the quasi-religious awe in which Epicurus was held (see on 1-30 above); cf. the superhuman feats of the *Graius homo* in slaying the monster of orthodox religion and traversing the infinite universe at I 62-79, the assertion of his status as *deus* at V 8, where he has conferred greater benefits on mankind than the traditional divine or semi-divine benefactors, and the allusion to his *diuina reperta* at VI 7. The attribution of divinity is, from an Epicurean point of view, in part literal: the Epicurean gods conformed exactly with the principles of Epicurean ethics, so achieving a life of perfect mental calm and serving as perfect models for human conduct (Introduction III); while Epicurus differed from them in his atomic constitution, his abode and his physical mortality, in this respect he matched them exactly. His implicit or explicit deification and the quasi-religious attitude towards him in the four Lucretian eulogies reflects the recurrent Epicurean paradox that Epicurean philosophy is more truly sacred and religious than orthodox religion.

proclaim the nature of the universe: *uociferari* is probably especially appropriate to prophetic utterance, thus fitting the implied antithesis with orthodox religion; cf. I 731-3, where the lavish praise elsewhere reserved for Epicurus is accorded to Empedocles, on poetic and philosophic grounds (*carmina quin etiam diuini pectoris eius / uociferantur et exponunt praeclara reperta, / ut uix humana uideatur stirpe creatus*). The echo of Lucretius' title in *naturam rerum* underlines the debt to Epicurus proclaimed in 3-8.

16-17 **the walls of the world part:** i.e. figuratively, thanks to Epicurean physics, which reveals the processes which take place beyond the limits of our own finite world and which are physically invisible to an observer on earth; cf. I 72ff., where Epicurus intellectually traverses the whole of the infinite universe beyond our world, and brings back as the prize of victory knowledge of scientific law, which enables him to triumph over the monster of conventional religion. Similarly here it is the revelation (*uideo* 17) afforded by Epicurean physics that banishes the two religious fears (*animi terrores* 16). *moenia mundi* is Lucretius' recurrent figurative phrase, rendered the more impressive by the alliteration, for the fiery shell of ether which formed the outermost limits of our world (and of the infinite number of others, more or less similar to it, which the universe contained: Introduction III).

the whole void: i.e. the infinite expanse of space, partly occupied and partly unoccupied, which is coextensive with the infinite universe.

18-24 The parting of the *moenia mundi* reveals first the true nature of the gods, who dwell in the *intermundia*, or spaces between worlds, and there enjoy self-sufficiency and ideal mental tranquillity; this revelation removes the fear that they control or intervene in the world or the workings of nature, for which they lack both the power and the motive. The passage is an adaptation of the Homeric description of the home of the conventional gods on Olympus at *Odyssey* VI 42-6:

ὅθι φασὶ θεῶν ἕδος ἀσφαλὲς αἰεὶ
ἔμμεναι· οὔτ᾽ ἀνέμοισι τινάσσεται οὔτε ποτ᾽ ὄμβρῳ
δεύεται οὔτε χιὼν ἐπιπίλναται, ἀλλὰ μάλ᾽ αἴθρη
πέπταται ἀνέφελος, λευκὴ δ᾽ ἐπιδέδρομεν αἴγλη·
τῷ ἔνι τέρπονται μάκαρες θεοὶ ἤματα πάντα

(where they say the abode of the gods stands safe for all time; never is it shaken by winds nor drenched by storm nor does snow come near, but a clear sky extends quite cloudless and above runs a white radiance; there the blessed gods take pleasure all their days). How literally Lucretius intends his picture of the physical surroundings of his gods is obviously rendered dubious by the passage's Homeric modelling; certainly it sheds no light on the question of the atomic basis of the Epicurean gods and their abodes in space (a full account is promised later, at V 155, but nowhere appears in the poem), or of their immortality, which they shared with no other category of atomic compound (Introduction III). By adopting Homer's picture of their peaceful environment and blessedness, and developing the latter in terms of self-sufficiency and mental tranquillity in 23-4, he is no doubt suggesting that it is here that traditional Olympian theology comes closest to the truth. Despite leaving vital philosophical questions unanswered, the passage is a poetic highlight; e.g. the slow, solemn rhythm of 18, with its 5 spondees, is appropriate to the awe-inspiring revelation, and the alliteration with harsh *n, c* and long *a* in 19-21a, where winds, storms and snow are described, gives way to more peaceful, liquid sounds, with *l* and long *u*, in 21b-22, which describe the positive features of the gods' peaceful environment. Tennyson echoes the passage both in his *Lucretius* (106-10), 'Where never creeps a cloud, or moves a wind, Nor ever falls the least white star of snow, Nor ever lowest roll of thunder moans, Nor sound of human sorrow mounts to mar Their sacred everlasting calm', and in *The Passing of Arthur* (427-9), 'The island valley of Avilion, Where falls not hail nor rain nor any snow, Nor ever wind blows loudly'.

18 **divine presence of the gods:** *numen*, from *nuo*, to nod, first denotes 'will', but is applied especially to divine will and then by extension to divine spirit or aura; its use here provides a more awe-inspiring phrase than plain *diui.* The latter is one of a number of second declension nouns which frequently retain the original form of the genitive plural (*-um* for *-orum*) in the classical period, like, e.g., *uir, deus* and *sestertius*.

20-1 **nor sullied:** the variation on the Homeric original, where snow does not 'approach', gives greater emphasis to the key point, the undisturbed peace of the gods' surroundings.

congealed by biting frost: Lucretius' scientific spirit leads him to add an explanation of the snow's formation, absent in the Homeric model; cf. West (1969) 32.

cloudless: *innubilus*, which looks back to *nec nubila . . . aspergunt* 19f., provides a sonorous equivalent for Homer's ἀνέφελος; it occurs nowhere else and is apparently coined for the purpose.

22 **beams . . . light:** the smile (*ridet*) here symbolises the benevolence of the environment. The line is reminiscent of I 8-9, *tibi rident aequora ponti,/ placatumque nitet diffuso lumine caelum*, where the sea's calm shimmering in spring is represented as a smile of welcome at the arrival of Venus. *diffuso* conveys a favourite Lucretian image, of light as liquid: cf., e.g., V 281-2, where the sun is a bounteous fountain of light flooding the sky. The light bathing the gods harmonises with the light imagery dominating the whole eulogy (see on 1-3 above): the gods have always enjoyed the light of the knowledge which Epicurus has for the first time made available to mankind, so enabling man to lead a godlike life (cf. on 28-30 and 322 below).

23-4 Lucretius here diverges furthest from Homer's description, explaining the gods' blessedness in terms of self-sufficiency and ideal mental calm; they thus have no motive to control or affect human life even if they could. The revelation simultaneously provides a model for human happiness: nature supplies all the gods' needs, just as, according to Epicurus, she usually supplies all human needs once unnatural and unnecessary desires have been put under control, and their self-sufficiency enables them to achieve freedom from bodily pain (ἀπονία) in addition to the freedom from mental turmoil (ἀταραξία) described in 24.

impairs: *delibare* here denotes 'to take away from' (cf. simple *libare* in 11) and so 'to diminish' or 'to spoil'; contrast the sense 'to take away' at 1088 and VI 621.

25-7 Epicurean philosophy banishes the fear of death through its revelation of the processes actually taking place below the earth, where the underworld of popular belief is non-existent.

nowhere . . . stand revealed: *nusquam apparent*, heralding the elimination of the second religious fear, answers *apparet* 18, which heralded that of the first.

realms of Acheron: *Acherusia templa* is an Ennian phrase (*Scenica* 98 Jocelyn). Acheron, one of the rivers of the traditional underworld, came to be used for the underworld as a whole. In Lucretius *templa*, though the word is applied to temples at VI 750 and 1274, usually has the archaic sense of 'regions' (originally areas of the sky marked off for augural purposes), but inevitably retains some of the religious overtones imparted by its augural sense and its classical usage: so here, Acheron is a source of religious awe for those ignorant of Epicurean philosophy. Though the context shows that the allusion is to the literal subterranean Hades of tradition, this could in turn symbolise any form of survival after death, which Epicurean *ratio* shows to be impossible; cf. 37, with note, and 86 below, where Acheron and its realms could be colourful symbols for death itself.

all the manifold processes . . . below: beneath his feet the Epicurean visualised first a flat earth at the world's centre, then the world's lower hemisphere, comprising first air and then the lower shell of ether encircling it (*moenia mundi* 18), and finally the infinite expanse of space beyond our world, containing an infinite number of worlds roughly similar to our own (Introduction III). *inane* (cf. 17) refers to the partly occupied space in all these areas.

28-30 **a sort of godlike pleasure and trembling awe:** eloquent testimony to Lucretius' almost religious feeling for Epicurus himself and for the majesty of nature which he has revealed. Pleasure, the Epicurean *summum bonum*, results because contemplation of the true nature of the universe removed the *animi terrores* and was in itself one of the highest pleasures open to the Epicurean. *diuina uoluptas* takes up *diuina mente* 15: Epicurus' godlike intellect has enabled the poet, and all mankind, to lead a godlike life of mental calm, as had Epicurus himself; cf. I 79, where Epicurus' victory over the monster of traditional religion has exalted mankind to the level of the gods. *horror* is particularly appropriate to religious awe, which in Lucretius' case is inspired not only by the magnitude of Epicurus' achievement in illuminating the whole of nature (29-30 take up the light image of 1-2 which has dominated the whole passage) but also by the majesty of the infinite universe which stands revealed; cf. V 1-2, on the impossibility of producing a poem worthy of the majesty of the theme and of Epicurus' discoveries (*pro rerum maiestate hisque repertis*).

31-93 ***Syllabus for the book and its importance***

The second part of the introduction to the book contains, as usual, a statement of its subject-matter (the nature of the soul and its two parts: 35-6) and purpose (the elimination of the fear of death: 37-40). But most space is devoted to the importance of this purpose: the striking claim that fear of death utterly spoils human life (38-40) is supported by two sustained illustrations, (a) (41-58) that of the professed, but non-Epicurean sceptics, whose old religious ideas of an after-life reassert themselves in time of stress, and (b) (59-86) that of the moral evils, starting with avarice and ambition and culminating paradoxically with suicide, to which, it is claimed, fear of death can lead or contribute. Structurally, the whole passage looks forward to the conclusion at 830-1094, which attempts to eradicate the fear of death whose effects are described here.

31-4 A summary of book I, which established the atomic nature of matter, and book II, which dealt with varieties of atomic motion and shape and their effect on compounds.

ultimate components: literally 'beginnings' (cf. the more frequent *primordia* and its metrical substitute *principia*: see on 236 below). The terms correspond to the Greek ἀρχή or ἀρχαί, applied not only by the atomists but by other Greek physicists to their concept of primary matter. Lucretius nowhere (cf. Introduction V) transliterates the Greek ἄτομοι, preferring less technical, more metaphorical terms: cf. *semina* (Greek σπέρματα) or 'seeds' at 127.

spontaneously, stimulated by ceaseless motion: the atoms moved naturally downwards, due to weight, but in other directions as a result of reverberation from collision and their tendency to slight, unpredictable swerve (Introduction III). *sponte sua* stresses that their motions result from their own nature, not from divine control.

different things: as often in Lucretius, *res quaeque* is used with reference to different types or species of thing, since objects of a given category behave, and are created, uniformly.

35-6 **it is clear:** *uideri* in Lucretius is always to be translated according to context: frequently (e.g. 164), though not always (e.g. 66), he uses it as a true passive, 'to be seen' rather than 'to seem', a sense comparatively rare in other authors. Since the poet is never in any doubt about his programme and its purposes, it is here to be taken as passive.

I must . . . illumine: the image of the light of philosophy dispelling the darkness of ignorance and fear, applied in 1-30 to Epicurus, is now picked up and applied to the poet, reflecting his relationship with his master and their common purpose: cf. I 933-4, where his poetry (*carmina*) is 'full of light' (*lucida*). The other half of the antithesis is taken up in *mortis nigrore* 39 (see on 38-40), where the blackness is the result of ignorance and fear.

the nature of mind and spirit: for the distinction between the two parts of the Epicurean soul, which emerges gradually from Lucretius' account at 94-416, see Introduction IV. *natura* here, as in 43 below, has its full force: contrast the periphrasis at 130-1 below (see note there).

37 **that fear of Acheron:** Acheron, like *Acherusia templa* (see on 25 above), is used in the first instance to sum up the traditional underworld or Hades, as is *Tartara leti* in 42 below. But there is no reason to suppose that the terms are restricted to the literal, still less that they allude specifically or exclusively to the primitive fears of punishment in Hades whose origin the poet seeks to explain at 978-1023. They could well be figurative, poetic expressions summing up the bogey of death in general, embracing not only ideas of any form of after-life but also Lucretius' own view of death as the end of consciousness, since the latter can inspire the instinctive reluctance to die which is one of the two central targets in the book's conclusion

(Introduction I and III). *metus Acheruntis* could thus well be a colourful poetic equivalent of *mortis formido* at 64 and 79.

38-40 **which . . . clouds . . . unsullied:** a sustained image, where human life is a clear pool or spring, sullied by the stirring up from below of black mud, symbolising fear of death and its miseries: see West (1969) 3. *mortis nigrore* 39 thus does double duty, contrasting not only with *claranda* 36 (see note above), but also with *liquidam puramque* 40, of the pure, unsullied pleasure which is denied. The harmonising images characteristically merge into one another, reflecting the poet's fertile visual imagination.

utterly: Lucretius often uses *funditus* in contexts which suggest, or play on, its root sense, 'from (or 'at') the bottom' (= *ab imo* here): cf. I 572, 620, 668 and 993, and V 497.

leaves . . . pure . . . : *relinquit* here governs accusative and infinitive by analogy with *sinit* or *patitur*, to which it approximates in sense; cf. I 515 and 703.

41-58 The example of the professed sceptics reflects the fundamental Epicurean tenet that it was not enough to accept the central Epicurean conclusions about the gods and one's fate at death: they had to be accepted on the basis of a firm understanding and acceptance of Epicurean physics (cf. 91-3 below), or they would crumble in time of stress; this made the study of Epicurean philosophy an essential ingredient in the recipe for human happiness. This in turn is of fundamental importance in assessing the audience Lucretius was seeking to convert: he sees his message as relevant not merely to the victims of primitive superstition, but to anyone who is not already a convinced Epicurean, however superstitious, religious or philosophical his beliefs (Introduction III).

41-2 **Certainly:** literally 'For as to the fact that', introducing counter-evidence, which 46ff. go on to discount.

a life of dishonour: *infamem* is technical, suggesting *infamia* resulting from criminal conviction and involving loss of civil rights, as 48-9 reflect.

the Tartarus of death: see on 37 above. The genitive is probably possessive, with Death the proprietor or occupant, rather than defining.

43-4 **the soul is composed of blood . . . wind:** i.e. material, and therefore, as Lucretius himself maintains, mortal. The sarcastic *si fert ita forte uoluntas* shows that these are popular ideas rather than formal philosophical theories, though each had a philosophical pedigree, the former apparently being asserted by Empedocles and the latter, as well as suggesting the breath or πνεῦμα of the all-pervasive world-soul of the Stoics, being attributed to Anaximenes. *animi* (or *animae*, if that is the correct reading), covering the sceptics' view of the soul, is 'non-technical'; cf. Lucretius' own inclusive use of the terms (Introduction IV).

45 **no need whatsoever:** *prorsum* is archaic for *prorsus* and *quicquam* adverbial accusative, 'in any respect'.

46 **you can tell:** the 'uncontracted' form of *animaduertas* draws attention to the root sense, of 'directing the mind' to something; cf. 54 below.

48-50 **these same people:** *idem* underlines their inconsistency; when overtaken by the *infamis uita* (48-9) to which they claimed death preferable at 41-2, they live on (*uiuunt* 50), instead of committing suicide as their own principles (though not

Epicurean moral theory, where suicide rarely became necessary or justified) would dictate.

51-4 Further evidence of inconsistency: they make offerings to propitiate or appease three classes of underworld beings in which they profess not to believe, (a) the ghosts of their ancestors (*parentant* 51), (b) the underworld deities (*di inferi*), including Dis (Pluto) and Proserpina (Persephone), for whom the black victims of 52 are appropriate (cf. Virgil, *Aeneid* VI 153 and Horace, *Satires* I 8.27), and (c) the deified spirits of the collective dead (*manibu' diuis* 52).

51 **wherever the wretches find themselves they still . . . :** i.e. although unable to make the offerings at the proper place, the ancestral tombs; this gives *tamen* most point. *parentant* is properly used of the annual offering at these tombs made at the *Parentalia* in February.

52 **spirits of the dead**: *manibu'* is one of some 40 examples in Lucretius of the suppression of *s* in a final short syllable in *-is* or *-us* before a consonant. This suppression, commoner in Ennius and regular in Plautus, had become old-fashioned by Lucretius' day and is avoided by his contemporary, Catullus. It indicates a weak pronunciation of the *s* in ordinary speech: according to Cicero, *Orator* 161, the dropping of *s* in final *-us* had once been considered a refinement, but was now (45 B.C.) considered rather provincial (*subrusticum*).

54 **religious ritual:** *religio* denotes (a) a feeling of religious awe, (b) the rites performed to settle this emotion (as here), and so (c) the organised worship of the gods. The most frequent sense in Lucretius is 'religious fear' or 'religious scruple' according to (a), suggesting in particular the fears of divine intervention and of death which are the poem's primary targets. The Romans derived the word variously from *relegere* (the ritual is regularly repeated) and *religare* (*religio* binds one): Lucretius favours the latter account at I 932, referring to the 'knots' of *religiones*, so suggesting an etymology for a key concept by a word-play. Whereas *religio* and *superstitio*, superstition, are normally distinct, Lucretius regards them as identical, and links them at I 62-5 by a word-play, where *religio* is a monster lowering (*super instans)* over mortals. In Lucretius the *e* is long (cf. *relicuo* 648 and *reliquias* 656), a relic of an original formation with *red-* (an alternative form of the *re-* prefix which survives, e.g., in *reddere*) and of subsequent assimilation to *rell-*.

55-8 The concluding psychological observation underlines the unreliability of professions like those of 41-5 above.

55 **doubt and trial:** *peric(u)lis*, 'perils', also fits the context in the original sense of 'testings'; the phrase recurs at 1076.

57 **this is the time when:** *tum demum* is literally 'then finally' and so 'then and only then'. The thought and language of the line is closely matched at Catullus 64.198, *quae* (sc. *querellae) quoniam uerae nascuntur pectore ab imo*.

58 **the reality remains:** the final monosyllable of *manet res*, an unsurpassed conjectural restoration of the text in two of the *Itali*, adds to the stark, dramatic effect.

59-86 Lucretius' second illustration, where fear of death contributes (a) to avarice and political ambition (59-73), resulting in the violation of all natural ties (70-3: cf. 83-6), and to their corollary, envy (74-8), and thence in turn (b) to suicide (79-86). The passage vividly reflects the contemporary Roman scene: the quest for riches and ruthless competition for power were the characteristic vices of the age and are amongst the poet's most constant moral targets.

59 **Again:** *denique* is most commonly used by Lucretius in enumeration (contrast the use in 50 above), not necessarily for the final point in a series.

avarice: classed by Epicurus, along with ambition, amongst the unnatural and unnecessary desires which were to be studiously avoided (cf. Introduction III). The rare form *auarities* is characteristic of Lucretius' archaising fluctuation between declensions (cf. *materies* 847 and 967) and is not without metrical convenience.

office: *honorum* is concrete, denoting the steps of the senatorial *cursus*.

60-3 **to reach the pinnacle of wealth:** presented as the goal not only of avarice but also of political ambition, an indication that the poet analysed the latter as stemming from the former and saw lust for power and office as springing ultimately from the opportunities which they offered for self-enrichment. Similarly in 70-1 below, civil war (*sanguine ciuili*) is presented as a direct means of amassing wealth, rather than of gaining power. 62-3 are repeated from II 12-13, with the substitution of *haec uulnera uitae* for *rerumque potiri* at the end of the second line.

sores of life: the same image is applied to the evils resulting from primeval religious delusion at V 1196-7.

64 **are nurtured in no small degree:** a restricted claim; fear of death is not said to *cause*, but to *contribute to*, the two *uulnera. minimam partem* is adverbial accusative.

65-7 The metaphor of contempt and poverty apparently lingering at death's portals is the key to the whole train of thought, which editors often find puzzling or illogical and sometimes use as evidence of Lucretian 'obsession' with the fear of death. The most satisfactory interpretation is that contempt and poverty *appear almost as bad as death*: their victims, devoid of position and riches, wrongly see themselves as deprived of security and pleasure (*dulci uita stabilique* 66), in short of what makes life worth living. To escape their virtual 'living death', they then (68ff.) seek the opposite extreme, embarking on a reckless pursuit of wealth, instead of living just lives in obscurity and cultivating Epicurean contentment. Their mentality then resembles that of the debased hedonists attacked at 912-8, and their revulsion from death stems not, as with the professed sceptics at 50-4, from fear of an after-life, but rather from fear of ceasing to exist and of thereby relinquishing the chance to enjoy life's pleasures: just as the professed sceptics illustrated the first, so the avaricious and ambitious illustrate the second of the two aspects of death which are addressed at 830-1094 (Introduction I and III). The parallel passage at 1053-75, where fear of death is at the root of another moral evil, restless dissatisfaction, which editors often find no less puzzling, is most satisfactorily explained along the same lines (see notes there). The traditional interpretation of the image of 67 is that contempt and poverty *appear likely to lead directly to death*, i.e. their victims see themselves as in imminent danger of murder and starvation, and so seek power and wealth to guard against these hazards. Certainly this idea is consistent with Epicurus, *Principal Sayings* 7, where desire for security (ἀσφάλεια ἐξ ἀνθρώπων), a goal properly achieved by abstinence from political life, conformity with justice and the cultivation of supportive friends, led some men to seek fame and prominence, and also with V 1120-2, where Lucretius presents the same point; this interpretation of the image, however, does not fit *dulci uita stabilique* 66, where *stabili*, applied exclusively to security from murder and starvation, would have to bear all the emphasis, and *dulci* would have no point, except to indicate the minimal pleasure of freedom from such drastic fates.

contempt . . . poverty . . . pleasure . . . security: the order is chiasmic, with *contemptus* opposed to *stabili*, which it seems to negate, *egestas* to *dulci*.

seem divorced: *semota* and *uidetur* take their gender and number from *egestas*, the nearer of the two subjects. The verb has its usual, rather than the 'Lucretian' sense: see on 35.

lingering . . . doors of death: however interpreted, the image, for which *quasi* apologises, influenced Virgil in his personification of the whole range of abstract concepts, including *turpis Egestas*, posted at the entrance to his Hades at *Aeneid* VI 273-81. *cunctarier* exemplifies the archaic passive or deponent infinitive in *-ier* for *-i*, used in some 1 in 10 instances by Lucretius, especially, as here, to provide a fifth foot dactyl. As with the *-ai* genitive (see on 83), Virgil's sparing imitations show that the form, in addition to its metrical convenience, could impart archaic dignity (Introduction V). The anastrophe, with *ante* following (and also separated from) *portas*, is also characteristic; cf. 140-1 and note.

68-9 **long to have escaped . . . removed themselves:** the construction exemplifies the occasional use of *uelle* with accusative and infinitive, rather than prolative infinitive, where the subjects are the same. A second *se* is to be supplied as object of *remo(ui)sse*, unless the verb is here intransitive through Lucretian fluctuation (see on 493). The perfect infinitives have point (cf. *cresse* 683), here stressing the subjects' eagerness to be free from their 'living death'.

70-1 **blood of fellow-citizens:** the civil wars of Marius and Sulla, witnessed by the poet in his youth, may be especially in mind. For the attribution of civil war directly to avarice, see on 60-3 above. The couplet involves variation and chiasmus, with *sanguine ciuili* taken up by *caedem caede accumulantes*, *rem conflant* by *diuitias . . . conduplicant.* A telling comparison is drawn between the amassing of wealth (*diuitias . . . auidi*) and the piling up of corpses (*caedem caede accumulantes*) which it entails; the long words *diuitiasque*, *conduplicant* and *accumulantes* (giving two successive pentasyllabic line-endings) and the juxtaposition *caedem caede* all help to mirror the sense of accumulation, exemplifying what West has called 'syntactical onomatopoea'.

72-3 The killing of fellow-citizens is now capped by the killing of kinsmen.

72 Virgil's adaptation at *Georgics* II 510, *gaudent perfusi sanguine fratrum*, which helps to confirm Macrobius' *fratris*, suggests that the context is still, as in 70-1, civil war. The antithesis between *gaudent* and *tristi* reflects the perversion of *pietas* (cf. 84 below).

73 **spurn in fear the tables of their kith and kin:** in case of poisoning; political now gives way to private crime. *consanguineum* is the old form of the genitive plural; see on 18.

74-8 Lucretius now turns to envy, the natural corollary of greed and ambition, illustrating it exclusively from the latter, and attributing it to the same source, *mortis formido* (*ab eodem saepe timore* 74).

75-6 **that . . . this man . . . this man:** the accusative and infinitive constructions are governed by *inuidia*; *illum* is used in anaphora, referring to a single imaginary rival.

stepping out . . . distinctions of office: suggesting an official appearance by a magistrate, with the appropriate robe and emblems.

77 **they themselves, they complain:** though *ipsi* is nominative, the idiomatic juxtaposition serves to emphasise the subject-accusative, *se*.

78 **lose their lives:** at the hands of jealous rivals, or by overreaching themselves in the pursuit of military glory.

in quest of statues and a name: cf. the scholium on Epicurus, *Principal Sayings* 29, where desire for crowns and statues is used to exemplify those desires which are neither natural nor necessary. For the archaic use of *ergo* as preposition, which adds a degree of solemnity, cf. V 1246.

79-86 The crowning paradox, whereby fear of death leads to suicide, is not peculiar to Lucretius, but goes back to Democritus, who claimed (Diels B.203) that in fleeing death men pursue it, while Seneca, *Moral Epistles* 24.22-3, cites three relevant pronouncements of Epicurus: *ridiculum est currere ad mortem taedio uitae, cum genere uitae ut currendum ad mortem esset effeceris* (it is ridiculous to rush to death out of revulsion from life, when you have created the necessity to rush to death by your life-style); *tantam hominum imprudentiam esse, immo dementiam, ut quidam timore mortis cogantur ad mortem* (men's foolishness, or rather their madness, is so great that some are driven to death by fear of death); *quid tam ridiculum quam adpetere mortem, cum uitam inquietam tibi feceris metu mortis?* (what is so ridiculous as to seek death, when you have made your life troubled through fear of death); cf. also Cicero, *De Finibus* I 49. In the Lucretian context, there is no problem in explaining the suicide as the outcome of the life of avarice, ambition and envy just described, which has initially been fostered by the fear of death; this life then brings such frustration and mental disturbance in its train that suicide results. The first of the sayings attributed to Epicurus in the Senecan passage cited above suggests that the master envisaged a similar chain of events.

81 **inflict:** *consciscere sibi letum*, primarily to decide on suicide, becomes a regular term for committing it.

82 **the source of their cares:** as traced in 63-4 ; see on 79-86 above.

83-4 Following Munro, I have supposed the loss of a line or lines after 82, which may have justified *fontem curarum* by reasserting the link between *mortis timor* and avarice and ambition, just as 83-4 ascribe the associated violation of *pietas*, which has been described in 70-3, to the same source. This removes the difficulties (a) of the switch to direct speech, with *hic timor* having to be supplied out of *hunc timorem*, and (b) of the use of *hunc . . . hunc* in 83 ('one man . . . another') with a different sense and reference from *hunc* 82. In order to take 83-4 as a continuation of the accusative and infinitive construction of 82, many editors emend the unexceptionable *suadet* 84, but of the many proposed replacements none is wholly satisfactory or convincing.

it persuades one man to betray . . . : for *suadere* with accusative and infinitive, replacing the prose construction of dative and an *ut* clause, cf. I 140-2 and Virgil,

Aeneid X 9-10. The idiom is facilitated by the analogy of verbs of similar sense, like *cogere* and *iubere*, which regularly govern this construction.

sense of honour: *pudor* denotes shame at things which should excite shame, thus approximating to conscience. There is elision (of *pudorem* before *hunc*) at the main caesura, a metrically unusual feature paralleled, in the third foot (as here), at 770 and 893, and in the fourth at 174 and 773.

friendship: highly valued in Epicurean moral theory (Introduction III), which adds to the seriousness of its violation. *amicitiai* exemplifies the archaic disyllabic *-ai* genitive of the first declension, which Lucretius uses slightly more often than the classical *-ae*; Virgil adopts it on four occasions. Lucretius is especially fond of it, as here, in polysyllabic words at the end of the line, where its sonority is more conspicuous.

in short: if the text printed in 84 is sound (see earlier note), *in summa* is here used by Lucretius for the only time with the sense of *denique* (cf. 50).

overturn the ties of duty: generalising from, and enlarging on, *uincula amicitiai rumpere*: *pietas* denotes duty wherever owed, whether to gods, country, family or friends.

85-6 Betrayal of country and parents to save one's own skin serves as a final, straightforward example of *mortis timor* undermining *pietas*. The violation of natural ties does not in this case (contrast 70-3) result from avarice and ambition, but the guilty remorse it might inspire makes it another potential source of paradoxical suicide.

have betrayed: for the short *e* of the perfect *prodiderunt* (the alternative, original, form), cf. 134 and 1028; the standard form, in each case, is metrically inadmissible.

seeking to avoid the realms of Acheron: *petere* here governs the prolative infinitive *uitare* by analogy with *conari*. For *Acherusia templa*, see on 25 above.

87-93 These lines appear also at II 55-61 and VI 35-41; 91-3 first occur at I 146-8. In each case they provide a transition from introduction to philosophical argument. Repetition of key lines and passages is not uncommon in Lucretius, and may be seen as evoking not only the repetitions of Homeric epic but also repeated religious formulae, so imparting an almost catechistic air. The passage is dominated by the light / darkness imagery so prominent in the poem, here in III taking up the motif which dominated 1-30 and recurred in 36-40.

88 **in daylight:** partly perhaps literal, like the contrasted darkness which surrounds the children, but clearly also figurative, alluding to the philosophical illumination brought by Epicurus in the opening eulogy, which has made it possible, for those who will only pay heed, to see the emptiness of their fears.

91-3 **must be dispelled:** Lucretius often uses *necesse (e)st* with the paratactic nominative and subjunctive, as here and, e.g., at 241-2, often with the accusative and infinitive, as, e.g., at 175, 204-5 (where *eam* is to be supplied) and 216.

bright shafts of day: a poetic elaboration of *radii solis*. The military image in *tela* suggests the 'routing' of the darkness, and fits the image of Epicurus as a warrior and monster-slayer which is built up in some memorable passages in the poem, especially at I 62-79 and V 1-54. The contrast between literal daylight (*radii solis*) and the philosophy (*naturae species ratioque* 93) for which it has served as an analogue suggests the superiority of the figurative light of philosophy, as if the light image is inadequate to do the philosophy full justice.

nature's outward appearance and its explanation: an approximation to Epicurus' φυσιολογία (natural science). The phrase implies an antithesis between nature's outward aspect and her inner (atomic) realities, and at the same time suggests the two main instruments of Epicurean scientific procedure, observation and reasoning on the basis of it (Introduction III).

94-416 THE SOUL'S NATURE AND ATOMIC CONSTITUTION

94-135 *Mind and spirit are each parts, not states, of the body*

At the beginning of his exposition, Lucretius not only clears the ground for the Epicurean view of the soul as a material part of the body, but simultaneously introduces the fundamental Epicurean distinction between its two parts (see Introduction IV) by arguing separately for the mind and the spirit. 94-5 and 106-16 immediately reflect that the mind is the organ of mental and emotional consciousness, 117-8 that the spirit is the organ of physical consciousness and situated in the limbs; the evidence for the bipartite soul lies essentially, as the argument reflects, in the different nature and location of the two categories of consciousness. Fuller details of the functions, placing and relationship of the two parts are to emerge gradually in the course of the subsequent discussion. The theory here opposed, that the soul was not a part but a harmonious state of the body, is advanced by Simmias in Plato, *Phaedo* 85e-86d, and attacked by Socrates, championing the immortality of the soul, at 91c-95a; it was later developed by two pupils of Aristotle, Dicaearchus and Aristoxenus, whose views are summarised by Cicero, *Tusculan Disputations* I 19-21. Though it leads to the very conclusion which Lucretius is concerned to establish, that the soul cannot survive death, it is vital for him to establish this conclusion on the firm basis of Epicurean scientific truth (see on 41-58 above); at the same time, his attack on the harmony theory enables him to introduce his own view of the soul not only as a part of the body but as a twofold part.

94-5 **mind, which we often call the intellect:** the 'rational part' of the Epicurean soul, embracing intellect, emotions and will (see Introduction IV). In normal usage, *animus* covers emotions as well as intellect, while *mens* refers more exclusively to the latter, but Lucretius treats the terms as interchangeable, sometimes pairing them, as at 139 and 142, or using *mens* for *animus*, as at 101, 152 and 228. The relative *quam* is attracted from the masculine to the gender of the predicate *mentem*, according to normal Lucretian usage after verbs of naming; cf. *harmoniam . . . quam* in 100 below.

rational and controlling power: i.e. intellect and will; *consilium* corresponds to Epicurus' τὸ λογικόν, *regimen* to his τὸ ἡγεμονικόν.

96-7 **no less than:** *ac* occasionally replaces *quam* after a comparative, by analogy with its use after words like *similis* and *alius*.

hand . . . foot . . . eyes: perceptible analogues for the physically imperceptible *animus*.

living being: Lucretius here, as often, suggests an etymology and uses it to reinforce his argument: a living (or animate) being (*animans*; cf. *animal*) is one that possesses a soul (*animus* or *anima* or both); cf. Cicero, *Tusculan Disputations* I 21, where the harmony-theorist Dicaearchus is reported as denying this very inference from such terms. Though *animantis* here picks up *hominis* and is restricted to man, this was not the only species endowed with *animus* as well as *anima* in Epicurean theory: e.g. at 296-306 the different temperaments of different species of animal are attributed to differences in the make-up of their *animus*.

98-101 **<Some . . . supposed>:** a rendering of Bailey's supplement for the line (or lines) lost before 98.

specific part: viz. the mind or *animus*; the denial that *animi sensus* is situated *in animo* is presented as an eccentric paradox.

a sort of life-giving state: *quidam*, commonly used to apologise for a bold expression or metaphor, here conveys sceptical scorn for the strange idea.

which the Greeks call a 'harmony': one of the poet's rare transliterations of a Greek technical term; cf. I 830-1, where he excuses himself on grounds of the dearth of Latin vocabulary (cf. 260 and note below). On the harmony theory, which identified the soul with a proper adjustment or attunement of the bodily parts, see introductory note to 94-135 above; for the attraction of *quam* into the feminine, see on 94-5. The indicative *dicunt* shows that the relative clause is treated as a Lucretian parenthesis, independent of the surrounding indirect speech.

a thing which causes us to have conscious life: the vague neuter *quod*, picking up *habitum* and *harmoniam*, reflects further scornful incredulity. The subjunctive *faciat* is generic-consecutive ('such as to cause'), as well as sub-oblique in the reported statement summarising the theory. The accusative and infinitive (*nos uiuere*) after causative *facere* is a rare, perhaps colloquial, alternative to *ut* with a subjunctive; cf. 301, and in prose Cicero, *Brutus* 142 (*nulla res magis . . . talis . . . oratores uideri facit qualis ipsi se uideri uolunt*: nothing is better calculated to make orators appear as they themselves wish to appear).

without the intellect residing: *mens* picks up *animi* 98 and is treated as its synonym; cf. on 94-5 above. *siet* is archaic for *sit*, as at II 962 and 1079.

102-3 **similarly:** literally 'as when'; the analogy provides a concluding illustration of the rival view, but, as 105 at once reveals, is in Lucretius' eyes quite false.

is . . . attributed to: literally 'is said to belong to', *corporis* being possessive genitive.

104-5 **Thus:** *sic* picks up the whole report of 98-103, not just the *ut* clause of 102-3.

in which they seem . . . astray: a characteristically confident assertion of rival error (cf. I 637 and 711), preceding the arguments designed to expose it. *mi* = *mihi*, as, e.g., at I 924.

106-16 Since mental experiences are often independent of, rather than matching, the bodily state, the mind must be an independent part, not a state, of the body. Two illustrations are adduced: (a) 106-11, where our emotions can conflict with, rather than matching and reflecting, our bodily state, as they would if they depended on it; (b) 112-6, where consciousness and emotions can be experienced in dreams when the body's activities are largely suspended; they cannot therefore depend on the total bodily state. Waking emotions and dream-consciousness are thus Lucretius' first evidence for the existence of the *animus* as a separate part of the body.

106-7 **So it is that:** i.e. because the facts are as Lucretius, contradicting the harmony-theorists, maintains.

ails: the verb *aegreo*, vouched for here by Macrobius' citation, is found in Latin only here and at 824 below.

when, nevertheless, we feel pleasure: as in 110 and 112-3 below, *cum* is used with indicative despite the concessive context, marked here and in 114 by *tamen*; cf. also 645-6 and, without *tamen*, 146, 150-1 and 653. The idiom may be explained in part as archaising, in part as stressing the temporal relationship; in the present passage, it is crucial to the argument that the contrasting physical and mental states are simultaneous.

another part, which is hidden: viz. the *animus*. The antithesis with *in promptu corpus quod cernitur* implies a characteristically Epicurean argument from the visible to the invisible; the visible body, which is sentient, provides an analogue for the invisible conscious mind.

108-9 **in turn the exact converse:** the combination of *retro*, *contra* and *uicissim*, each expressing the same idea, illustrates Lucretian pleonasm, a feature of his style symptomatic of his didactic energy and his quest for clarity.

wretched in mind: *ex animo* answers, and defines, *ex alia parte latenti* 107; contrast the idiomatic sense 'sincerely' at 914.

110-1 A characteristic analogy to reinforce the argument; the implication is that since the mind, like a part of the body (e.g. a foot), can suffer pain independently of the rest of the body, it must itself be a part of the body. For the argument from visible to invisible, cf. 106-7 above.

112-6 **Again:** introducing the second illustration of the central point; see on 106-16 above.

when our limbs . . . insensate: the suspension of physical activity and sensation in sleep is explained at IV 907-61 in terms of the disruption of the *anima* distributed throughout the body; part of it is supposed temporarily to withdraw from the body, the rest to be drawn deeper inside it.

something else in us: viz. the *animus*.

is . . . stirred by manifold impulses: i.e. experiences the dreams which arouse the joy and anxieties following. Dreaming is explained at IV 757-76 and 788-817 in terms of material effluences from objects making direct contact with the *animus*; see further on 430-3 below.

of the heart: the use of *cor* as a synonym for *animus* hints at the latter's location in the breast, the argument for which follows at 140-2, and may well be intended to suggest that language, which commonly refers to it as 'the heart', supports this location.

empty as they are: because they are experienced in dreams; like *omnis, inanis* qualifies both *laetitiae motus* and *curas*.

117-29 Lucretius here turns to the second component of the soul, the spirit or *anima*, and at 119ff. adduces two points against the harmony-theorists, though these merge into one another through compression. The first idea is that, as life can survive the loss of a large part of the body, and conversely be lost with the limbs virtually intact (119-23), mortality is not in proportion to the disruption of the bodily state (124-5), as it would be if life and sensation depended on bodily 'harmony'. The second idea is that at death the body loses heat and breathing ceases (121-3); this is taken as evidence that particles of heat and 'wind' are lost at death and that it is these (which the Epicureans regarded as two of the four elements comprising the soul: cf. 231-57 below), and not a bodily 'harmony', that are vital to conscious life (126-9).

117-8 **the spirit:** the 'non-rational part' of the Epicurean soul, responsible for bodily sensation (see Introduction IV).

also exists: i.e. has, like the mind, a physical existence, rather than being a state or 'harmony'. The emphatic position of *esse* confirms the existential sense: cf. 128 below.

situated in the limbs: *in membris* is especially applicable to the *anima*, which pervades the whole body (cf. *per totum dissita corpus* 143), but to the *animus* only as a synonym for *in corpore*; the force of *quoque* thus scarcely extends to the phrase.

119-20 **in the first place:** the second point emerges from the first and is accordingly not signposted; see on 117-29 above.

much of the body has been taken away: e.g. through amputation of limbs. The relative importance for life of *animus* and the *anima* housed in the limbs is a theme developed at 396-416.

121-3 **again, conversely:** *eadem* (sc. *uita*) is used idiomatically (cf. 48) to contrast the second situation with the first, and makes the same point as *rursum*; for the pleonasm, cf. 108 and note.

a few particles of heat: contrasting, together with the *aer* of 122, with the loss of 'much of the body' at 119. Heat, like air, was regarded by the Epicureans as an atomic compound.

have escaped: *diffūgēre* = *diffugerunt*.

air is given out through the mouth: the parlance is popular, rather than scientific; *aer* is here used as a synonym for *uentus* (126 and 128 below), though 231-6 later show them to be distinct (cf. VI 685), and to comprise, with heat, the first three of the soul's four elements. The words suggest the popular idea of the soul being 'breathed out' at death; the Epicurean picture of the process is provided at 254-5, where the parts of the *anima* escape through all the body's apertures, including the pores.

124-5 The couplet sums up the first point (see on 117-29 above); the disproportionate importance for life of the body's components shows that life cannot depend on bodily 'harmony'.

play an equal role . . . act as equal props: colourful imagery from the stage and from building enriches the technical argument; cf. 126-7 where the seeds are personified as 'ensuring' the continuation of life.

126-9 The second point; the crucial importance for life of heat and breath (which appears as 'air' in 122 above and 'wind' in 126 and 128 here) is taken as evidence of their existence as a life-giving part of the body, and thus, it is implied, as components of the *anima*. Naive though the reasoning is to the modern reader, the association of heat and wind with the soul was a popular ancient idea, all the more natural to a Roman in that *anima* denoted breath. Lucretius argues more formally for, and refines on, the popular view at 231-57.

seeds: for the metaphorical term *semina*, cf. on 31: Lucretius applies it not only to the atoms, but sometimes to compound component particles (cf. on 180), which he may have in mind here and in *corpora* 121 and 125.

warming heat: *uapor* in Lucretius is always a synonym for *calor*.

there exist in our body itself: i.e. as parts of the body, as opposed to a life-giving state.

130-5 Having demolished the harmony theory, Lucretius now criticises his rivals' use of terminology as he dismisses it.

the mind and spirit: literally 'the nature of mind and spirit'. Lucretius frequently uses the periphrasis with *natura* in referring to the soul and its two parts (contrast 35-6, where *natura* has its full force); as well as providing a metrically convenient variation, it is reminiscent of epic style (cf. on 8).

as it were: *quasi* apologises for the label *pars hominis*; though the passage has been concerned to show that mind and spirit are indeed parts of the living individual, they are highly unusual parts, being so refined as to be invisible, and having an intricate and unique relationship with all the other parts of the body.

give back the name 'harmony' . . . : to the musicians: cf. 135, where they are to keep it. The point is that *harmonia* is an improper term, which the rival theorists have misleadingly transferred to philosophy from music; Lucretius may here be thinking especially of the harmony-theorist Aristoxenus (see introductory note to 94-135 above), who was himself musician as well as philosopher. Such transferences contravened a precept of Epicurean Canonic or Logic, which laid down that words should be used in their basic, not in transferred or metaphorical senses - a rule not always observed by Epicurus himself, still less by Lucretius in his poetic medium (Introduction V). 132 (*ad organicos . . . Heliconi*) suggests that the term was musical in origin, 133-4 the alternative possibility that the musicians themselves drew it from some other source, making its use in philosophy doubly transferred and so doubly inappropriate. For the archaic genitive ending of *harmoniai*, here attached somewhat incongruously to a Greek word, perhaps to heighten the tone of mockery, see on 83. The pentasyllabic Greek word at the end of the line would have been admitted by Virgil, but in the context the effect is probably more mock-epic than epic.

borne down to the musicians from the heights of Helicon: a scornful allusion to the mythical idea that the Muses of Mount Helicon in Boeotia gave the musicians the term; myth, indeed, gave the Muses a daughter named Harmonia (Euripides, *Medea* 831-4). *organici* is the regular Lucretian term for musicians, replacing the metrically inadmissible *mūsĭcī*. *Heliconi* is ablative, illustrating the poet's occasional divergences from the classical norm in the ablative singular of the third declension; cf., e.g., *parti* 611 and *tripodi* I 739. The quadrisyllabic Greek name at the end of the line would, like *harmoniai* 131, have been acceptable to Virgil, but in the context probably has a mocking ring.

or perhaps: *siue* is used as if *siue delatum est* had preceded; the mocking tone of 132 suggests that Lucretius prefers the second possibility and that *siue* is corrective.

they themselves drew it from another source: i.e. the musicians, so far from being presented with the term by the Muses, transferred it to music from another field (probably carpentry), so that its philosophical usage is even more unjustified.

in their turn: just as the philosophers later drew it from music.
something which as yet had no name: i.e. musical 'harmony'.
let them keep it: *habeant* has the contemptuous force of *sibi habeant.*
do you listen: like *redde* 131, the imperative is addressed to Memmius (Introduction I) and through him to the general reader.

136-60 ***Mind and spirit are closely related to form a single entity, but mind is the dominant partner***

Having treated the soul's two parts separately in 94-135, Lucretius now provides an introductory summary of their relationship, adducing in the course of the passage two pieces of evidence for his two main points, their interaction and the mind's predominance in it: (a) at 143-4, where the spirit moves at the mind's behest, viz. in conscious acts of will, which, introspection suggests, occur in the mind, but which require the chain of command to be passed on to the parts of the body concerned by way of the spirit distributed throughout it; (b) at 152-60, where strong emotion in the mind, exemplified by extreme fear, can produce bodily symptoms and indeed total physical collapse, showing that the mind's distress has affected the spirit in the bodily parts involved, so disrupting their function. Whereas 94-135 treated the bipartite Epicurean soul in the first of its two crucial roles, as organ of consciousness, the two pieces of evidence presented here concern its second role, as initiator and controller of physical activity in the body; it was the human capacities for (a) consciousness and (b) self-determined motion that prompted the Epicurean view of the soul and provided the ultimate evidence for it (Introduction IV). The summary includes the first statement of the mind's location in the breast, together with argument (140-2), and points out that the mind, despite its close relationship with the spirit, can function independently of it (145-51). This preliminary account remains to be much amplified later; e.g. while 152-60 show mind acting upon spirit, their interaction was a two-way process, and 170-6 soon illustrate the converse; 396-416 reveal one specific aspect of the mind's dominance, its greater importance for life, while a fuller account of the mechanics of an act of will, alluded to in 143-4, follows at IV 877-906.

136-7 The double elisions in *anim(um) atqu(e) animam* and *inter s(e) atqu(e) unam* match the sense: the words merge into one another just as *animus* and *anima* merge to form a single entity. See further on 159 below.
in mutual union: *coniuncta* is neuter plural referring to nouns of different gender, a metrically convenient idiom commonly exploited by Lucretius (cf., e.g., 270, 283 and 287), especially with the pairing of *animus* and *anima* (e.g. 421 and 506-9), and occasionally extended to cases where the nouns are of the same gender (e.g. 601).
a single nature: viz. the soul.

138 **so to speak, the head . . . holds sway:** vivid, figurative language; *quasi*, apologising for *caput*, underlines that the *animus*, whose location (140) is in the breast, is not to be associated with the literal head.

140-2 The argument for the mind's location turns solely on the emotions, whose site, introspection suggests, is the breast, not on the intellect, which the modern reader associates more readily with the head. But ancient thinkers (see Introduction IV) normally linked intellect and emotions, placing them together either in the brain or in the breast (cf. Cicero, *Tusculan Disputations* I 19); the argumentation would thus have been less surprising to an ancient than to a modern reader.

in the central area . . . the vicinity in which: *in* and *circum* follow their cases, *media regione* and *haec loca*, in anastrophe, a metrically convenient device which is extended in poetry beyond standard prose usages like *mecum* or *Antio tenus*; cf., e.g., 67, 463 and 824.

143 **The rest of the soul:** viz. the spirit; as at 150, *anima* is here used non-technically, inclusively, of the soul as a whole, in anticipation of the linguistic point made in 421-4; see note there, and Introduction IV.

distributed throughout the whole body: further defining *in membris* 117; the evidence for the spirit's location lay in the whole body's capacities for consciousness and for action (see on 136-60 above).

144 **obeys . . . behest:** viz. in an act of will; see on 136-60 above. The language takes up the imagery of 138; *numen*, literally 'nod' and so 'will' (cf. on 18), fits the picture of the mind as 'head'; the addition of *momen*, etymologically connected with *mouetur*, helps to explain the metaphor. The line is remarkable for its assonance; that in *numen mentis momenque* links *momen* to *numen*, which it explains, and both words to *mentis*, suggesting that these are the mind's natural characteristics; that in *momen mouetur* seems to suggest that the mind's movement automatically moves the spirit, thus mirroring the latter's obedience.

145-51 The independent functioning of the mind described here introduces a qualification of the picture of interaction so far presented, though its intellectual capacity, summed up in *sapit* ('has wisdom') 145, represents another aspect of its predominance. Its capacity for independent emotion (*sibi gaudet . . . una* 145-6) has already been demonstrated in 106-11, where the argument turned on the independent experiences of mind and body (including the spirit contained in the body); indeed, the analogy of 147-51, in which the mind can experience emotion independently of the spirit just as parts of the body can suffer pain independently of the body as a whole, echoes that of 109-11 in which the mind can experience pain despite bodily well-being, just as a foot can suffer pain without the head being affected.

146 **when neither spirit nor body is . . . stirred by the process:** as Munro saw, *res* is specific, referring to the process by which the mind understands or feels joy independently, not indefinite (sc. *ulla*), 'anything'. The point is not that these independent mental activities require absence of sensation in body and spirit (as already shown at 106-11, mind and body can undergo simultaneous experiences of contrasting type), but that they do not simultaneously affect the body and the spirit contained in it; there is an antithesis with 152ff. where violent emotion in the mind does produce spectacular physical effects. The reading *ulla* for the adverbial *una* is thus based on a misunderstanding. *commouet* in the context has its root sense, 'moves together (i.e. with the *animus*)', reinforcing *una*; cf. *concruciamur* 148, *consentire* 153, and *una consentire* 168-9, and contrast *commota* 152 where the prefix has its more usual, intensive, sense. For *cum* used, as in 150-1 below, in a context which is concessive as well as temporal, see on 106-7.

148 **are not racked simultaneously:** *concruciamur* is a unique compound, apparently coined by Lucretius with the root sense 'are tortured together (i.e. with head or eye)'.

149 **the mind . . . on its own:** *ipse* has the same force as *sibi* and *per se* 145, and indicates that the emotions alluded to affect it alone, independently of the spirit in the limbs, as the *cum* clause of 150-1 goes on to specify.

150 **the rest of the soul:** for the sense of *animai*, cf. 143 and note above; for the archaic form of the genitive, much exploited by Lucretius with this technical word, usually as here at the end of the line, see on 83.

151 **no new impulse:** triggered by the mind's pain or joy.
frame: *artus* is synonymous with *membra*; Lucretius is fond of pairing the words, as at 703, II 282, IV 119, 888 and 1042, and VI 945.

152-60 The lines are antithetical to 147-51; more violent emotion in the mind affects the spirit, so producing physical symptoms. The passage thus concludes with a spectacular illustration of its two central points, that mind and spirit interact and that mind is the dominant partner.

152 The striking alliteration, with repeated *uē* and *m*, helps to convey the violence of the emotion described and to prepare for its violent physical effects in the sequel.

153-8 **we witness the whole spirit . . . suffering with it . . . :** *uidemus* here and in 157 below marks a characteristic Epicurean appeal to experience. The evidence that the whole spirit is affected lies in the physical symptoms so graphically described in 154-8, which show that it is failing to function properly in all the bodily parts concerned; thus the sweat and pallor of the whole body (*toto corpore* 154-5) provide evidence that the whole spirit throughout the limbs (*animam totam per membra* 153) is suffering with the mind. Similarities have been detected with Sappho's famous account of the physical symptoms of love (Lobel and Page, *Poetarum Lesbiorum Fragmenta* 31.7-15), adapted by Catullus in poem 51; whether or not Lucretius has any debt to Sappho here, he is at all times a keen observer and clinical reporter of such physical states (cf., e.g., the accounts of intoxication and epilepsy at 476-505), and not a single detail in his description is irrelevant to his scientific purpose. The increasingly stark succession of accusatives with infinitive in 154-6, with asyndeton in 156, builds up dramatically to the climax of collapse in 157-8. In this sequence, *sonere* 156, for classical *sonare*, exemplifies the poet's sporadic archaic fluctuation between conjugations.

159 The line is remarkable for its three elisions, *ess(e) animam*, *c(um) animo* and *c(um) animi*, two of them involving the monosyllable *cum*, first as preposition, then as conjunction; though Lucretius has fewer inhibitions than Virgil in eliding monosyllables and elides the conjunction *cum* elsewhere (e.g. 101), the elision of prepositional *cum* in epic is exceptional. As in 136-7, which introduced the topic, so in this conclusion the elisions match the sense of the close union of mind and spirit, the most striking elision being that of the *cum* linking *animam* and *animo*, the terms for the closely linked parts. In the context, the clash of ictus and stress resulting from the final monosyllabic word *ui* is not inappropriate to the forceful impact described.

160 **strikes and propels:** *propellit et icit* is a poetic inversion of the order of events (*hysteron proteron*).

161-76 ***Mind and spirit are corporeal***

For an Epicurean, the physical nature of the soul's two constituents followed inevitably from their status as parts, not states, of their possessor, and explicit allusion has already been made (121 and 126-7) to 'bodies' or 'seeds' of heat and wind, which, it was deduced, were vital constituents of the spirit. A formal proof of the soul's material nature, a point fundamental to the Epicurean arguments for its mortality, is now offered (cf. Epicurus, *ad Herodotum* 67): its interaction with the obviously material body, which it can set in motion and by whose distress it can be affected, would be impossible, were it not itself material. This depends in turn on the Epicurean principles that matter and void are the only categories of independent existence (I 430-2), and that the criterion of matter is that it can touch and be touched (I 434-6; cf. I 304) and so act and be acted upon (I 443), whereas void has none of these capacities. The Lucretian response to those believing, like Plato and Descartes, in an immaterial soul would have been to ask how such a soul differed from void, and how it could ever interact with the body. This interaction is here illustrated by two types of process, (a) at 162-4, where the soul acts on the body, and (b) at 168-74, where it is itself acted upon together with the body; in each situation, both mind and spirit are involved, with the spirit acting as intermediary between mind and body (see notes below).

161-2 **This same reasoning:** concerning interaction of mind and spirit, where mind has just been acting on spirit and spirit in turn on body; the echo of *propellit et icit* 160 in *propellere* 162 underlines the link.
mind and spirit are bodily in nature: literally 'the nature of mind and spirit is bodily'; for the periphrasis with *natura*, see on 130-1. *corporeus*, 'corporeal' or 'material', is the key-word in the argument; the responsions *corpoream / corpus* 162-3, *corpore / corporea* 166-7 and *corpoream / corporeis* 175-6 underline the logic of the central argument, that the soul's interaction with the body, or matter, proves its own bodily, material nature.

162-4 **they can be seen to:** *uidetur* is a true passive; see on 35.
propel . . . change . . . guide and steer: these processes are all initiated by the mind, whose impulse is transmitted to the appropriate parts of the body by the spirit; they thus provide further illustration of the mind as the dominant partner, holding sway in the whole body (138-9, 143-4). *regere ac uersare*, literally of directing in a straight line or turning, introduces a nautical metaphor; cf. IV 896-904, where, in the course of an account of the mechanics of the deliberate action alluded to here, the body / ship comparison is developed in detail. *mutareque* is one of some 25 Lucretian instances of the addition of the suffix *-que* to a short *e*, normally avoided by the Augustan poets for reasons of euphony, and sufficiently uncommon in Lucretius to show that he avoided it in the majority of available cases
arouse from sleep: in sleep (cf. on 112-6), the functions of the mind (except in dreams) and the spirit were suspended, the latter suffering physical disruption. Clearly the body's arousal was triggered by the spirit's reassembly, but how precisely this reassembly came about, and how far the mind played a part in it and how it was itself aroused, is not explained in any extant Epicurean source.

165-7 **we see:** *uidemus* echoes *uidetur* 164; the repetition of the verb at the end of successive lines emphasises that each step in the argument is patently valid and confirmed by experience.

without touch . . . without body: for the Epicurean principles involved here, for which Lucretius has argued at I 418-48, see introductory note to 161-76 above. They meant that all interaction, and all natural processes, depended on physical contact between corporeal objects. The corporeal nature of smells, sounds, heat and cold was demonstrated by a parallel argument at I 302-4: they must be material in order to stir the senses.

must it not be admitted: the rhetorical question, a feature of the poet's didactic style, adds urgency and apparent inevitability to the argument.

have a bodily nature: *corporea* takes up *nec sine corpore* 166; see on 161-2 above. The phrase, literally 'consist of a bodily nature' (or perhaps 'are of bodily nature': for *constare* in this sense, cf., e.g., I 245), was used in the parallel argument at I 302-3.

168-9 **What's more:** introducing the converse situation, where the soul is acted upon (see introductory note to 161-76 above).

you discern: insisting, like *uidetur* 164, that the appeal is to common experience.

our soul: since the processes of 168-74, no less than those of 162-7, involve both mind and spirit (which here communicates the body's distress to the central mind). *animus* here and at 175 below is most logically taken in the inclusive sense announced later at 421-4 (see Introduction IV, and cf. the sense of *anima* at 143 and 150 above).

is affected: Lucretius gives *fungi* (in classical Latin 'to perform' + ablative) the sense of 'to be acted upon', 'to suffer', corresponding to Epicurus' πάσχειν which is used in the parallel argument in *ad Herodotum* 67; cf. I 441 and 443, III 813 (= V 358) and, with an accusative object, III 734 and 801, and IV 947.

with the body . . . in the body: *cum corpore* and *in corpore* echo and re-echo *corpoream* 168, reinforcing the apparent relentlessness of the logic; cf. on 161-2 above.

suffers together with it: *consentire* = Epicurus' συμπάσχειν, and *una* reinforces the prefix; cf. *commovet una* 146 and note.

170-4 In this example a corporeal weapon damages the body and the spirit housed in it; the spirit then passes on its distress to the central mind. The faintness and collapse to the ground show that the spirit, especially in the knees, has suffered from the wound, the semi-consciousness (*mentis aestus*) and half-desire to rise that the mind in turn has been affected. The situation contrasts not only with 162-4, but also with 152-60, where mind affected spirit and spirit body; the pattern is here reversed.

driven inside: *intus* is occasionally applied to motion into, for the more usual *intro*; cf., e.g., I 223, II 711, Tacitus, *Histories* I 35 and Quintilian (despite his objections at I 5.50) XI 3.99.

fails to deal death: *si minus* is used for *si non*; cf. the regular *sin minus*, 'but if not', introducing an alternative conditional.

pleasant sensation of seeking the ground: Seneca, *Moral Epistles* 77.9, refers to 'a sort of pleasure brought on by a swoon' as familiar to those prone to such black-outs, and Montaigne, *Essais* II 6, to the pleasure of the fainting sensation he experienced as he fell from horseback.

a sort of vague desire . . . : both *quasi* and *incerta* express the vagueness of the impulse, which in turn reflects the distress of the mind, the seat of the will (*uoluntas*). The repeated *qu* in *interdumque quasi* produces a stuttering effect appropriate to the hesitant desire described, while as a result of the absence of a normal main caesura (see on 83 and 612) the line has an unusually high proportion of coincidence between ictus and stress, an effect appropriate to the drowsy context; cf. Virgil, *Aeneid* II 9, *suadentque cadentia sidera somnos,* and IV 486, *spargens umida mella soporiferumque papauer.*

175-6 The inference from the preceding example is now drawn.
the soul: for the sense of *animus*, see on 169 above.
must be: on the construction of *necessest*, see on 91-3.
corporeal weapons and blows: whose impact harms the body and the spirit in it, and so, through the agency of the spirit, the mind.

177-230 ***The soul's composition: (a) its constituent bodies are exceedingly small***

The account of the soul's structure, announced in 177-8, continues to 322 and falls into three logically arranged sections; here in the first its refined texture is established on the basis of two proofs. The first of these (182-207) concerns the mind exclusively, and turns on the swiftness of thought which was proverbial in antiquity; the mind, which has just been shown to be corporeal, must then be a very swiftly moving compound and must therefore comprise constituents which are (a) round and smooth, and (b) tiny and light. Liquidity in a compound has already been explained in terms of round, smooth components (II 451-61); smallness and lightness are now added as associated prerequisites, and the presence of all four qualities in the mind's constituents is demonstrated by analogies drawn from the more visible world (see on 189-99 below). This first argument presents difficulties if, as seems undeniably the case, Lucretius is here thinking of constituent atoms, and not, as Bailey and others suppose, of constituent particles, themselves comprising tiny groups of atoms and approximating to modern molecules: see on 180 below. The second proof (208-30), which depends on the premisses that the soul is material and leaves the body at death, is a straightforward appeal to experience: since there is no observable difference in the shape or weight of the body at death, the departed soul must comprise very small, lightweight constituents. This second argument is applied to both the soul's parts, but the main emphasis naturally enough now falls on the spirit, diffused as it is, in life, throughout all the bodily parts.

177-8 **what sort of matter:** *corpore* answers *corpoream* 175; having shown the soul to be material, Lucretius now moves on to the *nature* of its matter.
this soul: as in 169 and 175 above, *animus* is used inclusively; although the argument at 182-207 concerns only the mind, the discussion of 177-322, which is introduced here, also involves the spirit.
how it is made up: more literally 'from what it has been formed'; the perfect *constiterit* is virtually equivalent to present *constet* (or the synonymous *consistat*); cf. 440, and I 420 where Munro's note shows that the idiom is not confined to Lucretius.

179 **In the first place:** *principio* introduces the first of the three sections on the soul's structure.
exceptionally refined: *persubtilem* corresponds to Epicurus' λεπτομερές, 'of refined parts'; cf. *ad Herodotum* 63. The *per-* prefix is intensifying (cf. *perparuis* 216), with the same force as the adverbial *perquam* (180, 187, 204, 229); Lucretius

makes free use of such compounds, which are perhaps colloquial and are otherwise rare in poetry and, outside Cicero, in literary prose.

180 **bodies:** the terms *corpora* (cf. 195 and 205), *semina* (187, 217 and 230) and possibly *figurae* (190) are ambiguous, and applicable either to atoms or to compound particles, but the parallel argument at II 451ff. certainly concerned atoms, and the use of the technical term *principia* at 427 below with reference back to the present passage (which Bailey overlooks) shows that the same is true here; cf. also 241-6, where the argument of 182-207 is applied unambiguously to the atoms (*elementa* 244) of the 'fourth nature' in the soul. Because atoms are under discussion, the opening argument (182-207) is inconsistent with Epicurean theory, since it makes atomic speed vary according to atomic type, whereas Epicurus held that all atoms moved through void at the same rate, irrespective of their size, shape or weight (cf. II 238-9). Giussani suggested that Lucretius has here misrepresented his Epicurean source and that the original argument involved no inconsistency, since it concerned not individual atoms but 'molecules' (ὄγκοι), tiny compound particles, each made up of constantly moving atoms, but each with its own size, shape, weight and speed of motion. While this is not the only passage whose difficulties would be resolved if Lucretius has indeed confused atoms with 'molecules', (cf., e.g., II 381-97), there is no direct evidence for the 'molecule' concept in any extant Epicurean source, and it may be that the inconsistency goes back to Epicurus himself; if so, it can be paralleled from his astronomy, where some of the explanations of lunar eclipses which he has taken over from other thinkers are inconsistent with his own view of the relative sizes of earth, sun and moon.

181 **your mind may grasp:** after *animus* 177, the 'uncontracted' form of *animaduertas* (cf. on 46) imparts a deliberately playful touch, with the mind being directed to reflect on its own composition; cf. 239-40.

182-3 **We can see:** *uidetur* has its 'Lucretian' sense; cf. on 35.

as quickly: *adeo celeri ratione = tam celeriter.*

what the mind presents . . . initiates: the allusion is to an act of will, where the action is first pictured by the mind and then set in motion through the agency of the spirit; cf. IV 877-906. After *quam*, the relative *quod* is to be supplied as subject-accusative governed by *proponit*; for *sibi proponere* , confirming Wakefield's emendation, cf. 879.

184-5 **stirs itself into motion:** Lucretius' alternation beween *perciet* (cf. IV 563) and *percit* (303 below) illustrates archaic fluctuation between conjugations (cf. *sonere* 156).

any of the things which: *quorum natura* is periphrastic for *quae* (see on 130-1). As antecedent, *eorum* (partitive genitive) is understood with *res ulla*; for the sense-construction whereby *res* is treated as neuter, cf., e.g., I 57 and 450.

can be plainly seen before our eyes: there is a contrast with the invisible processes of the mind.

186-7 **has to consist:** *debere*, usually restricted in classical prose to moral obligation, is often used by Lucretius of logical, causal or scientific necessity; it not only provides variety with *necesse* or a gerundive, and sometimes a more convenient construction, but perhaps also suggests that objects have a duty to conform to nature's laws.

round . . . minute seeds: in the course of the opening argument, four qualities in the mind's seeds (i.e. its atoms: see on 180 above) are inferred from its mobility; they form two pairs, roundness and smoothness (the more perfectly round an atom, the smoother its surface) and smallness and lightness (the smaller an atom, the less its weight). *rutundus* is the usual spelling of *rotundus* in the Lucretian manuscripts.

188 **so that they can move . . . :** whereas greater weight and an irregular shape, which would cause them to get caught up in one another, would provide greater resistance.

a slight impulse: e.g. the images of smoke and mist witnessed in dreams at 430-3; see notes there. For the 'etymological' assonance *momine moueri*, cf. 144; the intervening plosives in *paruo possint impulsa* are not inappropriate to the impact under discussion.

189-99 The argument about the invisible is now supported by typically Epicurean analogies from the more visible, in two stages. The claim about the invisible atoms of the invisible mind is supported firstly by a comparison and contrast with the invisible atoms of *visible* compounds, water and honey respectively (189-95); the picture of the invisible atoms of water and honey is in turn justified from visible compounds, (a) the heap of poppy-seeds, where each seed resembles a water atom (and thus a mind atom) in being round, smooth, small and light; (b) the pile of stones or corn-ears, where each stone and each corn-ear partially resembles a honey atom, the stone in being comparatively large and heavy, the corn-ear in its irregular, spiky shape and consequent adhesiveness. These analogies are not mere illustrations, but constitute the evidence from experience for the principle on which the argument about the nature of the mind's atoms depends. The poppy-seeds also served as an analogue for water atoms in the parallel passage at II 453-5; since they, the stones, and the corn-ears are initially stationary in their respective heaps, they do not afford a complete or perfect Epicurean model of the atoms in compounds, which Epicurus, unlike his atomist predecessor Democritus, took to be in constant motion (cf. *aeterno motu* 33, and II 80-141 and 308-32).

189-90 **for example:** literally 'for indeed'; the analogy of water, the round shape of whose atoms was demonstrated at II 451ff., is used as evidence for the nature of the mind's atoms. The immediate echo of *momine moueri* 188 in *mouetur . . . momine* serves to emphasise the logic of the argument.

flows: *flūtat* is contracted from *flŭĭtat*; cf. *flutant*, restored by Turnebus at IV 77.

tiniest: the diminutive *tantillus* (= *tantulus*) occurs in Lucretius only here, but cf. the form *pauxillus* (I 835, 836 and III 229).

small shapes: *figurae* denotes atomic shapes, as at II 385 and 682, and III 246; see on 180 above.

which roll easily: i.e. round. The liquids in *uolubilibus* and *tantillo . . . flutat* 189 match the water's liquidity, the four dactyls in 190 its swift flow.

191-2 The five spondees in 191 provide a striking rhythmic contrast with the preceding line and match the hesitant flow of the more viscous honey. The fifth-foot spondee, common in the Greek hexameter and popular with Catullus and the Alexandrian school of Roman poets, is comparatively rare in Lucretius and in Augustan poetry; the other examples in book III are at 198, 249, 253, 417, 545, 907 and 963.

honey . . . is naturally: literally 'the nature of honey is'; *mellis natura* approximates to *mel* (cf. 130-1 and note).

thicker: *constans* is used in its root sense, 'standing together'; the comparative, like *cunctantior* 192, is not pre-Lucretian.

motion: for the fairly rare root sense of *actus*, cf. Virgil, *Aeneid* XII 687.

193-5 **undoubtedly:** Lucretius' frequent use of *nimirum* (never in an ironic sense) reflects his conviction of the validity of his conclusions.

does not consist of: *exstat* is here used idiosyncratically in the sense of *constat*.

smooth: *lēuis*, 'smooth', (cf. 200, 205, 244) is to be carefully distinguished from *lĕuis*, 'light' (cf. 196, 418).

refined: *subtilibus* corresponds to *minutis* 187 and *paruis* 190.

round: the full atomic picture was more complicated, since all compounds contained atoms of more than one type (II 581-99), and honey, in addition to the irregularly shaped atoms which explained its stickiness, also contained round atoms to explain its sweet taste (II 398-407); for other examples of a compound comprising atoms of contrasting or opposed types, cf. II 456-77.

196-9 **Again:** the second *namque* (cf. 189) marks the second stage in the appeal to the more visible world (see on 189-99 above).

with poppy-seed: *papaueris*, genitive with *aceruus*, is emphatically placed outside the *ut* clause to which it grammatically belongs.

you will find that: the 'ethic' dative *tibi* here expresses the interest of the second person in the outcome of the proposed experiment.

a slight, checked breath: *suspensa* suggests that this is a deliberately checked *human* breath.

a high heap: Giussani may be right in assuming the pile to have featured in a children's game, but it may equally, like the piles of stones and of corn-ears, have been assembled purely for the purposes of scientific experiment.

but . . . corn-ears: there is again a striking, expressive, rhythmic contrast; after the predominantly dactylic lines describing the rapid movement of the poppy-seeds (196-7), 198, like 191 above (see note there), has five spondees, and is the only Lucretian line without a dactyl in the last four feet. *conlectum* is a necessary correction of the manuscripts' *coniectum*, as at IV 414. In the context, the *-que* of *spicarumque* has the force of *-ue*, a common Latin idiom: cf., e.g., 150, 284, 797 and 841.

it can in no way: as subject, *aura* is to be supplied, and, with *potest*, *cogere* to govern *conlectum*. *noenu* is a strong, archaic, form of *non*, from *ne* + *oinom* (= *unum*), used also at IV 712.

199-202 **Therefore:** the only Lucretian instance of *igitur* placed first in its sentence.

bodies: the propositions advanced here are valid in Epicurean theory for all bodies save the atoms, which moved at a constant rate irrespective of their shape or weight; see on 180 above.

in proportion to their smallness and smoothness: as exemplified by the poppy-seeds (and water atoms). *proquam* (cf. classical *prout*) is found only in Lucretius (cf. II 1137, VI 11), and here provides a variation on standard prose constructions for proportion (e.g. *quo minora et leuiora sunt, eo mobiliora sunt*). For the probably colloquial *paruissima* for classical *minima*, cf. I 615 and 621, where the classical form was reserved to express the idea of a technical minimum.

but on the other hand . . . : as at 191 and 198, there is expressive rhythmic contrast; after the primarily dactylic line and a half appropriate to swiftly moving bodies, spondees predominate for the appearance of the heavier bodies in 201, while the final monosyllabic word in 202 serves appropriately to weigh down the line.

the greater their weight and roughness: as exemplified by the stones and corn-ears respectively. *magis cum pondere magno* = *ponderosiora*; the indefinite *quaecumque* (literally 'whichsoever prove heavier . . .') again provides variation on the standard prose construction (*quo ponderosiora et asperiora inueniuntur* . . .).

206-7 Epicurus similarly warns the disciple of the importance and value of key points (*ad Herodotum* 52 and 47b), as did Lucretius at I 331.

good sir: *o bone*, corresponding to the Greek ὠγαθέ, is addressed in the first instance to Memmius, and through him to the general reader (cf. 135 and note): its rather colloquial tone scarcely proves, as suggested, e.g., by Townend (1978) 276, that this cannot be the case.

prove: *cluere*, literally 'to be spoken of' (cf. I 449), often approximates in sense to *esse*.

208-10 **Again . . . also:** *quoque* . . . *etiam* is another instance of Lucretian pleonasm; cf. 108 and note.

proclaims its nature: i.e. the soul's. Since the first argument concerned the mind alone, whereas the second, which begins here, concerns both its parts (as 212 and 228 confirm), there is some awkwardness in the use of *eius*, which is most naturally taken as referring back to *animus* in the technical sense, covering mind alone, at 203, and not to *animus* in the inclusive sense, covering both parts, at 177. Despite the problem, which would probably have been ironed out in revision, there is no overall ambiguity. For the personification of facts or things as declaring or proclaiming (the first sense of *dedicare*) scientific truths, cf., e.g., I 365, 367 and 422.

how tenuous is its texture: i.e. comprising tiny, well-spaced atoms. *dedicat* governs (1) *naturam* and (2) the indirect question of 209-10; the construction is of the biblical 'I know thee, who thou art' type.

if it could be gathered together: i.e. if the tiny atoms of the rarefied compound could be assembled; such a condensation is imagined, purely for the sake of argument, at 533-47. The rare compound *conglomerare* is attested in Ennius.

211-5 **that . . . autopsy reveals:** the *quod* clause, expressing 'the fact that . . .', defines *haec res* 208. *cernas*, literally 'you would discern', is subjunctive because the second person is indefinite; the graphic *ibi*, 'there', suggests first-hand experience.

the carefree peace of death: the description anticipates the conclusion which it is the book's central aim to establish. Death, or its peace, is here personified as taking possession of the deceased.

the substance of his mind and spirit: for the periphrasis, see on 130-1.

judging by: *ad*, 'in relation to', indicates the twin criteria.

safeguards: death is again personified; *praestare* is here used of safeguarding goods for which one has stood surety.

the consciousness of life: for the close association of life and consciousness, cf., e.g., *uiuere cum sensu* 101; *uitalem sensum* recurs at 527 and 635.

heat: for the sense of *uapor*, see on 126. For heat as one of the soul's four elements, see 231-6.

216-20 **the spirit as a whole:** as specified in 212 and 228, the argument applies to both parts of the soul, but in drawing the conclusion Lucretius concentrates on the spirit for which it has the greater cogency; whereas the mind might be expected to escape from the recesses of the chest without damage to the bodily contours, even if there was a discernible loss in weight, the spirit's distribution throughout the whole body made the preservation of the bodily contours at its departure the more remarkable.

exceptionally small seeds: i.e. atoms; see on 180. For the compound *perparuus*, which recurs at V 588, cf. *persubtilem* 179 and note.

woven as it is . . . : the phrase reinforces the argument; since the spirit is so widely distributed through the body (as established, e.g., at 117 and 143), its constituents must indeed be especially refined to leave the body without discernibly affecting its contours or weight.

veins . . . flesh . . . sinews: in this list of bodily tissues, which recurs at 566-7 and 691, *uiscera* has its regular Lucretian sense; cf. also 249 and 266.

in so far as: *quatenus* is causal, as always in Lucretius (cf. 424); the clause restates the argument of 211-5 in terms especially appropriate to the *anima.*

completely . . . whole body: *omnis* and *toto*, like *nexam . . . neruos* 217, reinforce the argument by focusing on the large area occupied by the spirit in life.

the outer contour: *extimus* is a rare alternative form of *extremus*, and *circumcaesura* (literally 'a cutting round'), which occurs in Latin only here and, in the same phrase, at IV 647, is a translation of the Greek περικοπή, illustrating the poet's complaints of the dearth of Latin technical vocabulary at I 136-9 and 260 below.

is . . . preserved intact: *praestat* with reflexive and agreeing adjective does not carry the same commercial metaphor as in its use at 215 above (see note there).

no tittle of weight is lost: *hilum*, an old word of uncertain derivation, denotes something tiny. Lucretius normally combines it with a negative; for exceptions, cf. 514 and note. *defit* is an old, middle, form of classical *deficio*; cf. II 1141.

221-7 The argument concludes with corroborative analogies, where the soul's departure from the body is compared with the loss of scent or flavour from a compound.

It is like this when: *quod genus* is a common Lucretian formula for introducing an analogy, comparison or example; with *est cum* here and at 597, it approximates to *ita*, the *quod* of the adverbial accusative being connective (= *hoc*), whereas at 266, 276, 327 and 431 it approximates to *ut* or *uelut*, the *quod* introducing a subordinate clause.

the bouquet of wine: for this sense of *flos*, apparently a less standard metaphor than the modern 'bouquet', cf. Plautus, *Curculio* 96; it is not without poetic advantage, in suggesting a comparison of the departing soul with a fading flower. The use, or misuse, of Bacchus in the 'faded' sense to denote wine, his province, is justified by Lucretius at II 655-60, provided that such devices (which contravene the rule of Epicurean Canonic that words should be used in their primary senses) do not contaminate the mind with conventional religious ideas.

sweet breath of an unguent: the bold use of *spiritus* for the unguent's scent emphasises the parallel with the soul of a man, which Lucretius identifies, at least in part, with his breath.

flavour: *sucus*, normally 'juice' or 'sap' (whose loss from objects would produce *discernible* differences), here denotes the flavour contained in it; for this extended sense, cf. II 458.

seems no smaller to the eyes . . . from its weight: just like the body after the soul's departure; cf. 213-4 and 219-20. The adverbial accusative *nil* with the comparative is a variation on the usual construction with the ablative of measure of difference (cf. *nihilominus).*

many minute seeds: the size of the seeds (i.e. the atoms, as at 217 above) is the main point at issue; *minuta* answers *perparuis* 216 and is taken up by *pauxillis* 229. Editors complain that whereas flavours and scents, the soul's analogues, are here the product of *many* atoms, the soul at 278 comprises *few* atoms. However, the terms are relative and there is no serious inconsistency: the atoms responsible for scents, for example, though few compared with the other atoms in the compound, had to be numerous enough to diffuse the odour constantly and over a wide area (even if scents normally had a shorter range than sights or sounds); the soul-atoms in turn, though numerous enough to produce life and sensation throughout the whole body, were few relative to the number of body-atoms (cf. 370-95). The mechanics of taste and smell are explained at IV 615-705.

in the total mass of the objects: the rest of the mass comprises a far greater number of larger atoms.

228-30 The conclusion of the second argument is now confidently reasserted.

Therefore . . . again and again: this insistent formula occurs some thirteen times in the poem; cf. 576 and 686.

one can see . . . that: Lucretius uses *scire licet*, the uncontracted form of *scilicet* ('obviously'), governing the original accusative and infinitive construction, almost half as often as *scilicet* itself; cf. 866 and 873.

the substance of mind and spirit: cf. 212 and note.

tiny: on the rare diminutive *pauxillus*, see on 189.

no weight: *nil ponderis* echoes *nec . . . ponderis hilum* 220.

231-57 *The soul's composition: (b) its four elements*

Having demonstrated the soul's generally refined atomic constitution, Lucretius now seeks to prove that it contains four specific types of atomic compound, or elements, heat, wind and air, three of the most refined elements known to experience, whose effects on moods and temperaments are to be described at 288-322, and a fourth, nameless element which was more refined still, and which was postulated to account for physical and mental consciousness. The passage concludes (245-57) with an account of the mechanics of physical sensation: the atoms of the fourth element in the *anima*, because of their refinement, are first to respond to a stimulus (e.g. a pin-prick) and take on new motions which are passed on to the other soul-elements, heat, wind and air, in ascending order of grossness, and similarly in turn to the body-tissues, blood, flesh and, in the most extreme cases, bones and marrow. Sensation is thus explained as a by-product of atomic motions occurring in the soul-body compound; as already explained at II 865-990, individual atoms are devoid of sensation, which is a secondary quality of animate compounds. The body's participation in sensation is further emphasised later, at 333-6 and 350-69. Though no account of mental and emotional consciousness is offered here, the process must clearly have been triggered in a parallel way, with the fourth element passing on its motions to heat, wind and air, this time in the *animus*. The passage, however sketchy, is of great importance, since the explanation of consciousness in material terms is one of Lucretius' most serious problems, if his account of the soul's nature in III and its processes in IV is to carry conviction, while the account of consciousness presented here carries vital implications for the all-important conclusion that it must cease at death.

231 **This substance:** *haec natura* refers to *mentis naturam animaeque* 228; the four elements are present in both parts of the soul. The theory of certain German scholars, that the fourth element was present only in the *animus* (or was identical with it), was convincingly refuted by Giussani, *Studi Lucreziani* (1896) 183-217.

232-3 A refinement on the picture suggested at 121-9 above, where heat (*calor* 121, *uapor* 126) and wind (*uentus* 126, but loosely termed *aer* in 122) were vital parts of the soul; air (*aer* 233) is now added to wind (*aura* 232) and heat (*uapor* 233) as a third, distinct component. At VI 685 wind results when air is set in motion, which suggests that wind and air comprised the same types of atoms, which performed more violent patterns of motion in wind than in air. As at 121-9, the presence of wind and heat in the soul is rather naively inferred from the cessation of breathing and the loss of bodily heat at death.

a sort of tenuous breath: *quaedam* (cf. 241) adds vagueness, probably suggesting that the breath or wind contained in the soul is not quite identical with that of everyday experience. The *u* of *tenuis* is here consonantalised, so that the word scans as a trochee; cf. 243, 383 and 448, and for the converse process see on 330.

234-6 The presence of air in the soul is now justified on theoretical grounds: heat, or fire, an especially rarefied compound, must contain a high proportion of air in its interstices; cf. the claim at VI 1034-6, that all-encircling air must be contained within the fabric of all compounds.

there is no heat: *quisquam*, normally a pronoun, is used adjectivally for *ullus*, as at I 1077, II 857 and III 875.

because it is rarefied in nature: literally 'because its nature is rarefied'; *constat* here approximates to *est* or *semper est. rara* is placed first, outside its clause, for emphasis.

primary particles: *primordia*, literally 'first beginnings', and *principia*, 'beginnings', which replaces it in the genitive, dative and ablative where it is metrically inadmissible, are Lucretius' standard terms for the atoms, once the atomic nature of the ultimate particles has been demonstrated in book I. On his choice of these terms, and their Greek basis, see on 31.

237 **the soul:** *animi* is inclusive, as earlier at 169, 175 and 177; see Introduction IV.

threefold: *triplex* is antithetical to *simplex* 231.

238-44 The presence of the fourth element is now deduced on the theoretical grounds that wind, heat and air cannot account for consciousness, either physical or mental.

240 **the motions that carry sensation:** i.e. physical sensation, involving the *anima* in the parts of the body which are affected; the phrase recurs, with the same reference, at 245, 272 and 379, though in the only other instances, at 570 and 924, it also embraces mental consciousness. For the compound *sensifer* (unique to Lucretius), cf. *florifer* 11 and note.

and the manifold reflections of the mind: the corrupt text in the manuscripts clearly conceals an allusion to mental consciousness, involving the *animus*, which Frerichs' emendation, adopted by Bailey, supplies as well as any. To avoid the repetition of *mens* from 239, Bernays and Munro there emended to *res*, 'the fact of the case', but, whatever the precise text in 240, there is probably a deliberately playful touch in the picture of the mind reflecting on the source of its own processes; cf. 181 and note.

241 **some sort of fourth substance:** *quaedam* (cf. 232 and note) freely acknowledges the shadowy nature of this component. Though the idea may owe something to the Aristotelian concept of the soul as the fifth nature, or quintessence, in the body, there is the fundamental difference that, whereas this quintessence was supra-material, the Epicurean 'quartessence' was indubitably material.

242 **altogether nameless:** because it is quite unlike any compound known to experience.

243-4 **more tenuous:** for the consonantalisation of the first *u* in *tenuius*, making the word dactylic, cf. on 232.

composed of smaller, smoother basic components: *elementa* (Greek στοιχεῖα), primarily denoting 'first principles' or 'rudiments', is applied technically by Lucretius to the atoms, as a variant on *primordia / principia* (see on 236); cf., e.g., II 393, 411, 463 and 981 and III 374; this usage is not of course to be confused with that of the derivative 'elements' for the four types of atomic compound which make up the soul. *elementa* is also the appropriate Latin term for the letters of the alphabet, and its application to the atoms is all the more appropriate in the light of Lucretius' favourite analogy, which was probably traditional to the atomists, between the atoms in compounds and the letters in words: cf., e.g., I 196-8, 823-9 and 907-14, where the double sense of the word is exploited at 828 and 913. The association of the mobility of the fourth component with the size and smoothness of its *atoms* helps to confirm that it was the *atoms* of the soul in general which were under discussion at 182-207; see on 180. The phrase *e . . . elementis* is adjectival, with *e* and *ex* serving as Lucretian shorthand for *factum e*; the repetition of the preposition (with the same two adjectives, together with synonymous nouns) is paralleled at VI 353-4, and there is no need to emend either *e* or *ex* (despite VI 330) to *est*.

245-57 On this account of physical sensation and the role of the fourth element in it, see introductory note to 231-57 above.

245 **throughout our members:** *per artus* shows that, as in 240 above, *sensiferos motus* is applied exclusively to physical sensation, even though the fourth element must clearly have triggered mental processes in a parallel way.

246 **to be stirred:** resulting in rearrangement of the motions of its atoms.

being made up: the participle is used causally.

shapes: synonymous with *elementis* 244 and so indubitably denoting *atomic* shapes; see on 180 and 190.

247-8 **heat . . . wind . . . air:** the other three elements in the *anima* in ascending order of grossness.

with its unseen power: for this type of periphrasis, see on 8 and 130-1, and cf. 269, 277 and 286-7.

take up the movements: i.e. their atoms adapt their pattern of motion.

everything is set in motion: i.e. the atoms of all the bodily tissues adapt their motions in turn. For completeness or graphic effect, Lucretius takes what he admits in 256-7 is an extreme and rare case, where the sensation extends beyond the blood and flesh to the bones and marrow, with potentially fatal results (249-55).

249-51 **blood . . . all the flesh . . . bones . . . marrow:** like the elements in the *anima*, the bodily tissues are affected in ascending order of grossness. The shock of the effect on the flesh is conveyed by the fifth-foot spondee in *persentiscunt* (see on 191), its completeness by the *per-* prefix and the emphatically placed *omnia* in 250.

pleasure . . . its searing opposite: *contrarius ardor* is literally 'the opposite flame (or 'heat')'. The allusion reflects that, in Epicurean moral theory, every sensation (and every experience) involved a feeling of pleasure or pain, which were the basic moral criteria, in so far as pleasure was to be pursued and pain avoided, even though Epicurus qualified this doctrine in various crucial ways (Introduction III).

252-5 **pain . . . its keen torment:** *dolor* defines *contrarius ardor* 251. The implication is that extreme pleasure can penetrate as far as this *without* fatal consequences.

cannot lightly: i.e. without the dire effects described in the *quin* clause; *temere*, 'rashly' or 'heedlesly', virtually personifies *dolor* and *acre malum*.

as far as this: i.e. to the bones and marrow. *penetrare* and *permanare* emphasise the deep penetration involved in such a process.

without everything being . . . disturbed: i.e. without the whole soul-body compound being disrupted. *quin* = *ita ut non*. The fifth-foot spondee in *perturbentur* (cf. *persentiscunt* in 249 above) again helps to convey the shock involved, while the repeated prefix in *permanare / perturbentur* conveys that the depth of shock matches the depth of penetration.

parts of the spirit: cf. 396-416, where, although the *anima* is less vital for life than the *animus*, its total loss proves fatal and results in the departure of the *animus*.

all the body's apertures: the allusion is primarily to the pores; the popular account of the soul being breathed out through the mouth, suggested at 122, is here modified to conform with orthodox Epicurean theory. At the same time, *caulae*, basically 'little hollows', could *include* the mouth. At 702, it is applied to *internal* bodily apertures.

256-7 **the motions:** pleasure-bringing motions no doubt reached bones and marrow as infrequently as those which brought pain, but *hanc ob rem . . . ualemus* shows that the allusion must be exclusively to the latter, potentially lethal, category.

as it were: *quasi* apologises for the imprecise *in summo corpore*, which is used to sum up the blood and outer flesh.

258-322 ***The soul's composition (c): interrelationship and effects of its four elements***

The introductory complaint about the poverty of Latin prepares the reader for difficulties ahead, but the opening point, that the soul's four elements are inextricably intermingled to form a unique compound, in which the qualities of its four components are inseparably combined (262-5), emerges clearly enough, and is illustrated with the analogy of the various secondary qualities which are inextricably combined in a piece of meat (266-72). At 273-81, the point is developed in connection with the 'fourth nature', now strikingly described as 'the soul of the soul'; i.e. its role in the soul matches that of the soul in the living being. Three main points of comparison lie behind the metaphor or analogy: (a) the fourth nature is intermingled throughout the soul, as is the soul-compound throughout the body; (b) it is the most refined element in the soul, as is the soul in the living creature (this refinement is now expressed in terms of a scale of imperceptibility, of being below the ken of the senses; hence the language of hiding - *latere* 273, 277 and 280 - and the spatial terms *subest* 273, *penitus* 273 and *infra est* 274); (c) it initiates consciousness in the soul, as does the soul in the living being (cf. 246ff. above), and, because of this, is said to 'hold sway in the whole body' (281). Lucretius now turns to the three other elements and first (282-7) reiterates their intermingling in the soul-compound (for a problem of interpretation in these lines see on 284 below); he then alludes to their role in moods (288-93) and temperaments (294-313), associating heat with anger, wind with fear and air with placidity. Such explanations of moods and temperaments are not confined to the Epicureans, but can be paralleled from Greek medical writers, from Aristotle and from the Stoics, who, however, all placed the elements responsible in the body, rather than, like Epicurus, in a corporeal soul. While *calidi plus* 294 suggests that temperamental differences are caused by differences in the proportions of the three elements present in different souls, the way in which a given element comes to predominate in a mood is left unexplained - a somewhat surprising omission even in the summary to which the poet is restricting himself (261). The passage concludes with the addition of two important riders; 314-8 reveal that more detailed differences in human temperament depend on further differences in the atomic types present in the soul, which are too complicated for discussion; this shows that Epicurus had worked out this branch of his psychology in considerable detail, although the Lucretian outline is the fullest account of it which has survived. Secondly, since the account of human character has shown (307-13) that it is to some degree ineradicable, the reader is assured that Epicurean philosophy can temper faults of character sufficiently to allow him to lead the ideal Epicurean moral life and so to achieve happiness (319-22).

258-61 This introduction looks forward to both the main topics in the passage, (a) the interrelationship of the four soul-elements (summed up in *inter sese mixta* and *compta* 258-9), and (b) their functions or effects (summed up in *uigeant* 259), viz. the fourth element's role in triggering consciousness, and the contribution of heat, wind and air to moods and temperaments.

the poverty of my native tongue: this famous complaint is repeated from I 136-45 and 830-2. Though interpreted more generally by Pliny, *Letters* IV 18.1, it is primarily a complaint about the lack of ready-made technical vocabulary in Latin for the expression of Greek philosophical ideas: the problem is first raised (I 139) in the context of the novelty of the poet's subject-matter (*rerum nouitas*), and at I 830-2 the difficulty (solved, for once, by recourse to transliteration) is the lack of an equivalent for Anaxagoras' technical *homoeomeria.* Cicero, *De Finibus* III 3, similarly complains of having to improvise his own philosophical vocabulary and to assign new names to new concepts, though in Lucretius' case, as I 143 reflects, the problem is twofold: he has to devise not only vocabulary (*dicta*) but metrically (and poetically) admissible vocabulary (*carmen*). But even if the complaint primarily concerns technical terms, the poet's various coinings of non-technical words may indicate that he found more general limitations in the language, at least for the purposes of hexameter verse composition. The intricate subject-matter of the present passage presents him with general difficulties, but specific problems arise at three points: (a) at 273-80, in expressing the elusive, refined nature of the nameless element, for which spatial terms and the language of hiding are adopted (see introductory note to 258-322 above); (b) at 284, a line of disputed interpretation which most probably alludes to a comparative prominence of heat, wind or air which affects moods and temperaments (see note there); (c) at 314-8, where the lack of terms for the great variety of atomic shapes in the soul which affect temperament and character precludes further discussion. As at I 136-45 and 830-42, the language and metre of the passage seem calculated to illustrate the problem, and also the poet's versatility in coping with it; thus the use of the vague *ea* (literally 'those things') for the elements in 258 at once highlights the poet's lack of a generic term for them (cf. *nil unum* 263 and note), while the absence of a proper main caesura in 258 is the first of several reflections of the metrical problems involved. Similar, illustrative, linguistic and metrical 'licences' in the immediate sequel include the tmesis *inter . . . cursant* and the juxtaposition of *primordia* with its metrical alternative *principiorum* in 262, the metrically convenient archaism *secernier* for *secerni* in 263, the use of *fieri diuisa* as a metrical alternative for the inadmissible *dīuĭdī* in 264, the highly unusual archaism *uis*, = *uires*, in 265, *uiscere* in its standard Lucretian, but archaic, sense of 'flesh' in 266, and the very rare *augmen* ('bulk'), a possible Lucretian coining, in 268 (see notes below).

262-5 **rush to and fro among one another:** the compound *intercursant* is divided by tmesis. Lucretius' examples of the licence are less extravagant than are sometimes to be found in Ennius, but less restricted than Virgil's, who only separates the *in-* prefix, and then only with the suffix *-que*; Lucretius separates other prepositional prefixes, usually with *-que*, but occasionally, as here and at 860, with *enim* or, as at V 287 and 299, with *quasi.* While the licence reflects the vocabulary problems imposed by the poetic medium, it may also, as in other cases (cf., e.g., 860, I 452 and 651 and V 287 and 299), be seen as fitting the sense: the parts of the word are intermingled in the line as are the atoms of each of the soul-elements in the soul-compound; cf. 283, where word-order produces a similar effect.

with the motions proper to them: literally 'with the motions of primary particles'; *principiorum* replaces the metrically inadmissible *primordiorum* (see on 236). The juxtaposition not only illustrates the terminological difficulty, but mirrors the juxtaposition of different types of atom as they intermingle in the soul-compound. G.B.Kerferd, *Phronesis* 16.1 (1971) 90-1, suggested that *principiorum* depends on *primordia* and is here uniquely used as a generic term for the soul's four elements. While this application of the term is not inconceivable in the context of the complaint of lack of vocabulary, one would expect it to be confirmed by repetition elsewhere in the passage, and this interpretation also leaves *motibus* intolerably weak and isolated.

no single element: more literally 'no single thing'; as with *ea* 258, the vagueness of the Latin reflects the lack of a specific term.

be isolated: for the archaic form *secernier* (= *secerni*), cf. *cunctarier* 67 and note.

its powers: *potestas*, like *uis* 265, denotes the effects, functions or qualities of each element, which are no more isolable in the soul-compound than are the elements themselves.

spatially divided: parallel in sense to *secernier* 263. *fieri diuisa* = *diuidi* (see on 260 above).

they form, so to speak: as subject of *exstant*, supply *ea* and / or *potestates eorum*, alluding to the elements and / or their qualities. The apologetic *quasi* reflects the difficulty of expressing the idea behind the line.

many forces: the form *uis* for *uires* is found only in Lucretius, at II 586 and V 1033 in the accusative, here alone in the nominative.

of a single body: i.e. the soul-compound, which, unlike each of the elements in it, comprises a single entity: *unius corporis* contrasts with *nil unum* 263.

266 **Just as:** *quod genus* here = *uelut*, and is picked up by *sic*, corresponding to *id genus*, at 269; see on 221. The analogy introduced here (contrast e.g. 189-99) is purely illustrative.

267 **smell, taste, and a particular colour:** for this list of secondary qualities, cf. II 680-1; such qualities were possessed by atomic compounds, not by the atoms themselves (II 730-1022). Lambinus' correction of *calor*, the reading of the manuscripts, is essential, since, in view of *sapor* ('taste'), the allusion can scarcely be to living flesh; again, heat, unlike smell and taste, would itself exemplify the soul-elements, rather than providing an analogy for them. The smell and taste which are part and parcel of the meat are to be differentiated from the bouquet, perfume and flavour more readily lost to their compounds at 221-3, where the atoms responsible for these qualities were more readily detachable.

268 **a single bodily bulk:** *unum . . . corporis augmen* is answered by *unam naturam* 270, and also looks back to *unius corporis* 265.

269-72 **by the combination of:** *mixta*, like *commixta* 283 and *diducta* 287, is neuter plural; cf. 136 and note.

the unseen power of wind: the periphrasis, repeated from 247 (see note there), closely associates the element with its qualities; cf. *potestas* 264.

that volatile force: i.e. the fourth, nameless, element. The term *uis* (cf. 265) closely links this element in turn with its qualities.

distributes: *diuidit* (contrast *diuisa* 264) serves as a synonym for *didit* 245.

to them: i.e. to heat, wind and air (cf. 247-8). Lucretius and the Augustan poets occasionally use the archaic form *olle* (= *ille*), which here provides variety with *illa* at the end of the preceding line.

the beginning: as at I 383 and II 269, *initus* provides a metrical alternative for *ĭnĭtĭum.*

which is the initial source of . . . : literally 'whence first arises'; the clause defines *motus* 271, with *unde* equivalent to *e quo.* 271-2 sum up the two stages of the process described in more detail at 247-51, 271 the distribution of the impulse throughout the soul-elements, 272 its communication to the body-tissues, represented here by *uiscera.* Only at this second stage does the soul-body compound experience sensation (cf. the emphasis on the body's participation at 333-6 and 350-69); hence the emphatic position of *sensifer*, outside its clause, in 272.

Many editors take the clause as continuing the description of *mobilis illa uis*, with *unde* = *e qua*, but this leaves *motus* 271 implausibly undefined, yet with the same reference as *sensifer motus* 272.

273-4 **This substance:** i.e. the fourth, nameless, element (*mobilis illa uis* 270-1).

you see: the explanatory *nam* reflects that, as at 246, the fourth element's ability to trigger the initiation of consciousness follows from the refinement of its texture.

lies most deeply hidden and buried . . . unobtrusive: the terms *penitus latet*, *subest* and *infra* are used to express remoteness from perceptibility; cf. 277 and 280, and see notes on 258-322 and 260. The fourth nature never manifests any trace of secondary qualities, as do heat, wind and air in moods and temperaments (288-313).

275 **the soul of the complete soul:** *anima* here and at 280-1 is used inclusively, as the combination of *animus* and *anima* in the explanation of the image at 277 confirms; cf. Introduction IV, and 143 and 150 above. For the three main points of comparison behind the metaphor, omnipresence, refinement and the initiation of consciousness, see introductory note to 258-322 above.

276-8 **Just as:** for the use of *quod genus*, cf. 266 and note.

in our limbs and our whole body: despite the mind's location in the chest, the description is valid for the complete soul (mind + spirit), whose omnipresence in the body matches that of the fourth nature in the soul.

force of the mind . . . power of the spirit: these periphrases for *animus* and *anima*, involving *uis* and *potestas* rather than *natura* (see on 8 and 130-1), seem to have been suggested here by *uenti caeca potestas* 247 and 269 and the use of *uis* 271; they link abstract with concrete, associating *animus* and *anima* with their qualities or powers, and reappear, e.g., at 397, 499, 558, 583, 600, 638, 674, 680, 747, 771 and 844.

latently: *latens* is answered by *latet* 280; refinement in texture is the chief point of comparison. For the terminology, see on 273.

because they are formed: the clause explains *latens* 277.

a few small bodies: though the main emphasis so far has been on the size of the soul-atoms, their paucity has been implied in *persubtilem* 179; cf. also the allusion to the few seeds of wind and heat which escape at death in 125-6. *paucis* is a comparative term; the soul-atoms are few in relation to the number of body-atoms; see on 226.

279-81 **I can assure you:** the 'ethic' dative *tibi* again enlivens the argument; cf. 197.

this nameless substance: *nominis expers* echoes 242; for the use of *uis*, cf. 271 and note.

being made of minute bodies: the participle is used causally (cf. 246); the phrase answers the *quia* clause of 278, just as *latet* answers *latens* 277.

as it were: *quasi* here apologises for the arresting metaphor of 275, now that its point has been explained.

holds sway in the body as a whole: in that it initiates consciousness in the soul, as does the soul in the body. The same phrase is used of the soul at 709 (see note there); contrast 138-9, where it was applied quite differently to the mind, to express its dominance in the mind-spirit relationship.

282 **Similarly:** i.e. to the fourth element, which fulfils its function (the triggering of consciousness: 271-2) whilst pervading the whole soul-compound (just as the soul pervades the whole body: 276-7).

283 **intermingled with one another . . . produce their effects:** *inter se uigeant commixta* echoes *inter sese mixta . . . uigeant* 258-9. The word-order, with *uigeant* placed between *inter se* and *commixta*, matches the physical intermingling described; cf. 262 and note.

284 **with one more unobtrusive or more prominent than the others:** the interpretation of the line is disputed. *subsit* clearly takes up from 273-80 the idea of remoteness from perceptibility, and many editors, including Bailey, assume an allusion to the relative refinement of heat, wind and air in terms of the size of their respective atoms (cf. *facta minutis corporibus* of the fourth element at 279-80). However, the allusion to the effects, or functions, of heat, wind and air (*uigeant* 283) suggests that it is their secondary qualities, not the sizes of their respective atoms (which in any case have no relevance to the sequel in 285-7), that are here under discussion, and that the line looks forward to the account of their effects on moods and temperaments (288-313), referring to a relative prominence which one or other of the three may gain, temporarily or more permanently, in the soul of a given individual. Such an interpretation does not require Brieger's emendation of *aliis* to *alias* ('with one more unobtrusive, or more prominent, at one time, another at another'), which would make the line applicable only to moods (288-93), not to temperaments (294-313). For the use of *-que* with the sense of *-ue*, cf. 198 and note; *aliis* is either ablative of comparison or dative with the two verbs.

285 **yet in such a way that:** as the *ni* clause of 286-7 makes clear, *ut* = *ita tamen ut*, introducing a limiting consecutive clause; a soul-element cannot become so prominent as to disrupt the soul's unity.

they all clearly go to make up: despite the triple subjects in 282-3 and 286-7, *ab omnibus* presumably includes the fourth element, whose participation is implied by *consimili ratione* 282 and *sensum* 287; cf. 265 and 269-71. *uideatur* is here a true passive (cf. 35 and note), 'is seen to' (not physically, but by inference from experience).

286-7 **otherwise . . . would:** literally 'in order that . . . may not'; *ni*, from *nei*, is an old form of *ne*, and not to be confused with *nisi*. Like *olle* (cf. 271), it is of no metrical advantage, but imparts archaic variety for its own sake.

air along with its powers: for the periphrasis with *potestas*, cf. 247, 269, 277 and notes.

each be isolated: i.e. each separate out from the soul-compound, and respectively display the full qualities of heat, wind, and air. *sorsum* is repeated with the third subject to emphasise the key idea of separation, which is taken up again in *diducta*.

disrupt and destroy sensation: because they would no longer interact with the fourth element whose function is to trigger consciousness.

288-9 **The mind:** the discussion so far has been applicable to the complete soul (mind + spirit), but in describing the effects of heat, wind and air on moods and temperaments, Lucretius now turns to the *animus* as the seat of the emotions. At the same time, the *anima* too must have played its part to produce the physical signs of the emotions concerned (e.g. the blazing eyes in 289).

you see: with Faber's *etenim,* the greater or lesser prominence of heat, wind and air (284) is now exemplified from moods and temperaments. *etiam*, the reading of the manuscripts, which, on alternative interpretations of 284 (see note above), leaves the transition to moods and temperaments intolerably vague, may have arisen from confusion with 292 below; for *etenim* postponed to second position, cf. VI 912.

seethes in anger: *in ira* goes closely not only with *sumit* but also with *feruescit*: the standard metaphor (cf. 295) lends support to the association of anger with heat.

fire flashes from the fierce eyes: the physical manifestations of the various moods and temperaments, which receive considerable emphasis and are vividly described throughout, provide a degree of evidence from experience for the whole Epicurean theory; *ardor*, 'heat' and 'brightness', is a partial synonym for *calor* 288. Lambinus' *acribus* is to be preferred to the manuscripts' *acrius* ('more fiercely <than normal>'), not so much on the strength of the imitation at *Aeneid* XII 102, since Virgil is quite capable of adapting his models, as because an allusion to fire flashing at other times is beside the point.

290-1 **the abundance of chilling breeze:** i.e. wind; its association with cold (cf. *frigida mens* 299 and *gelidas auras* 300) fits the cold sweat and trembling limbs which are amongst fear's physical symptoms. *multa* suggests that the quantity of the element concerned determines the mood (as, on the evidence of *calidi plus* 294, it determines temperament), but how such temporary quantitative superiority is brought about is left unexplained.

makes the flesh creep and the limbs tremble: the same physical manifestations are described in 300-1.

292-3 **Again . . . also:** for the pleonastic *etiam . . . quoque*, cf. 208.

tranquil state of air: literally 'state of tranquil air'. Atomic motion was less agitated in air than in wind (see on 233), hence its association with placidity, which may have been supported by physical indications like the steady breathing of the carefree individual contrasted with the rapid panting of the victim of fear.

when the heart is at peace: an allusion to the Epicurean ideal of ἀταραξία, freedom from mental disturbance.

294-313 The discussion now moves on from moods to temperaments (i.e. permanent predisposition to such moods), which are illustrated first from the animal kingdom, then (307ff.) from man.

294-5 **hearts . . . temperament:** *corda* and *mens*, like *animus* 288, denote the seat of the emotions, which in turn affects the *anima* to produce the physical manifestations.

boil over in anger: cf. 288-9 and note above.

a greater quantity of heat: a clear indication that differences of temperament are attributed to quantitative differences in the soul-elements; see introductory note to 258-322 above.

296 **A prime example of this:** literally 'Amongst the first of this sort'; *quo genere* is ablative of quality.

violent breed of lions: for the periphrasis with *uis* (literally 'might'), cf. *fortis equi uis* 8.

297-8 The alliteration with *p* and *r* helps to convey the vigour of the roars described.

waves of their passions: the uncontrollable waves of anger sustain the image of hearts boiling over in anger in 294-5.

299 **chilly hearts:** as in 295, *mens* denotes the seat of the emotions, reflecting that beasts, though denied a rational faculty by Epicurus, possessed at least a rudimentary *animus*.

possess more wind: *uentosa magis*, literally 'more windy', implies a higher proportion of the element (cf. *calidi plus* 294).

300-1 The predominantly dactylic rhythm matches the speed and agitation described.

arouse cold breezes in their flesh: through the agency of the *anima*, which produces the bodily symptoms of the emotion (see on 288 above). These breezes make the flesh creep (*ciet horrorem membris* 291).

causing a trembling motion to manifest itself . . . : cf. *concitat artus* 291. For causative *facere* with accusative and infinitive, see on 100-1.

302 **But cattle . . . calm air:** the somewhat strained Latin (literally 'The nature of cattle lives more with calm air', a variation on *bobus plus est placidi aeris*; cf. 294) reflects the problems alluded to at 260. *magis* is not to be taken with *placido*, since Epicurean air, by definition, is always calm.

303-4 **are . . . stirred:** for the fourth conjugation form *percit*, see on 184.

the smoky torch of anger: the vivid image is not only poetically effective, but up to a point scientifically appropriate, in so far as the soul of the irascible creature is literally fiery.

enveloping them in a pall of blinding darkness: though the smoke from the torch is purely figurative, the image conveys the idea of anger clouding the judgment of its victim.

305 **numbed . . . cold shafts . . . :** a vividly contrasting image for fear; the connection with wind is suggested by the allusions to the cold associated with it (cf. 290, 299-300). The alliterative pattern in *torpet telis perfixa pauoris* adds to the effect.

306 **they form an intermediate between . . . :** *interutrasque* is an adverb found only in Lucretius, who uses it on at least five other occasions (e.g. V 472). The accusatives *ceruos . . . leones* are governed by the *inter-* prefix, making Avancius' *inter utrosque* unnecessary.

307-9 **So it is with the human race:** i.e. they display the same temperaments (however much education may modify them).

education: *doctrina*, which at II 8 was applied to Epicurean philosophy, here denotes general education, which gives its recipients a superficial civilised polish, and contrasts with *ratio* (Epicurean philosophy) in 321.

certain of them: i.e. those who receive it or benefit from it.

it . . . leaves behind: *illa*, referring to *doctrina*, emphasises the contrast with *ratio* 321. It can scarcely be neuter plural ('those traces just observed in animals'), since the traces left behind in men are traces not of animal but of natural human temperament, and the preceding discussion has in any case concerned animal temperament in general, not traces of it.

natural temperament: literally 'nature of the mind'; for the use of *animus*, cf. 288 and note.

310-3 **it must not be supposed . . . :** the lines may be partly directed at the Stoics and their view of the ideal Stoic sage as perfectly virtuous, or equally at the Platonic and Aristotelian idea of the completely wise man as completely good. Epicurus saw human nature as less perfectible, even though he saw happiness as within the reach of most people, given the right standards.

311 **so as to stop:** *quin* = *ita ut non*.

too precipitately: *procliue* suggests motion on a downward path; the comparative shows that anger is not always a fault (*malum* 310), thus allowing for righteous anger.

fits of fierce anger: the plural *iras* denotes separate instances of the emotion.

312 **a little too quickly:** implying that in some circumstances a degree of fear is a natural and excusable reaction (even though religious fear, the target of the poem, is invariably a *malum*).

313 **with more than reasonable forbearance:** although placidity was an aspect of the mental tranquillity (ἀταραξία) which was the Epicurean moral goal (cf. 292-3 and note), forbearance was more a Christian than a Greco-Roman virtue, and could, in the poet's eyes here, be carried too far.

314-8 For this significant point, see introductory note to 258-322 above. The attribution of more detailed differences of character to the soul's atomic make-up further limits the degree to which traits of character can be changed or eradicated; hence its inclusion here, before the concluding reassurance that Epicurean philosophy still leaves ideal happiness within reach.

in many other details: i.e. apart from the three main character-types so far discussed.

but I cannot now reveal the hidden causes . . . : as Munro suggested, the poet may well be drawing on Cicero, *Aratea* 234, *quorum ego nunc nequeo tortos euoluere cursus*, but there is no reason to suppose, with Kenney, that the motif is purely literary or that Lucretius is not here omitting a technical discussion found in his Epicurean source.

for all the shapes of the primary particles: with *quot sunt*, supply *figurae*; for *principiis* replacing the metrically inadmissible *primordiis*, see on 236.

which are the source: *unde* = *ex quibus*, referring back to the atomic shapes.

variety in character: *uariantia* is apparently coined by Lucretius as a metrical equivalent for *uărĭĕtas*; cf. I 653, where *rerum* is also coupled with it but has a more concrete sense. Lucretius has no qualms about the repetition of *res* in varying senses in 314, 318 and 319.

319-22 Since the argument from 282 has suggested that moods and temperaments lie to some degree outside human control, reassurance is very necessary, and is resoundingly provided, in this conclusion.

I see I can assert: i.e. on the basis of experience of Epicurean evangelism. *potesse*, the archaic, original form of *posse* (from *pote*, a weakened form of *potis*, + *esse*), contrasts with *nequeo* 316; as subject-accusative, supply *me* (cf., e.g., IV 457 and V 390). *firmare* has the force of *affirmare* or *confirmare*.

traces . . . which are left: by general education (*doctrina* 307: *uestigia linqui* echoes *relinquit . . . uestigia* 308-9), rather than by Epicurean philosophy (*ratio* 321); the picture is that *doctrina* leaves traces of temperamental faults which *ratio* can further reduce to a tiny, negligible, minimum.

philosophy: i.e. the true (Epicurean) philosophy, the *uera ratio* proclaimed at I 51; cf. *ratio tua* 14. The ethical code, for which the Logic and the Physics provided an indispensable basis (Introduction III), was of especial importance for the correction of faults of character, with its insistence, e.g., on the limitation of the desires.

so very slight: *usque adeo . . . paruula = tam paruula.*

living a life worthy of the gods: i.e. leading the ideal Epicurean moral life, of which the gods afforded the perfect model (cf. on 15). Epicurus similarly promises the disciple that he will live as a god among men, *ad Menoeceum* 135. The words are thus quite literally intended; the *d* alliteration adds to the impressiveness of the phrase. The inspiring prospect is strategically placed at the end of the long, technical passage, spurring the reader on to further study.

323-49 ***The interdependence of soul and body***

This important passage prepares for, and foreshadows, many of the proofs of the soul's mortality which follow at 417-829. It makes two, mutually complementary, points: (a) soul and body are mutually indispensable, in that neither can exist, survive, or feel without the other (323-4; 326-30; 333-43; 347-8); (b) they are intimately connected structurally, right from the moment of conception (325; 331-2; 344-6; 349). The interwoven presentation of the two points illustrates their complementary nature in Lucretius' mind, as does his deduction of either of them from the other; though for most of the passage he argues from the close structural union to mutual indispensability (logically enough, since the former has already been implied and foreshadowed in the preceding discussion), this pattern is conspicuously reversed in the last two lines, as if to illustrate that the two points are as interdependent as soul and body themselves. Though the arguments that neither partner can function or survive without the other are more convincing for the body than for the soul, the poet obviously does not regard the passage as constituting a cast-iron case, or the long sequence of proofs of the soul's mortality at the heart of the book would be superfluous; he is rather suggesting the general probability that, if the body depends on the soul, the converse is also true, and that neither of such intimately linked partners could survive the loss of the other.

323-4 **This . . . substance:** i.e. the soul (*animus + anima*), whose constitution has been the subject of 177-322.

is housed: i.e. is held in and protected (cf. Epicurus, *ad Herodotum* 63-5, where the body acts as its covering, τὸ στεγάζον); the description foreshadows the key image of the body as the soul's vessel or container (*uas* 440).

by the whole body: which the *anima* pervades. Though the inclusion of *ab*, which normally expresses agent rather than instrument, could here be seen as personifying the body in its role as the soul's protector, superfluous prepositions are a feature of Lucretian style, and of Latin poetry in general; cf. 429, 522 and 820.

is itself the guardian: the converse of *tenetur* 323. In his inscription of Epicurean doctrines made in the second century A.D., Diogenes of Oenoanda in Lycia sums up the reciprocal relationship by speaking of the soul being bound and binding in return (Chilton 37.1.10).

325 **they cohere . . . having common roots:** a striking image, with soul and body pictured as two plants, not with interwoven roots but growing from the same roots. The line recurs at V 554, where it is applied to the earth and the cushion of air which mysteriously supports it from below, whose relationship is explicitly compared with that of body and soul.

326 **obviously cannot be plucked apart:** as in 333 and 338 below, *uideri* is a true passive (see on 35); Lucretius in each case appeals to experience to support his claim, even though the soul's destruction when 'plucked apart' is less obvious than that of the body (see introductory note to 323-49 above).

327-30 The first of two illustrative analogies for the soul-body relationship; this positive comparison is followed by a negative comparison at 339-43.

Just as: for the use of *quod genus*, cf. 266 and note.

it is not easy: an ironic understatement, in the case of both frankincense and the soul; cf. 361.

pluck . . . from: *euellere* echoes *diuelli* 326, emphasising the parallelism.

without its whole nature also being destroyed: i.e. without the destruction of the frankincense. As in the analogy of the piece of meat (266-8), the smell or scent is here integral to the compound; contrast the analogy of the compounds which lose their flavour, and the atoms reponsible for it, much more readily (221-3). *quin* = *ita ut non*, as at 311.

the substance of mind and spirit: *naturam* in this periphrasis echoes *natura* 328; this, together with the repetition of *haud facile est quin*, further underlines the parallelism.

the whole fabric: i.e. of soul and body; the neuter plural *omnia* covers *animus*, *anima* and *corpus*.

being dissolved: the *u* of *dissoluantur* is vocalised, giving a fifth foot dactyl (cf. 706 and 815); the spondaic fifth foot (see on 191) is comparatively rare in Lucretius and normally reserved for special effect. The *u* almost certainly also counts as a vowel at 455, 470, 578, 612, 758 and 903, but is consonantal at 438, 602, 613, 701, 756 and 818.

331-2 **with their primary particles so intertwined with one another:** a reassertion of the structural union expressed in the still stronger image of 326, again supporting the contention of their mutual indispensability. *inter se* belongs to *implexis*, the words of the phrase being intertwined with others like the atoms they describe (cf. 262 and 283).

from their earliest origin: since conception, as 346 makes clear.

a life which they share as co-heirs: a legal image in which life is an inheritance (*sors*) shared between them.

333-6 The discussion reverts to mutual indispensability, here illustrated from consciousness, for which each partner is required.

it is clear that: because the dead body shows no sign of consciousness and because experience tells us that the body participates in sensation, not just the soul in it; the latter, important, point is elaborated at 350-69. *uidetur* is again a Lucretian passive (cf. 35 and note).

neither body nor soul: *animus* is here used inclusively (see Introduction IV), to cover both mind, the organ of mental consciousness (which was possible only while the body acted as the mind's container), and the spirit which triggered physical consciousness. However, as 335-6 are concerned exclusively with the latter process (as *per uiscera* makes clear), it is perhaps surprising that Lucretius did not write *animae* (cf. 341 and 344). For the periphrases with *potestas*, whose root appears also in *posse* 333, see on 277. *quaeque* here denotes each of two, replacing the usual *utra* or *altera*, perhaps because of the influence of the reflexive *sibi* with which it is often combined.

is kindled and fanned: *conflatur* and *accensus* introduce another vivid image to the passage.

the motions shared between them: as described in detail at 246-51. With *eas*, understand *potestates*.

337-8 Mutual indispensability is further illustrated from the common birth and growth of the two partners, and the body's decay on the soul's departure.

obviously never endures: *uidetur* marks a third appeal to experience; cf. 326 and 333.

339-43 The positive analogy of 327-30 is now supplemented by a negative comparison: the body cannnot survive the loss of the soul as water can survive the loss of its heat. This was because soul and body were integral parts of a single compound, whereas hot water was a mixture, heat being an atomic compound which constantly passed into and out of others. The heat present in the soul came into a very special category, since it was integral to the soul-compound (258-87), whereas in other cases heat was much more readily detached.

liquid water: for the characteristic periphrasis (literally 'the moisture of water'), cf., e.g., *liquidus umor aquai* 427.

abandoned limbs: because the *anima* has departed (see the following note).

divorce from the spirit: here and in 344 below, *anima* is best taken in its technical sense; though the contention would apply equally to the complete soul, the allusions to the limbs (*artus* 342) and to mutual contacts of body and *anima* (345) show that Lucretius is thinking of the spirit which pervades the whole body. *discidium*, commonly used of the sundering of persons in divorce, is sometimes applied technically by the poet to the dissolution of an atomic compound (e.g. I 220 and 249), but here denotes the soul's separation from the body, as its use in 347 below, of the sundering of one partner from the other, confirms; cf. also 581 and 839, where the sense is primarily the same.

wrenched apart: *conuulsi* is opposed to *neque . . . conuellitur* 340.

rotting completely away: for the tmesis *conque putrescunt*, cf. 262 and note. The division of the word is not inappropriate to the physical disintegration described. The *p* alliteration and the repeated *con-* prefix (which like *penitus* emphasises the thoroughness of the process) add to the impact of the description.

344-7 The structural union of soul and body is once more invoked to support the interdependence just claimed.

body and spirit by their mutual contacts learn: literally 'the mutual contacts of body and spirit learn', a bold use of abstract for concrete. *contagia* (neuter plural) is probably a Lucretian coining to replace the inadmissible *contāgĭō*; cf. 471 and 740, and Virgil, *Eclogues* 1.50. The interweaving of words in this 'golden' line, comprising adjective (a), adjective (b), verb, noun (a) and noun (b), may well, as Kenney suggests, 'reflect the mutuality of the body-soul contact'. For the sense of *anima* here, see on 341 above.

while still contained . . . womb: further explaining *ab origine prima* 331 and *ex ineunte aeuo* 344.

their divorce: see on 342 above.

without doom and disaster: *sine peste maloque* has a proverbial ring.

348-9 The preceding pattern of arguments is now dramatically reversed at the end of the passage, illustrating the complementary nature of its two central points (see introductory note to 323-49 above).

the cause of their well-being: *causa salutis* echoes 324 above, making the inversion of the opening argument in 323-6 the more conspicuous.

their natures are linked also: i.e. they are structurally linked to form a single atomic compound.

350-69 ***The body participates in physical sensation, not just the soul in it***

The major aspects of the soul's nature and constitution have now been covered; the three remaining passages in this part of the book are in the nature of footnotes or appendices on comparatively specialised points. The first two are each polemical; they form a natural sequel to 323-49, in that they each concern the body-soul relationship. The first, which is much the most important of the three for Lucretius' later purposes in the book, is an emphatic corroboration of the point implied at 246-57 and asserted explicitly at 333-6 above, that the body shares in physical sensation; this means that the soul, even if it could survive without the body, would be incapable of sensation without it. 350-8 concern the sensation of touch throughout the body, triggered by the *anima* in the part affected; 359-69 concern the sensation of sight (probably representing all four localised senses, including taste, smell and hearing), triggered by the *anima* in the eyes (or other sense-organs). In each case, the argument depends primarily on an appeal to experience, the ultimate criterion of knowledge in Epicurean Logic: introspection clearly reveals that the body, and the sense-organs (represented by the eyes), themselves actually feel (modern physiologists, by contrast, would suggest that the sensation takes place, if anywhere, in the brain, which constructs a model of the body and allocates sensations to various places on that model, sometimes with a slight margin of error). The whole passage is aimed in part, but not necessarily exclusively, at the Stoics, who restricted sensation to the soul and regarded the eyes as windows through which the soul looked out; the latter theory, set out by Cicero, *Tusculan Disputations* I 46, may go back to Heraclitus and is attributed also to some Peripatetics (Sextus Empiricus, *Aduersus Mathematicos* VII 129 and 350).

350 **To continue:** literally 'As to what remains', a formula of transition, especially frequent in the later books, which reflects the urgency of Lucretius' didacticism.

disputes: for this sense of *refutare* (usually 'to disprove'), cf. V 727; the present is perhaps conative, 'tries to disprove'.

351 **the spirit, intermingled throughout the whole body:** Lucretius attributes to his potential opponent his own view of the soul as having two parts with different functions and locations.

352 **refer to as:** *nominitamus* is an iterative form apparently coined by the poet for the inadmissible *nōmĭ nāmus*; he uses it in four other places.

353 **against the quite manifest truth:** the word-order, with *res contra* between *manifestas* and *uerasque*, throws emphasis onto the two adjectives.

354-5 **who will ever explain . . . :** the rhetorical question makes the assertion of the primacy of experience the more impassioned; for a similar appeal, cf. I 422-3. *adferet* = *rationem adferet* and so governs the indirect question *quid sit . . . sentire.*

what bodily sensation is: *corpus sentire* involves a bold extension of the substantival use of the infinitive, and does the work of the abstract *corporis sensus*; the expression is loaded, anticipating the Lucretian view that the body's sensation is actual, not merely apparent.

if it is not what: after *si non*, understand *id est.*

356 **You may claim:** *at* is equivalent to *at enim*, introducing a dramatised objection.

the body is totally devoid of sensation: and therefore, the opponent infers, can never have experienced it in life; the argument is compressed, this step being merely implied, not stated.

357 **but this is because . . . :** Lucretius accepts the opponent's premiss, but denies his inference; the body experienced sensation in life, but lost it because it never possessed it in its own right, as a *proprium*, or permanent property. The idea is that physical sensation is a property of neither body nor *anima*, but of the soul-body compound.

358 **like many other features . . . :** e.g. heat and motion, whose loss at death does not mean that the body never possessed them, any more than the loss of sensation proves that the body never felt.

359-61 **the mind looks through them:** for this theory, see introductory note to 350-69 above. *animus* is to be taken, like *anima* 351 and 356 above, in its technical Lucretian sense, with his own view of a bipartite soul again attributed to his rivals. This argument concerns the *sensation* of sight, which Lucretius placed in the eyes and the *anima* in them, not the interpretation of the visual image, which was the sphere of the *animus*. In the rival theory as presented here, the sensation of sight is placed in the central *animus*.

through open doors: more literally 'when doors have been opened' or 'by way of open doors'.

is not easy: for the ironic understatement, cf. 328.

the sensation in them leads in the opposite direction: i.e. it is a matter of common introspective experience that sight is localised in the eyes. Sensation, the ultimate criterion of knowledge, is characteristically personified and presented as leading the observer to the truth; the image is developed in *trahit* and *detrudit* 362.

362 **to the very pupils:** as the location of sight. For *acies* = *pupula*, a sense developed from the word's application to the keen edge of sight, cf. 411.

363-6 A corroborative point: bright lights dazzle the eyes, but have no such effect on doors, proving the falsity of the analogy.

especially as we are . . . unable: the indicative with causal *cum* is an archaic construction; cf. 441, and, for concessive *cum* with indicative, note on 107.

brightness of our vision . . . brightness of the light: *lumina* (as often in poetry) denotes the eyes, *luminibus* lights; the 'word-play', or verbal conceit, emphasises the paradox of the situation in which light hampers vision; for a very similar effect, cf. 387 and note.

doorways through which: *qua* (sc. *uia*) = *per quae.*

we ourselves: as opposed to our *animus*, which on the rival theory looks out through the 'doors' of the eyes.

any pain: resulting from dazzling light. The argument not only seeks to prove the rivals' analogy false, but continues the appeal to experience, since Lucretius would certainly maintain that the pain of being dazzled manifestly occurs in the eyes, not in the central *animus.*

367-9 A concluding *reductio ad absurdum*, with which Lucretius often likes to end a polemic (cf. I 919-20 and II 976-84), although a serious point, which is further developed at 624-33, lies behind it; if the soul survives death, it will be incapable of what we understand as sensation, to which physical sense-organs like the eyes are clearly indispensable.

obviously ought to have a better view: *uidetur* is again a Lucretian passive (see on 35), and *debere* is characteristically applied to logical necessity (see on 187).

with the doorposts and all taken away: i.e with the surrounding tissue also removed, to allow a still wider view. The use of *ipse* in this ablative absolute construction echoes the Greek idiom with αὐτός in comitative dative phrases like αὐτοῖς (τοῖς) ἀνδράσιν , '(the) men and all'.

370-95 ***The atoms of soul and body are not arranged alternately***

In this second 'appendix' (see introductory note to 350-69 above), which like the first concerns an aspect of the soul-body relationship, Lucretius seeks to correct the view of Epicurus' atomist predecessor, Democritus, that the atoms of soul and body alternated in an ABAB pattern. This is ruled out (a) on the grounds that the soul-atoms are both smaller (177-230) and fewer (278 and note) than the body-atoms, and must accordingly be more widely spaced; this is confirmed (b) by our insensitivity to certain very small and very light objects, which touch the body's surface too far from a soul-atom, and also too lightly, for sensation to be initiated (see further on 381-90). Though 372 suggests that Democritus applied his theory to the whole soul, Lucretius' argument primarily concerns the *anima* (see on 372 and 374). The passage reinforces the Epicurean idea of the soul's exceedingly refined texture (177-230).

370-1 **In this connection:** i.e. the relationship of soul and body, the central topic since 323. For the recurrent formula *illud in his rebus*, cf., e.g., 319 and 900.

one can: the subjunctive *possis* is of indefinite second person, as also in 377 below.

the view posited . . . : literally 'that which the revered view of the hero Democritus posits', with *sancta* poetically transferred from the philosopher to his theory. 371 recurs at V 622, in introducing a valid astronomical theory of Democritus. Lucretius' reverence reflects Epicurus' debt to the atomist pioneer; *sanctus* is applied also to Empedocles, whom Lucretius admired both for his achievement in philosophical poetry and for certain aspects of his philosophy itself (Introduction V), in a passage of lavish praise at I 730.

372-3 **soul:** since the sequel mainly concerns the *anima*, *animus* is here clearly inclusive (cf. 334). However, although Democritus' distinction between mind (νοῦς) and soul (ψυχή) roughly corresponds with the Epicurean distinction between the two parts of the soul, it is difficult to see how he can have applied the principle of alternation with body-atoms to the concentration of atoms which formed the mind, as Lucretius surprisingly suggests here.

juxtaposed . . . alternate variation: three Latin phrases, expressing one-to-one juxtaposition, alternation and interweaving, are used to clarify the ABAB arrangement posited by Democritus. *priuis*, an adjective used by Lucretius in the sense 'each single one' (cf. its application to single footsteps in 389 below), is dative with *apposita*, and replaces the metrically inadmissible *sīngŭlīs.*

374-5 **the basic components of the soul:** on *elementa* as a term for the atoms, see on 244. Since the atoms of both *animus* and *anima* were smaller and fewer in number than the body-atoms (cf. 177-230 and 278), *animae* here, and hence also *animai* 380 and 392, is best translated as inclusive, even though the rest of the argument, from *rara per artus dissita sunt* 376-7 to the end, applies only to the technical *anima.* There is hiatus, with the final *-ae* of *animae* remaining long and unelided before the following vowel, for which *loci opus* VI 755 provides the only Lucretian parallel; contrast cases where the hiatus shortens the preceding vowel sound (e.g. II 404, V 7 and 74), or which involve monosyllables ending in *-m* (cf. 1082 and note).

much smaller: as demonstrated at length at 177-230.

which make up: for the anastrophe of *quibus e*, see on 140-1.

376-7 **fewer in number:** as implied, e.g., in *persubtilem* 179; cf. the allusion to the *pauca corpora* forming the soul at 278.

dispersed . . . throughout our limbs: *per artus* shows that the discussion is now restricted to the spirit.

378-80 The thought is very compressed. The unstated premiss is that tiny objects to which we are insensitive touch our bodies in the spaces betwen soul-atoms. These spaces must therefore be roughly the size of the tiniest objects to which we are sensitive; if the spaces were larger, these objects could fit into them, and so fail to produce sensation; if the spaces were smaller, we should be sensitive to still tinier objects, which would no longer fit into them. For complications in the argument, see on 381-90 below.

the ultimate bodies which comprise the soul: for *exordia* as a term for the atoms, see on 31; the addition of *prima* (balancing *prima* 378: see note below) gives a still closer correspondence with *primordia.*

are at intervals which match the size of: literally 'preserve intervals as great as'; the diminutive *quantula* reflects that the comparison is of relatively small sizes.

the smallest bodies: literally 'the first bodies' (sc. on an ascending scale of size). *prima . . . corpora*, which was announced as a technical term for the ultimate particles at I 61 (cf. 438 below), is here differently applied, but is deliberately echoed in the technical *exordia prima* 378, as if to underline the logic of the argument, that the intervals between the *prima exordia* (or *prima corpora*) of the soul match the size of the *prima corpora* to which we are sensitive. The combination of *corpora* with *in corpore* is equally calculated, mirroring the impact of one type of body on another.

381-90 These examples of objects to which we are sometimes insensitive show that 378-80 have oversimplified, and that weight, as well as size, can be a crucial factor. Two distinct categories are adduced: (a) objects both tiny and light, like the particles of dust, chalk and mist in 381-3; (b) much larger objects, which are still very light, like the gossamer threads in 383 and the feathers and thistle-down in 386. Insensitivity to this second category is most easily explained if the soul-atoms are pictured, as Giussani suggests, as always below the body's surface, so that, even if a long gossamer thread touches the body at a number of points which are each immediately above a soul-atom, the impact is in each case too slight to be communicated to the soul-atom by the body-atoms above it. With the first category, while contact with the body's surface immediately above a soul-atom would produce sensation, contact above the *spaces* between the soul-atoms would not be sensed, as the impact would then be too slight to be communicated to the nearest soul-atoms by the body-atoms which had been touched. This sort of explanation, though not made explicit, fits the concluding description of the requirements for sensation at 391-5. The picture becomes still more complicated in that, according to Epicurus (though not to Democritus), the atoms of soul and body were already in constant motion before any external impulse produced new, potentially sense-bearing, patterns of motion. Though this idea can be reconciled with Lucretius' argument, he may possibly have overlooked it here, as seems to be the case in some of his discussions of the atoms in compounds in book II (cf. on 189-99).

381-2 **Sometimes:** whether a tiny object touched us directly above a soul-atom, or above the spaces between them, was to a large extent a matter of chance, so that our insensitivity to such objects must vary considerably on the Lucretian theory. *interdum* possibly acknowledges this, as does the allusion to the *individual* footsteps of insects at 389-90.

dust clinging to our body: the abstract *pulueris adhaesum*, where *adhaesus* is a Lucretian coining which he uses on three other occasions, is preferred to the concrete *puluerem adhaerere*, which would balance *sidere cretam*. For the local ablative *corpore* attached boldly to a noun, a type of construction much more natural in English than in Latin, cf., e.g., II 51 (*fulgorem . . . ab auro*) and V 300-1 (*ab . . . ignibus . . . origine flammae*).

sprinkled chalk settling: *incussam* suggests deliberate sprinkling, and hence an allusion to chalk used as a cosmetic (cf., e.g., Martial VIII 33.17). After *incussam*, *sidere* (the infinitive of *sido*) most probably denotes the moment of impact, not, like *adhaesum*, the resultant state ('resting on').

383-4 **the spider's slender threads:** the *-ei* of *aranei* scans as a single syllable by synizesis (cf. 877 and 918); *tenuia* also is trisyllabic, the *u* being consonantalised (cf. 232 and note).

we are enmeshed: humans are playfully compared with the insects snared by the spider. The compound *obretimur* is apparently another Lucretian coining; the *ob-* prefix reinforces, from *obuia*, the idea of the obstacle lying in our path.

385-6 **shrivelled coat:** an allusion to the spider's moult, a chitinous coat which it sheds on several occasions between emergence from the egg and maturity: see Wellesley (1974-5) 34-6, and for *uestis* similarly applied to the skin shed by a snake, cf. 614 and IV 61. The rare *uietus* appears to suggest both fragility and decay.

on our head: the picture must be of the moult, the feathers and the down falling on the hair, whose insensitivity was presumably put down to an absence of soul-particles in it; this is another complication in the argument, indicating how compressed and simplified the account is. *supera*, an old form of *supra*, provides an extra dactyl.

thistle-down: *pappus* more literally denotes down from any plant.

387 **lightness . . . a heavy task:** there is a word-play, or verbal conceit, based on the two senses of *grauatim*, 'heavily' and so 'with difficulty'; it also brings out the paradox whereby lightness acts as an obstacle and presents difficulty; cf. 364 and note.

388-90 **every single creeping creature:** the smallest might steer a path above the spaces between the soul-atoms, and the lightest might pass directly above soul-atoms without the impact reaching down to them.

each individual footstep: implying that we feel some, but not all of the footsteps, depending on whether they are planted directly above soul-atoms or above the spaces between them; cf. on 381 above. *priua* = *singula*, as in 372.

the other insects: a discreet veil is drawn over further unsavoury examples.

391-3 **many things have to be stirred:** *multa* alludes to the body-atoms. *multa ciendum est* is used for the normal *multa cienda sunt*; Lucretius is fond of this construction (cf. 626, and, e.g., I 111), in which the impersonal use of the gerundive, normal with intransitive verbs (e.g. *legibus parendum est*), is extended to verbs which govern a direct object.

begin to feel the shaking of the primary particles: i.e. of the body-atoms stirred by the external impulse. *primordia concussa* is best taken as an *ab urbe condita* type of construction ('the shaken atoms' = 'the shaking of the atoms'), rather than as accusative and infinitive (sc. *esse*: 'that the atoms have been shaken'), since the atoms of the *anima* have no cognitive qualities. The inceptive *sentiscere* is found only here, and at IV 586 where it is used absolutely (cf. the compound *persentiscere* at 249); the subjunctive, like *possint* 394, is normal after *prius . . . quam* in the context of requirement. Exception has been taken to the vagueness of *multa* 391 and to the supposedly confusing word-order in 392-3 (where the subject, *animai semina*, is postponed for greater emphasis), but Marullus' transposition of 392 and 393 ('So true is it that many seeds, immingled in our bodies throughout our frame, have to be stirred in us, before the primary particles of the soul are shaken and begin to feel') results not only in tautology, since the *semina . . . immixta* are identical with the *primordia animai*, but in the dubious claim that the soul-atoms themselves feel, whereas 350-69 have maintained that sensation is experienced not by the *anima* but by the soul-body compound.

394-5 **exchange repeated blows:** *tuditare* is a very rare iterative form of the root *tundere*. As 395 shows, the allusion is to the repeated blows of the soul-atoms on one another; these occur as they communicate the motions which initiate sensation to one another, as described at 245-8, before these are passed on in turn to the body-tissues. The full picture is thus that the body-atoms on the body's surface pass on an external impulse, provided that it is strong enough, to the soul-atoms, which then interact with one another, initiating sense-bearing motions which are communicated to the body.

over such large intervals: Wakefield's *tantis* (for *quantis*, the reading of the manuscripts) is as satisfactory an emendation as any; the intervals between the soul-atoms are large, compared to those between the body-atoms. The ablative is of a circumstantial type.

396-416 ***Mind is more crucial to life than is spirit***

In this third and final 'appendix' to this part of the book (see introductory note to 350-69 above), Lucretius turns from the relationship of soul and body to that of the soul's two parts. The mind has already (136-60) been shown to be the dominant partner in that, as the seat of the will, it can set the body in motion through the agency of the spirit, and also communicates strong emotion to the spirit; a further aspect of its predominance is now added, its greater importance for the retention of life, which can survive the loss of a large part of the spirit but not the loss of the mind. These propositions are stated rather than argued for, though the former, given the Epicurean view of the soul, is supported by experience in that the loss of spirit involved in, e.g., the amputation of limbs is not necessarily fatal. On what basis damage to the mind was assumed to be fatal (e.g. the frequency of death from wounds to the chest which housed it) must remain a matter of conjecture; there is no exact parallel for the passage in other Epicurean sources. Though in the nature of a footnote, it provides a natural transition to the arguments for the soul's mortality which follow, with its account of the two situations from which death inevitably follows, (a) loss of, or damage to, the mind, and (b) loss of the whole spirit.

396-7 **the bolts of life:** for the impressive metaphor, which has a measure of scientific justification in the interlocking union of the atoms of mind, spirit and body, cf. I 415 and VI 1153.
more dominant: *dominantior* looks back to *dominari in corpore toto*, of the mind's generally predominant role, in 138.
as regards life: i.e. for its preservation.
the spirit: on the periphrasis with *uis*, see on 277.

398-9 **mind and intellect:** on these terms and their pairing, see on 94.
no part of the spirit . . . any short spell of time: considerably overstated, since at 713-40 particles of spirit left in the body supply the souls of the maggots which infest the decomposing corpse.

400-1 **follows as its companion:** perhaps, as Kenney suggests, sustaining the image of *dominantior* 397, with the spirit in the mind's retinue.
leaving the limbs cold: by removing the heat which is one of the soul-elements; cf. 121, 126, 215 and 233.

402 **has remained . . . remains alive:** *manet* and *remansit* contrast with *nequit residere* 398 and *linquit* 401, *in uita* with *in leti frigore* 401.

403-4 **however lacerated is the trunk:** the trunk, in which the *animus* is to be found, is differentiated from the surrounding limbs, which normally contain *anima*. *quamuis* is here used with the indicative instead of the original, paratactic jussive, subjunctive, as at 705-6 and IV 426 (contrast 307-8 and 874); the construction, facilitated by analogy with *quamquam*, becomes increasingly common in post-Lucretian poetry and in Silver prose.
surrounding limbs . . . surrounding spirit: the repeated *circum* (literally adverbial, 'round about') emphasises the link between the two processes: the mutilation of the victim's limbs results in the loss of the parts of the spirit housed in them.

released from the limbs: an explanation of *adempta*; the spirit which has been lost has escaped through the wounds inflicted on the mutilated limbs, which are thus left paralysed. If *remota* is the correct reading, the allusion cannot be to limbs which have been totally severed, since the spirit's departure from them after their loss would be quite irrelevant to Lucretius' point; an allusion to amputation can only be obtained by reading *remotis* ('with the surrounding spirit lost and the limbs removed'), but the description then culminates in the loss of the limbs instead of the loss of the spirit housed in them, which is the point at issue.

405 **the heavenly breaths:** a poetic, rather than a scientifically precise, expression, since breathing took place in the lower atmosphere which comprised air (*aer*), not the fiery upper atmosphere of ether (*aether*).

406-7 **if not totally:** a qualification of the picture so far suggested; total loss of the spirit is fatal. *omnimodis* (= *omnibus modis*) does not occur before Lucretius; here, it replaces *omnino*.

408-15 An illustrative analogy with the eye, in which the mind corresponds to the pupil, the spirit to the rest of the eye-ball, and life to sight: damage to the pupil, or to the whole of the rest of the eye-ball, is fatal to sight, as the loss of the *animus*, or of the whole *anima*, is fatal to life. In the presentation of this analogy, the pattern of the preceding discussion is deliberately inverted: 408-12 correspond to 402-7 and 413-15 to 398-401 in a calculated chiasmic arrangement.

408-9 **the surrounding eye has been lacerated:** *lacerato oculo circum* answers *circum caesis . . . undique membris* 403 and *adempta anima circum* 404.

the pupil has remained undamaged: *pupula mansit incolumis* answers *mens animusque remansit* 402.

the lively power of sight survives: the periphrasis with *uiuata potestas* (which is applied to the body-soul compound at 558 and to the soul at 680) reinforces the analogy, in which sight corresponds to life. *stat . . . uiuata potestas* answers *manet in uita* 402, *uiuit . . . auras* 405 and *in uita . . . haeret* 407. *cernundi* illustrates the older form of the gerund (and gerundive) of verbs of the third and fourth conjugations, which Lucretius sometimes prefers; cf., e.g., 626 and I 59.

410-2 **provided only . . . leave it isolated:** the clause answers *si non omnimodis* 406. The force of *ne* extends from *corrumpas* to *caedas* and *relinquas*; the three verbs are indefinite second person.

eye-ball . . . pupil: for *lumen* used of the eye, cf. 364; *orbem* here excludes the pupil, whereas *orbis* 415 includes it, as the context in each case makes clear. For *acies* = *pupula*, cf. 362.

that too . . . : i.e. in addition to the total loss of the *anima*, which also results in the destruction of the two parts concerned.

without their destruction: i.e. of eye-ball and pupil, for which *anima* and *animus* are the respective analogues. *eorum* is neuter plural, applied to things (*pupula* and *orbis*) of different gender (cf. 136 and note).

413 **if that middle part . . . is eaten away:** the clause answers *sine mente animoque* 398.

414-5 **light of the eye . . . fades . . . darkness falls . . . gleaming ball:** the double sense of *lumen* (cf. 364 and note) and of *occidit* is exploited to introduce an imaginative comparison between eye-failure and sunset. *occidit lumen* primarily denotes the death or failure of the eye, but simultaneously suggests the setting of the sun, an idea reinforced by the juxtaposition of *lumen* and *tenebrae*; the image is sustained in *splendidus orbis* 415, primarily denoting the eye-ball but simultaneously developing the comparison between it and the setting sun.

however unimpaired: with *quamuis*, supply *est* (cf. 403) or *sit* (cf. 307-8); for the ellipse, cf. VI 1194.

in other respects: i.e. apart from the pupil.

416 **have spirit and mind . . . been bound:** *uincti* replaces the more usual neuter plural (cf. 136 and note), perhaps because *animus* and *anima* are personified in the political image contained in *foedere*.

417-829 THE SOUL'S MORTALITY

After a short but important introduction (417-24), Lucretius presents the long sequence of arguments which forms the kernel of the book. They fall into two main categories: (a) 425-669, designed to show that the soul dies with the body; (b) 670-783, designed to show that the soul is born with the body and had no previous existence; these are followed (c), 784-829, by a short passage of more general argument against its eternity, which is applicable both to its continued survival and to its pre-existence. The reason for this essentially twofold approach is itself twofold. Firstly, from the Epicurean point of view, birth and death implied one another: birth was the formation of an atomic compound, and no atomic compound (with the sole exception of the gods) could escape resolution into its components, i.e. death; anything that had been born must die, and anything that died must previously have been born. Lucretius' two main lines of argument thus complement and corrroborate one another throughout; the same principle is applied in the arguments for our world's destructibility at V 235-415. Secondly, ancient believers in the soul's immortality went rather further than their modern counterparts, and tended to believe not only in its eternal survival after death but also in its eternal pre-existence before this life, as in the Pythagorean theory of the transmigration of souls or in Platonic philosophy; Lucretius' second category of arguments has an especial relevance to such views.

This whole section of the book introduces comparatively few new ideas: its conclusions follow for the most part from the view of the soul established at 94-416. The arguments are designed, as often in Lucretius, to have a cumulative effect; many of them amount to different, always vivid, illustrations of the same underlying premiss, while those aimed against pre-existence are often the exact converse of those aimed against survival. Three types of argument are especially prominent: (a) those which depend on the close structural union of soul and body throughout life, an idea established at 323-49 above; (b) those which turn on the soul suffering in the body, where suffering on the one hand is a general symptom of mortality (in that things which suffer all ultimately die), and on the other (like its converse, cure) involves change, which on Epicurean principles entails mortality; (c) those designed to show that the soul can be divided, where division is a form of change and of destruction, which will eventually prove fatal. A high proportion of Lucretius' 'proofs' falls into one or other of these three groups.

The arrangement of proofs within the three subsections identified above, dealing in turn with survival, pre-existence and eternity, has sometimes been thought haphazard, in that related proofs are not always placed side by side. This has sometimes been attributed to incomplete revision, which some of the older editors sought to remedy by large-scale transposition: more probably, as Heinze suggested, Lucretius deliberately separated a number of closely related proofs to provide maximum variety.

417-24 ***Introduction***

This short opening appeal to Memmius (Introduction I and II) not only reflects the importance of this section of the book, but also (417) foreshadows its two main subdivisions (see introductory note to 417-829 above) and (421-4) adds a vital terminological and philosophical point.

417-8 **Come now:** the formula, paralleled in Greek didactic poetry, and used some fifteen times by Lucretius, reflects the urgency of his didacticism.

insubstantial: the lightness of the soul's fast-moving atoms has been implied at 201-2.

of living creatures: another indication that man is not alone in possessing a soul; indeed, the collocation *animantibus . . . animos animasque* suggests that an *animans* is to be defined in terms of the possession of some form of *animus* and / or *anima*; cf. 97 and note.

subject to birth and to death: on these mutually complementary ideas, which look forward to the two main categories of arguments to follow, see introductory note to 417-829 above. The two final spondees in 417, *et mortalis*, (cf. on 191) underline the solemnity and importance of the subject-matter, and throw additional weight onto the second of these key ideas.

419-20 **to set out:** cf. I 52, alluding to the poetic / philosophical gifts spread by Lucretius before his dedicatee.

long research: caused by the difficulties of devising (a) technical vocabulary and (b) metrical and poetic expression, as described at I 136-45; cf. 260 and note.

pleasurable toil: for the phrase, cf. II 730, and for a similar virtual oxymoron cf. *noctes uigilare serenas*, of spending tranquil nights awake in composition, at I 142. The pleasure involved arises in part from the pursuit of Epicurean philosophy, the highest pleasure open to an Epicurean. For Lucretius' delight in his poetic task, cf. also I 924-8.

worthy of your career: for the lavish compliment to Memmius' public achievements, cf. I 26-7, where Venus, his patron goddess, has endowed him with every excellence; on his career, see Introduction II.

421-4 The primary function of the lines is to announce that *animus* and *anima* may each henceforth be used inclusively, for the soul as a whole, a usage which has already been anticipated on a number of occasions (Introduction IV): it should also be borne in mind that, after this announcement, the terms continue quite often to bear their technical senses. Editors have not however always appreciated that the lines also carry a philosophical implication. While some of the ensuing proofs concern both parts of the soul, some concern only one of them: Lucretius is clearly claiming that if he proves the mortality of either part, the mortality of the other follows automatically from it, since together they constitute a single entity and a united compound (424); this has been demonstrated in the preceding section at 136-60, as has their identical atomic constitution (177-322), so that the mortality of one must entail that of the other.

421-3 **make sure that you link . . . :** the periphrasis with *fac* and the subjunctives is less peremptory than the straight imperatives *iunge* and *crede*.
say: *uerbi causa* may well involve a Lucretian word-play, suggesting (a) 'for example', *animus* being the other possibility, and (b) 'in order to find a term' (i.e. for the complete soul).

424 **they make up . . . are:** *sunt* is in each case attracted to the number of the singular predicate.

425-669 ***(a) The soul dies with the body***

425-44 **Proof 1: the liquid, volatile soul cannot survive without the body to act as its container**

This fundamental argument depends primarily on the soul's exceptionally refined structure which was demonstrated at 177-230; it also takes up, from 323-49, the theme of the body as the soul's protection, this time with the poet's favourite image of it as the soul's vessel or container (*uas* 440). The importance of this opening argument is reflected in the recurrence of its themes at, e.g., 508-9, 555-7 and 570-5.

425-7 **I have shown:** literally 'since I have shown' (i.e. at 177-230); the opening *quoniam* clause is interrupted by a long parenthesis (*nam . . . feruntur* 428-33), and the second (434-6) does not resume the first, but adds a second basis for the conclusion.
that it is refined: the allusion is to the whole soul, whose two parts have the same atomic constitution. *eam* is to be supplied as subject-accusative, referring either to the inclusive *animam* in 422 or to *coniuncta . . . res* 424. *tenuem* takes up *persubtilem* 179 and *tenui textura* 209.
much smaller primary particles: *principiis* shows that the argument of 179-207 concerned atoms: see on 180.
water's liquid moisture: in this periphrasis, *liquidus* has scientific point, reflecting that water itself comprises small, round atoms (cf. 189-90). The normally short first *i* of the adjective is here long, as at I 349, and at IV 1259 where both quantities are found in the same line in the appropriate context of *mixing*. With the nominatives after *quam*, understand *factus* (or *facta*) *est*.

428-33 The parenthesis repeats and amplifies the argument of 182-205, where the speed of thought showed that the mind comprised tiny (round and smooth) bodies.

428-9 **excels them in mobility:** cf. 184-5, where the mind moves more quickly than any visible object.
by the impact of a more refined impulse: cf. 188-9, where mobility is associated with susceptibility to a slight impact. On the redundant *a* with *tenui causa*, see on 323; *tenui* answers *tenuem* 425, reflecting that the refinement of the substance is in proportion to the refinement of the impulse that can stir it.

430-3 **images of smoke and mist:** in the earlier argument, the 'refined impulse' was the *animus* itself, which stirred itself into motion (184); an example of an especially subtle *external* impulse is now added, in anticipation of the doctrines of book IV. The 'images' (*imagines* 430 and *simulacra*, Lucretius' more usual term, 433:

Epicurus' εἴδωλα) are the thin films or effluences of atoms which in Epicurean theory constantly streamed from the surface of objects; they initiated (a) sight, when they reached and stirred the *anima* in the eyes, and (b) thought and dreams, when they permeated the chest-wall and made direct contact with the *animus.* Since all *simulacra* were far more refined than the objects which discharged them, and smoke and mist were themselves especially volatile, rarefied compounds with tiny, well-spaced atoms, Lucretius here presents a *tenuis causa par excellence*; again, the images which stirred the *animus* in dreams, which provide the crowning illustration in 431-2, were, like those which stirred it in thought, even more rarefied than those which stirred the *anima* in the eyes and so produced sight (IV 752-6). On the *simulacra* and their role in general, see IV 26-268 and 722-822.

as when: *quod genus* here = *ut* or *uelut*, introducing a specific example (from dreams, rather than from vision or thought); cf. 266 and note.

altars . . . : deliberate irony may lie behind the choice of a dream of a traditional religious observance as part of the evidence for the 'anti-religious' conclusion that the soul is mortal.

breathing out their hot smoke and carrying it: literally 'breathing out heat and carrying smoke', but the verbs are equally appropriate to one another's objects, as is *alte* to both verbs; *uaporem*, which rather than denoting 'steam' has its constant Lucretian sense (see on 126), is thus linked with *fumum* in a virtual hendiadys. For *ferreque*, with *-que* appended to short *e*, cf. 163 and note.

433 **for that these images are carried to us . . . :** best taken as a general assertion of the validity of the doctrine of the images, which awaits demonstration in book IV, with *haec simulacra* referring to the images of smoke and mist specified in 430, and through them to the *simulacra* in general as the source of sight, thought and dreams. Creech's *feruntur*, for the manuscripts' *geruntur*, is confirmed by the application of the verb to *simulacra* some eight times in books IV and VI; Lambinus' *genuntur*, 'are generated', though the verb is correctly restored at IV 143 and 159 (cf. 797 and note), does not fit the context here. Bentley, supposing an assertion that dream-images reach us from the external world rather than being generated by the mind, unnecessarily emended *haec* to *hinc*, 'from these sources (viz. altars and their hot smoke)'.

434-6 **since you see:** the second *quoniam* clause (see on 425-7 above) is independent of the first, adding a new step in the argument. *cernis* marks an appeal to experience, to a visible analogy for the soul's fate at death.

liquid . . . its moisture: *umorem et laticem* takes up *liquidus umor aquai* 427.

once its vessels are shattered: preparing for the image of the body as the soul's vessel (*uas* 440), which recurs at 555 and 793, and was not peculiar to the Epicurean school: cf., e.g., Cicero, *Tusculan Disputations* I 52 and Aristotle, *Historia Animalium* 521b6.

dissipated . . . dispersed in all directions: the repetition of the *dis-* prefix emphasises the scattering of the compound on its escape from its containers.

mist and smoke disperse: *nebula ac fumus* takes up *aut nebula aut fumus* 428; the repetition of *discedit* (cf. *discedere* 435) underlines the parallel behaviour of water, mist and smoke.

437-9 **the soul:** *animam* is non-technical; see on 425 above.

drains away . . . dissolves: the compounds with *dis-* echo those of 435-6, and reinforce the parallel; *diffundi*, of being poured in different directions, fits the analogy with water in 434-5.

much more swiftly . . . more quickly: because it is much more refined atomically (425-8).

into its original particles: the soul's fate is finally expressed in atomic terms. *corpora prima* = *primordia*; contrast 378-9, and see note there.

escaped and departed: *ablata recessit* exemplifies Lucretian pleonasm (cf. on 108), both verbs denoting the same process; the indicative shows that the clause is treated as independent of the indirect speech governed by *crede* 437.

440-3 **when the body . . . cannot:** the postponement of *cum* is not arbitrary, but serves to emphasise *corpus . . . eius* in preparation for the contrast between it and air (*aer* 443) as 'containers' for the soul. *cum* is not merely temporal but causal; for the archaic indicative construction, cf. 363 and note.

which comprises its vessel, so to speak: for the image, see on 434; the apologetic *quasi* reflects that it was not scientifically perfect, in that, as 556-7 later concede, soul and body were more intimately interwoven than a liquid and its container. For the perfect *constitit*, cf. 177-8 and note.

once it has itself been shattered: *conquassatum* echoes *quassatis* 434; the picture is of the body suffering violent injury and the soul escaping from its wounds.

become less dense through the loss of blood from the veins: a slower process, where prolonged bleeding leaves apertures in the body through which the soul escapes; in terms of the analogy, the vessel becomes porous.

how are you to suppose: *qui credas* introduces a rhetorical deliberative question; *qui* is the old ablative of the interrogative.

ever be held together by air: literally 'be held together by any air'; Kenney well compares the early and colloquial use of *nullus* as a stronger form of *non*. For the archaic form of the passive infinitive, see on 67.

444 **which is . . . less capable of holding it together:** with Bergk's *incohibensquest*, the relative clause describing air's unsuitability as a container forms an effective rhetorical contrast with *quod uas quasi constitit eius* describing the body as the soul's natural container in 440, and *incohibens*, a presumably coined Lucretian negative like *inolens* II 850, provides a pointed concluding contrast with *cohiberier* 443 (cf. *cohibere* 441); *magis* applies to *incohibens* no less than to *rarus*. *incohibescit*, the reading of the manuscripts, which would involve a presumably coined inceptive compound, is unsatisfactory, since Lucretius would not describe air as beginning (or striving) to hold the soul together. Lachmann's *is cohibessit* makes the line a separate question ('Is that, which is more rarefied than the body, to hold it together?', with *cohibessit* archaic for the perfect subjunctive *cohibuerit* in a repudiative question). Despite the uncertainty as to the precise text and punctuation, the general point behind the line is clear. *rarus* looks back to *rarefactum* 442.

445-58 Proof 2: the parallel growth and development of body and intellect show that they must die together

This argument primarily concerns the *animus* (see on 455 below); like the last, it has a connection with 323-49, where the mutual interdependence of soul and body was explained in terms of their close structural union throughout the whole of their existence. While applying primarily at the level of general probability, as an inductive argument from experience (body and mind are observably similar in their development, so that the similarity is likely to extend to mortality), it can also be interpreted in terms of some of the crucial principles which emerge later: suffering and decline imply destructibility, and at a certain point must prove fatal (484-6, 602); indeed, any form of change (growth, as well as decline) implies destructibility (513-20).

445-6 **we perceive that the mind is born:** something of an overstatement, since 670-783 are devoted to proving this very point. The observable evidence alluded to here includes, e.g., the mind's immaturity and lack of memory at birth. *sentimus* (cf. *uidemus* 457) is used partly to mark a contrast with the more theoretical opening proof which has preceded.
simultaneously . . . together . . . simultaneously: the adverbs emphasise the parallelism at each of the three stages.

447-8 **immature physique . . . judgment . . . slender:** the verbal correspondences in *tenero* and *sententia tenuis* underline the parallelism between the physical and mental states. For *tenuis* scanned as a disyllable, cf. 232 and note.

449-50 **physical strength . . . mental powers:** the sequence *uiribus . . . uis* again underlines the parallelism.
rational faculty: for this aspect of the *mens* or *animus*, cf. 95 and note.

451-3 **shattered:** *quassatum*, echoing *quassatis* 434 and *conquassatum* 441, acts as a reminder of the image of the body as the soul's vessel.
pressing power of time . . . their powers blunted: physical *uires* now prove no match for the metaphorical *uires* of time, which are made more impressive by the *u* alliteration. For the sense of *obtundere*, cf. IV 355 and 613, and VI 399.
intellect limps . . . tongue strays . . . mind totters: the decreasing length of the three limbs of the tricolon adds to the starkness of the description. *claudicat*, *delirat* (originally of straying from the furrow in ploughing) and *labat* (Lachmann's brilliant and virtually certain restoration) are all physical terms, whose transference to the mind (and its spokesman the tongue) graphically reinforces the parallelism betwen mental and physical decline.

454 **everything:** i.e. both mental and physical powers; the line sums up the point of 451-3.
at the same time: *uno tempore* corresponds to *pariter* and *una* in 445-6.

455-6 **it is natural:** literally 'it is appropriate' (i.e. logically).
the whole substance of the soul: the argument has been based on the *animus*; Lucretius now exploits the principle established at 421-4, of deducing the mortality of the whole soul from that of either of its parts. At the same time, the *anima* plays a part in some of the stages of bodily development and decline that are cited as

parallel to those of the *animus*; e.g. the staggering of the young limbs in 447 is due in part to the immaturity of the *anima*, which fails to control the body properly.

in turn: literally 'also' (i.e. as well as the body), but the force of *quoque* does not extend to *ceu fumus in auras*, which fits only the soul.

dissolves: *dissolui* should be scanned as quadrisyllabic: see on 330.

like smoke . . . : the *manner* of the soul's destruction follows not from the present argument, but rather from the volatility demonstrated in proof 1 (cf. the allusion to smoke at 428 and 436). The comparison is not exclusively Epicurean, but goes back to Homer, *Iliad* XXIII 100; cf. also, e.g., Plato, *Phaedo* 70a. With *fumus*, *dissoluitur* is to be supplied.

457-8 **since we see that . . . :** the premiss is restated from 445-6; the passage ends on the note on which it began. As subject-accusative, understand *ea* (neuter plural agreeing with *fessa* 458), referring to *corpus* and *anima* in the inclusive sense of 455; though *corpus* has not been mentioned since 452, body and soul (represented primarily by the mind) are the twin subjects of thought throughout the passage.

grow together: as shown at 447-50.

as I have shown: at 451-4.

gape wearily with the chinks of age: a colourful variation on *senescere* 446. *fessa* and *fatisci* are etymologically connected; *fessa*, of physical tiredness, suggests an equation between the cracks of decay, expressed by *fatisci*, and the yawning of the physically tired. *fessa fatisci* reappears at V 308, where it is applied to crumbling shrines of the gods.

at the same time: *simul* provides a final variation on *pariter*, *una* and *uno tempore* (445-6, 454 and 457).

459-525 Proofs 3-7: the soul's sufferings during life, and its cure by medicine, reveal its mortality

The close connection between these five proofs is reflected in the conclusion at 521-5, which embraces them all. The first four turn on various forms of distress suffered by the soul, or one of its parts, in life, while the fifth turns on the converse, its cure. As in proof 2, the argument applies at more than one level. Proofs 3-7, like proof 2, involve an analogy with the body; since the soul suffers, or is cured, like the body, it is likely to be equally mortal. Proofs 3-6 also involve the idea that suffering is a symptom of mortality, in that things which suffer can all be observed eventually to perish. But in addition to these more general arguments, other more specific fundamental ideas are introduced: (a) suffering, if increased, must bring destruction (484-6); (b) change implies destructibility (513-20); (c) division implies destructibility (500-1). Underlying all these points are the Epicurean principles that only atomic compounds can suffer or be changed or divided, and all atomic compounds, barring the gods, are destructible.

459-73 *Proofs 3 and 4: the mind (a) suffers its own pain and disease, in the form of painful emotion, and (b) suffers in bodily diseases, which can lead to delirium and coma*

Proof 3, which concerns the parallel sufferings of mind and body, is a natural sequel to proof 2, which depended on their parallel development and decline; proof 4 moves on to sufferings which mind and body share, a theme continued in proofs 5 and 6. The argument from the mind's own pains (proof 3) is attributed by Cicero also to the Stoic Panaetius (*Tusculan Disputations* I 79).

459-61 **There is the additional point that:** more literally 'In addition to this comes the fact that', a formula of transition used some nine times in the poem.

we see: for the appeal to experience, cf. *sentimus* 446 and *uidemus* 457 in the preceding proof.

for its part: *ipsum* underlines that mind behaves just like body.

keen anxieties, grief and fear: from the point of view of an Epicurean, whose goal was freedom from mental disturbance (ἀταραξία), such painful emotions, which the true philosophy could at least reduce, were especially akin to diseases.

462 **therefore it is natural . . . :** a parallel inference to that at 455-6 above, similarly introduced by *conuenit*. As subject-accusative, understand *eum* (= *animum*); the mortality of the *anima* follows automatically (421-4), as also at 470 below.

463-4 **What's more:** *quin etiam*, introducing proof 4, suggests that the shared sufferings which follow are even stronger evidence than the parallel sufferings of 459-62; proofs 3-7 form a climactic sequence, as the evidence adduced becomes increasingly spectacular.

reason deserts it: *dementit*, which is not found before Lucretius and may well be coined by him, vividly expresses the mind's loss of faculties, so that it ceases to act as *mens* at all. The *animus* is virtually personified at this point, in so far as *dementit* and *delira fatur* are directly applicable to persons; cf. *madet mens* 479, with note.

its utterances are delirious: cf. *delirat lingua* 453 as a symptom of mental decline. The original sense of *delira* (see note there) sustains the image of *auius errat* 463.

465-6 **by overpowering drowsiness:** *lethargus* in Greek is the technical term for the coma (Latin *ueternus*) to which allusion is made.

as the head nods and the eyes droop: literally 'as the eyes and the nodding droop'. *nutu* is abstract for concrete (= *nutanti capite*); the picture seems to be of the head first nodding, then falling motionless.

endless sleep: the allusion is clearly to a terminal coma, as 467-9 below confirm; this provides a perfectly adequate illustration of the mind suffering in bodily disease, as it suffers the damage of loss of consciousness while still in the body, before the moment of death. The description of the sleep as eternal is characteristically loaded and tendentious, as it anticipates Lucretius' conclusion while he is still stating the argument; cf., e.g., *leti secura quies* 211. There is thus no need to strain *aeternum*, as do many editors, by taking it either as 'seemingly endless' (i.e. to the bystanders) or as 'unbroken'.

467-9 **is able to:** *potis est* is archaic for *potest*; cf. 319 and note.

recalling the victim to life: the phrase no doubt includes an allusion to the *conclamatio*, a week's period of mourning during which the deceased was summoned back to life; lack of response afforded the final criterion of death.

bedewing their faces and cheeks with tears: a similar phrase was used at II 977, in a *reductio ad absurdum* of the view that atoms can be sentient. There may be a sardonic note here too, suggesting that the mourners' grief is exaggerated; cf. 904-11 and notes.

470-1 **Therefore you must confess:** a stronger assertion of the conclusion than in the corresponding line at 462 (cf. 455) with *conuenit. fateare necessest,* where *fateare* = *fatearis*, a paratactic jussive subjunctive (cf. 91-3 and note), is a favourite Lucretian formula, used on some twelve occasions in the poem.

is dissolved: for the scansion of *dissolui,* cf. 455 and note.

the contagion: *contagia* (see on 345) here, like its derivative, denotes infection, as also at VI 1236.

472-3 These lines provide further corroboration for both preceding proofs; not only do the parallel and shared sufferings of mind and body suggest that they are each liable to the same fate, but these sufferings are themselves symptomatic of mortality and pave the way for death.

pain and disease: whether physical or mental; *dolor* and *morbus* were similarly combined at the beginning of the passage in 460. Proof 3 illustrated the mind's *dolor*, proof 4 its sharing of bodily *morbus*.

artificers of death: for this sort of oxymoron, cf., e.g., *discidium parere* I 220 and *stragemque propagant* I 280.

as we well know: an appeal to everyday experience and to deaths accelerated by pain and disease.

476-86 *Proof 5: the soul suffers in intoxication*

In this graphic and accurate account of the successive stages of drunkenness, a topic much discussed by ancient philosophers, its physical symptoms are attributed to the *anima*, which is affected by the wine as it is absorbed into the body through the veins, and so fails in its function of controlling the body which it occupies; the central *animus* also suffers in its turn. Since the *anima* here, as also in proof 6 below, passes on its distress to the body, the process is to some extent the converse of that in proof 4, where the body passes on its distress to the other part of the soul, the *animus.*

476-7 **Again, why is it . . . that . . . :** the long rhetorical question adds impact and inevitability to the explanation advanced in the *quod* clause which concludes the sentence in 482-3. For the sense of *denique*, cf. 59 and note.

when the keen potency . . . : the conspicuous alliteration and assonance in *uini uis penetrauit* (cf. *uemens uiolentia uini* 482) and *discessit diditus ardor* add to the vigour and vividness of the description.

spread and been distributed into the veins: cf. II 1125 and 1136, and IV 955, where all food is distributed to the body by this route. The repeated *dis-* prefix in *discessit diditus* emphasises the idea of distribution.

478-80 A climactic sequence, as the symptoms are described in progressively shorter, starker expressions, culminating with the tricolon of nouns (*clamor singultus iurgia*); for a smaller-scale example, cf. 453, whose pattern closely matches that of *praepediuntur . . . mens* in 478-9.

heaviness of the limbs: because the *anima* fails to support them properly.

grows slurred: *tardescit*, 'becomes slow', is probably a coined Lucretian inceptive; its slow rhythm, with three long syllables, matches the sense. The *anima* in the tongue here fails to work properly.

his mind is saturated: the wine now permeates and drenches the *animus* in turn. *mens* is here virtually personified, in that *madere* and *madidus* are often applied to the victim of intoxication himself (cf. 464 and note).

his eyes swim: because the wine drenches and disturbs the *anima* in them.

shouting, sobbing and quarrelling: though *singultus* is also applicable to hiccuping, the nouns more probably denote the noisy, maudlin and aggressive stages of inebriation, which further reflect that the *animus*, the seat of the emotions and reason, is now affected.

481-3 **why are there all those other . . . symptoms of this sort:** a discreet veil is drawn over other unpleasant signs of intoxication; cf. 390 and note. *cetera de genere hoc* (cf. 744) is a formula used some thirteen times in the poem. *cur*, introducing the last limb of the rhetorical question, is postponed, and *cetera* and *ea* make up the grammatical antecedent of the *quaecumque* clause.

accompanying: literally 'whichsoever now follow'; *iam* goes closely with *sequuntur*.

wreak disorder on the soul: *animam* is highly emphatic; the crucial point is that the soul is affected in the processes described. Though the physical symptoms just traced result mainly from the disruption of the *anima* proper, the allusion to *mens* 479 makes it clear that *animam* is here inclusive and covers both parts of the soul.

while it is actually in the body: the implication is that, if the soul suffers so violently while still in the body, it will fare far worse outside its 'container' after death; cf. 506-9 and 603-6, where the point is developed more fully in connection with epilepsy and fainting fits.

484-6 A corroboration of the general idea that suffering implies mortality: severe suffering must ultimately prove fatal, an idea reinforced by Epicurean atomic theory (see introductory note to 459-525 above). The point is applicable to all the soul's misadventures adduced in proofs 3-6, not only to those occasioned by intoxication.

anything . . . demonstrates: for the personification of things or facts as proclaiming or revealing the truth, cf. 208 and note.

suffer disorder and impediment: *conturbari* takes up *conturbare* 483, and *inque pediri* (= *et impediri*: for the tmesis cf. 262 and note) answers *praepediuntur* 478 (where the impediment is passed from *anima* to legs).

infiltrated: *insinuare*, whose root suggests winding a way in, denotes entry which is devious or difficult, and is a favourite Lucretian term for atomic permeation; it can, as here, be sinister, suggesting pernicious, disruptive infiltration. It is used in the active either, as here, of entering or, as more usually, of causing to enter. On its application to the entry of a pre-existing soul into the body, see on 671.

487-509 *Proof 6: the soul suffers in epilepsy*

Epilepsy and its dramatic effects provide the fourth, culminating illustration of the soul's distress during life; the symptoms are attributed to the disruption of both parts of the soul by a poisonous secretion in the body (see on 502-3). The graphic, detailed account affords no evidence for the idle speculation of some critics that the poet himself suffered from the affliction, whose spectacular effects made it a natural choice for inclusion. In addition to his main purpose of demonstrating the soul's mortality, Lucretius may have the subsidiary, purely incidental motive of explaining away the superstition attaching to the disease by providing a scientific account of its symptoms; this superstition is reflected in its two names, *morbus sacer*, the accursed disease, and *morbus comitialis*, because its occurrence at the *comitia* or popular assembly led to adjournment. Similarly, the preceding proof (476-86) may serve the additional, purely incidental purpose of countering the view of intoxication as a god-given state induced by a literal Bacchus.

487-8 **What's more:** as at 463 above, *quin etiam* marks a still stronger example in this climactic sequence.

before our very eyes: the phrase marks an appeal to experience, but also helps to emphasise the dramatic suddenness of the attack.

as by the impact of a thunderbolt: the comparison with the traditional weapon of Jupiter suggests the popular view of epilepsy as a divine visitation, which the poet is incidentally countering.

489-91 As in 478-80, the short, parallel clauses add to the drama and vividness of the account. Four main verbs are placed in each of the first two lines, reflecting the violence of the attack, only one in the third, as if to mirror the exhaustion there described. Celsus III 23 confines himself to the first two of the nine symptoms detailed here: *concidit, ex ore spumae mouentur.*

his limbs shake: literally 'he trembles as to his limbs'; *artus* is an adverbial accusative of part affected, a Greek construction commonly imitated by Roman poets, though usually with a passive rather than, as here, with an active verb.

his senses desert him: like *dementit* 464, *desipit* shows that the *animus* is affected, as 499-501 go on to explain.

his muscles grow rigid: *extentare* is a rare frequentative form of *extendere*.

492-4 The manuscripts are corrupt here; the text adopted explains the symptoms of 489-91, in particular the foaming at the mouth, in terms of the disruption of the *anima*. Brieger's *ui*, which was perhaps the original reading of O, is a certain correction of *uis* in 492, since *distracta* must, as at 501, 507, 590 and 799, apply to the *anima*, in order to provide a reference for *ut docui* 500. In 493 *agens spumas* is supported by *spumas agit* 489, and the lengthening of the final short *a* of *anima* before the *sp* of *spumas*, though unparalleled in Lucretius, is justified by the triumphant emphasis which falls onto the word, which is the key to the argument. Catullus has examples of such lengthening at 17.24, 44.18, 63.53 and 64.186 (*nulla spes*); Lucretius occasionally (e.g. I 372) allows such vowels to remain short, but the poets normally avoid such collocations altogether. [Alternatively, if *animam* is retained in 493, a line or lines (e.g. *turbatur natura animae grauiterque laborat*) must be assumed lost before it; *nimirum quia* would then begin a new sentence, whose main clause, *turbat agens animam spumas* (or *spumans*) would describe the victim: 'he disturbs foam as he drives out his spirit ' (or 'he is in turmoil as he drives out his spirit, foaming').]

his *spirit*: as *per artus* makes clear, *anima* is here technical; the *animus* is brought in later, at 499.

is in turmoil: *turbare* is used intransitively, as at II 126 and 438, V 502 and 504, and VI 370; such fluctuation between transitive and intransitive senses is a feature of Lucretian style.

driving foam before it: *agens spumas* takes up *spumas agit* 489, but with the root sense more prominent; the picture seems to be that part of the disrupted spirit, in the form of breath, escapes violently from the mouth, whipping the saliva into foam.

just as . . . the winds: the comparison is not gratuitous poetic adornment; the action of the winds on the sea presents a scientific analogue for that of the *anima* (spirit or breath) on the saliva. The repeated sibilants in 493-4 are appropriate to the splashing of the foam described, the *u* alliteration in 494 to the violence of the winds.

495-501 After the general explanation of the symptoms, with especial emphasis on the foaming at the mouth which is the most characteristic of them, specific explanations of two of the others are now added.

495-8 **Groaning:** *gemitus* takes up *ingemit* 489. The symptom is explained partly as a voluntary response to pain, partly as an involuntary emission of unarticulated sounds by the speech-organs, whose *anima* is in disarray.

the seeds of his voice: in speech, atoms were emitted from the throat (IV 524-48) and moulded together into a succession of appropriately shaped compound particles by the tongue and lips (IV 549-52).

are all expelled together . . . carried out . . . *en masse*: instead of being formed into the succession of differently shaped compound particles required for articulate speech. The context suggests that *omnino* is boldly used to make the same point as *glomerata.*

where their habitual route lies: with *consuerunt* (= *consueuerunt* = *solent*), *ferri* is to be supplied.

so to speak: *quasi* apologises for the metaphor of the route contained in *munita uiai*.

a paved path: *munita uiai* (= *munita uia*) exemplifies Lucretius' fondness for the neuter plural of an adjective or participle with the genitive of a noun, a poetic idiom which spreads to Silver prose and often expresses an abstract idea. The genitive is in origin partitive, but participle and noun are here co-extensive; cf. *strata uiarum* (= *stratae uiae*) I 315 and *uera uiai* (= *uera uia*) I 659.

499-501 **Loss of his senses:** *desipientia* takes up *desipit* 490.

the functions of mind and spirit: the periphrasis with *uis* adds to the sense; not only are mind and spirit disrupted, but so are their functions. It is primarily the disruption of the *animus*, here introduced into the passage for the first time, that occasions *desipientia.*

as I have shown: at 492-3, which described how the *anima* was *distracta*.

divided and separated, thrown apart and torn asunder: the repeated *dis-* prefix, further reinforced by *seorsum*, lays great emphasis on the soul's disintegration; division was an automatic sign of mortality (cf. 640-1). *seorsum* is trisyllabic, as at 551 and IV 491; elsewhere in Lucretius, it is disyllabic by synizesis, and usually spelt without the *e*, as at 286 and 334.

that same poison: which occasions all the symptoms of the disease; the allusion is to the venomous secretion (*acer corrupti corporis umor*) of 503.

502-3 **has turned back:** *reflexit* is here intransitive; for such fluctuation, cf. 493 and note.

venomous secretion . . . has returned to its lair: ancient medical writers attributed epilepsy to an overflow of one of the three 'humours' of the body, bile, serum and phlegm (cf., e.g., Plato, *Timaeus* 82e; similarly, fever is attributed by Lucretius to an excess of bile at IV 664). *latebras*, as Ernout points out, suggests the image of a venomous snake; cf. *ueneno* 501 and *reflexit* 502. *redīt*, contracted from *rediit*, is perfect; cf. *obit* 1042.

504-5 **gets . . . to his feet . . . regains full consciousness:** cf. Celsus III 23, *deinde interposito interuallo ad se redit et per se ipsum consurgit. redit* 505 echoes *reditque* 502, reinforcing the logic of the account: one type of return leads automatically to another.

unsteadily: *uaccillans* is literally 'swaying' or 'staggering'; *quasi* apologises for, or tones down, the strong expression. The spelling with double *c*, which may arise from false derivation from *uacca*, gives a long first syllable and is unparalleled in poetry; contrast 479, and cf. *cuppedine* = *cupidine* at 994.

recovers his soul: the phrase suggests that part of the disrupted soul has been lost during the attack, as 493 (see note there) also implies. Similarly, part of the *anima* left the body during sleep and was somehow replaced at wakening; cf. IV 916-49. In view of the allusion to both *animus* and *anima* in 499, *animam* should here be taken in its inclusive sense. For the rare frequentative form *receptat*, cf. *extentat* at 490.

506-9 These lines develop the point which was more briefly hinted at in connection with intoxication at 483; see note there. The argument is applicable to all the sufferings of the soul adduced in proofs 3-6, and serves also as a reminder, and reinforcement, of proof 1, concerning the soul's inability to survive without the body's protection.

mind and spirit: *haec*, like *eadem* 508, is neuter plural referring to *animus* and *anima*, which were paired at 499.

are buffeted . . . and racked: though, in view of *credis* 508, the subjunctives could be explained as sub-oblique, IV 195 suggests that they are causal after *ubi*, a construction apparently, as Kenney notes, unparalleled elsewhere.

such great maladies: i.e. those set out in proofs 3-6, in 459-505.

torn asunder: for *distracta* of the soul or its parts, cf. 492 and 501.

in wretched wise: for this perhaps colloquial form of adverbial expression with *modus*, cf. *modis . . . miris* I 123.

without the body, in the open air: *sine corpore* is antithetical to *corpore in ipso* 506, and is immediately developed by *in aere aperto*, which recalls air's unsuitability as a container for the soul (443-4) and the image of the body as the soul's protection (323) and vessel (440).

the buffeting breezes: which would quickly reduce mind and spirit to their component atoms.

510-25 *Proof 7: the mind can be cured by medicine*

The climactic sequence of the soul's sufferings is now capped with the ultimate paradox: the mind's cure, by drug therapy, is another indication of its mortality. The proof depends on the Epicurean axiom, introduced at 519-20, that any form of change (which cure exemplifies) entails mortality.

510-2 **like the ailing body:** at one level the argument depends on the analogy with the body: see introductory note to 459-525 above.

by medicine: e.g. by hellebore, an almost proverbial remedy in antiquity for mental disorders.

foretells that its life is mortal: *praesagit*, a word associated with divination, is characteristically appropriated for scientific prediction. The oxymoron in *mortalem uiuere* is equally characteristic; cf. 472 and note.

513-6 The idea that change, which cure involves, must entail the addition, subtraction or rearrangement of parts depends ultimately on the Epicurean idea that only atomic compounds, which apart from the gods are all destructible, can undergo such processes.

it is fair to assume that one is adding . . . if one: literally ' it is reasonable that whoever . . . should add . . .'.

transposing: *traiecere* is an old spelling of *traicere*; cf. *eiecit* (= *eicit*) II 951.

something, however minuscule: *hilum* (cf. 220 and note) is used by Lucretius without a negative only here and at IV 515; *prorsum* intensifies it, as at 1087.

is entering on an attempt to alter . . . seeking to sway: *adoritur*, *infit* and *quaerit* are roughly synonymous, and govern the prolative infinitive by analogy with *conari* or *coepisse*; cf. 86 and note.

517-8 **allows neither . . . :** *neque . . . uult* virtually personifies the immortal object as refusing any type of modification.

rearrangement . . . addition . . . ebbing away: *transferri*, *tribui* and *defluere* answer *traiecere*, *addere* and *detrahere* 513-4. The compound *defluere*, which introduces a liquid image, is used by Lucretius only here.

519-20 This recurrent Epicurean axiom, whereby change entails death, appears also at I 670-1 and 792-3 and II 753-4, with reference in each case to the need for an unchanging substratum of matter, which was provided by the atoms. The Epicureans may well have derived it from the criticisms of the earlier physicists made by Parmenides and the Eleatic school.

whenever an object . . . this automatically involves: literally 'whatever object . . . this is immediately', with a slight grammatical *non sequitur*, or anacoluthon.

its natural bounds: i.e. the limits of its nature, which make it what it is. For the image, cf. the eulogy of Epicurus at I 75-7, where he has revealed the limits imposed by scientific law on different types of object, and how each has a deep-set boundary-stone (*alte terminus haerens*).

521-5 A conclusion to the whole sequence of proofs from 459-520.

the mind: since proofs 3-7 have all involved the mind, with which proof 7 has been exclusively concerned, *animus* is best translated technically here, even though the *anima* has played a central role in the sufferings adduced in proofs 5 and 6.

whether . . . or whether: the placing of the alternatives at the beginning and at the end of the sentence adds impact to the inescapable dilemma.

as I have shown: in proofs 3-6, at 459-509.

swayed by medicine: for the redundant *a* (contrast 511 above), cf. 323 and note.

truth . . . false reasoning: the two are graphically portrayed as adversaries in a duel, from which the latter tries unsuccessfully to escape; for the imagery of conflict, cf. Epicurus as monster-slaying hero and all-conquering general at I 62-79 and as philosophical warrior superior to Hercules at V 43-51.

be seen to confront: *uidetur* is again a Lucretian passive: see on 35.

triumph over falsehood: editors have not appreciated that *conuincere* is appropriate both literally and metaphorically, combining the senses 'to prove' (the usual connotation: cf., e.g., V 728) and 'to defeat thoroughly (in the figurative duel)' (cf. V 1178). The simple verb, to which Lucretius sometimes gives the normal sense of the compound (e.g. II 748, VI 498), combines the same two senses at IV 481, *ueris . . . uincere falsa*. For the metaphor of proof as verbal conquest, cf. the combination of *uincere* with *dictis* or *uerbis* at I 103, V 99 and V 735.

with double-edged refutation: an allusion to the dilemma of 521-2, but *ancipiti* sustains and develops the military image by suggesting a double-headed axe with which false reasoning is felled by truth. The spondees in the third and fourth foot, with surrounding dactyls, help to convey the effort that goes into the deadly blow. *refutatus* is apparently one of the poet's fourth declension coinings.

526-47 Proof 8: in death by creeping paralysis, the soul must be divided and is therefore mortal

This is the first of a number of arguments (cf. 580-614 and 634-69) which turn on the Epicurean axiom, formally presented later at 640-1, that division, like change (cf. 519-20), implies destructibility and is indeed a form of destruction; its occurrence here may have been suggested by the allusion to the soul's division in epilepsy at 492-3 and 499-501, and there is certainly no need to resort to arbitrary transposition in order to group the arguments from division more closely together. Death by creeping paralysis is here attributed to the progressive loss of the *anima*, which rendered the body capable of sensation and (when the *animus* dictated) of movement, and is treated as a manifest example of the *anima* being divided, and leaving the body piece by piece (526-32): in the remainder of the passage, a rival analysis of the process is dismissed as both false and irrelevant. Though the passage concerns the *anima*, it should be remembered that the *animus* too would depart with the last remnants of the *anima* (cf. 406-12).

526-30 The similarity, pointed out by Lambinus, to Plato's famous account of the death of Socrates after drinking the hemlock (*Phaedo* 117e-118a) is probably deliberate; to use the death of the champion of the soul's immortality as evidence of its mortality would be entirely characteristic, capping the preceding paradox where the mind's cure proves it destructible.

526-7 **pass away gradually . . . limb by limb:** *ire* = *obire*. Lucretius is fond of adverbs in *-tim* (cf., e.g., *summatim* 261): *paulatim* is here developed by *membratim*, and later by *tractim* (literally 'draggingly') 530 and *particulatim* 542. The five spondees in 527 are appropriate to the slow advance of the paralysis described.

529-30 **the other members:** *alios* appears to be used loosely for *ceteros*, as at 550 and 1038.

chill footsteps of death: literally 'footsteps of chill(ing) death'. Despite his insistence that death is not to be feared, the poet's imagery not unnaturally sometimes reflects instinctive human revulsion at the prospect; cf., e.g., *leti sub dentibus ipsis* I 852, where death is pictured as an all-consuming monster.

531-2 **And since the spirit's substance is *severed*:** though Lucretius does not elsewhere postpone *atque* (or *et*), the triumphant emphasis on *scinditur*, the key-word in the argument, which is accordingly placed outside its clause and first in the sentence, justifies the exception (cf. also the unparalleled placing of *igitur* at 199); Munro's *itque* is beside the point, since the argument turns not on the soul's departure, but purely on its division, while Bernays' *aeque* implies that the body is divided as well as the *anima*, and Lambinus' *atqui* is too strong and not elsewhere found in Lucretius. The manuscripts' *animo haec* perhaps arose from an original *animo* with an alternative *-ae* termination; the argument certainly concerns *anima*, not *animus*.

does not depart as a whole: for *exsistit* = *exit*, cf. II 796 and V 212; for *sincerus* (usually 'unmixed', 'unalloyed') = *integer* or *incolumis* (i.e. in one piece, a sense which *uno tempore* helps to clarify), cf. 717.

533-9 A rival analysis, whereby the soul escapes division by concentrating in a single spot within the body, is now refuted on the grounds that such a spot would be hypersensitive. Who, if anyone, held this theory is unclear: it may be suggested simply to show that there was no feasible alternative to the Epicurean account.

533-4 **it can draw itself inside:** instead of gradually *departing* (*exsistit* 532). *ipsam* is subject-accusative (see on 77), and suggests deliberate activity, as opposed to the division undergone passively in 531-2.

535 **this is why:** rather than because of the successive loss of its fragmented parts.

537 **is being concentrated:** for the root sense of *cogere* (= *co-agere*), cf. I 1020 and VI 274.

ought to be manifestly more sensitive: because the spirit is the organ of physical sensation. *debere* is again applied to logical necessity (see on 187) and *uideri* is again a true passive (see on 35); for their combination, cf. 368. *in* here expresses 'in a state of', as at 295 (*in ira*).

538-9 **as we have already said:** at 531-2 above; having eliminated the alternative analysis, Lucretius now reasserts his own account. *dilaniata* and *dispargitur* repeat the idea of *scinditur* and *nec . . . sincera*, *foras* of *exsistit*, and *interit ergo* of *mortalis habendast*. The spelling of *dispargere* with *a* rather than *e*, preserved here and in some other places in the Lucretian manuscripts, provides a clearer reminder of the root sense, 'is scattered in different directions', which is crucial to the argument.

540-7 The claim that even if the rival hypothesis were true the spirit would still be mortal is an effective debating point to conclude the Lucretian case.

540 **even if we chose to allow:** *si iam* indicates a hypothesis accepted simply for the sake of argument (cf., e.g., I 396, 968 and 1071); *libeat* makes the concession a matter of arbitrary whim.

541 **that the spirit can be condensed:** sc. without producing a hypersensitive spot, the absence of which provided the evidence that such concentration was impossible.

543 **you must . . . concede:** with *necesse*, *est* is to be supplied; though this is the only instance of its omission in this formula (for which see on 470), the manuscripts exhibit the same ellipse with the gerundive of obligation in several places, e.g. 796.

544 **perishes by being scattered to the breezes:** as Lucretius maintains; *dispersa per auras* takes up *foras dispargitur* 539. J.D.Duff's conjecture *per artus* is accordingly misconceived.

545 **grows numb after contracting its parts:** as on the rival analysis, in which it concentrates within the body (*introrsum* 534, which is antithetical to *foras* 539 and *per auras* 544). The two concluding spondees (see on 191) provided by the rare inceptive *obbrutescat* ('becomes dull' or 'stupid') slow the line down and fit the progressive numbing which is described. *obbrutescat* is justified in so far as the opponent imagines the *anima* gradually contracting within the body yet with a steady loss, rather than gain (cf. 537), in sensitivity; while a rival would doubtless claim that the concentrated soul eventually escaped from the body, the Lucretian retort would be that this in turn could not be effected without its division (cf. 580-91). The word is thus less 'question-begging' than, e.g., Bailey and Kenney maintain.

546-7 **the victim as a whole:** *hominem totum* alludes to the soul-body compound, which, unlike body or soul alone, enjoyed life and sensation as properties: cf. 357 and note.
loses more and more . . . less and less of life remain: *magis ac magis undique* and *minus et minus undique*, identically placed in their respective lines, well express the relentlessness of the progression. The comparatives take up *paulatim* and *membratim* at the beginning of the passage, just as *sensus* and *uitae* take up *uitalem . . . sensum* 527.

548-57 Proof 9: the mind cannot survive apart from the body any more than can the sense-organs

The mind, the organ of mental consciousness, is here treated as analogous to the organs of the physical senses. The passage contains no really new idea, turning primarily on the analogy between the body and the soul, or one of its parts, on which proofs 2-7 (445-525) at least partially depended; the last three lines return also to the key image of the body as the soul's container (cf. 434-44) and the close structural union of soul and body (cf. 323-49).

548-54 There is no formal apodosis to the opening *quoniam* clause (548-50); a second *quoniam* clause is replaced by the comparative clause with *ueluti* at 551-3, and the main clause is accordingly introduced by *sic* at 554. For the anacoluthon, cf. 425-439.

548-9 **is a specific part:** as demonstrated at 94-116.
in a set place: i.e. the chest, as demonstrated at 140-2.

550 **all the other sense-organs:** *sensus* here, as at 626 and 630, is given the concrete sense of the Greek αἰσθητήρια, an indication of the dearth of Latin technical terms complained of at 260. The indefinite suffix of *quicumque* is separated by tmesis, as at 940 and 1075. For *alii* = *ceteri*, cf. 530 and note.
guide our lives: the poet is fond of the nautical metaphor contained in *gubernare*.

551 **a hand:** serving as the representative organ of touch.
nostrils: replacing *aures* in the previous list at 549, probably, as Giussani pointed out, because hearing can survive the loss of the ear-flap.

552 **when removed:** for the neuter plural *secreta* applied to nouns of different gender, see on 136.

553 **in a short time:** for the redundant *in*, which in prose would give *tempore* a non-temporal sense (e.g. 'crisis'), cf. 323 and note.
in decay: the *e* of *tabe* may be arbitrarily lengthened as at I 806; cf. 732 and note.

554-5 **cannot exist:** much less experience mental consciousness: at 552 the sense-organs, which provide the analogue for the mind, cannot *feel or* exist in isolation.
as the body is clearly: the neuter relative *quod* refers back to *corpore*, which the intervening *et ipso homine* has further defined. *uidetur* (cf. 35 and note) is again a Lucretian passive.

556-7 **or whatever else you care to picture . . . intimate bonds:** the admission that the key image of the body as the soul's vessel, introduced at 440, is not wholly adequate strengthens the argument from it: something more intricately linked with its contents than a container with its liquid would be all the more incapable of preserving those contents once it was broken. While the spirit which was interwoven throughout the body was more intimately physically linked with its container than the mind which is the subject of discussion here, the 'intimate bonds' between mind and body are illustrated, e.g., by the mind's ability to set the body in motion through the agency of the spirit which pervaded it, or by the communication of sufferings described in 463-73.

558-79 Proof 10: the structural union and mutual interdependence of soul and body show that the soul cannot survive in isolation

The arguments applied to the mind in proof 9 are now extended to the complete soul. The central ideas, the close structural union in which the body acts as the soul's container, are taken up from 555-7, and the passage serves to reinforce the arguments of 323-49 and 434-44 respectively. 563-5 also apply to the whole soul the same sort of analogy that was applied to the mind as the basis of proof 9 (see note below).

558 **body and soul, with their lively powers:** since this argument concerns both parts of the soul, *animus* and *anima* are to be taken inclusively throughout it, except when paired as in 565 and 578-9. For the periphrasis with *uiuata potestas* , cf. 277 and 409 and notes.

559 **thrive . . . by virtue of their mutual ties:** *coniuncta* takes up *coniunctius* 556, and re-introduces the theme of 323-49 (cf. *coniunctam . . . naturam . . . eorum* 349). The participle is used causally; it is neuter plural, and the verbs plural, as if *corpus atque animus*, rather than the periphrasis with *potestas*, had preceded (cf. on 136).

560-1 **the soul . . . cannot . . . generate:** though *animus* is inclusive (see on 558 above), Lucretius is probably here thinking especially of the technical *animus* as the initiator of motion in the animate being. *edere*, literally 'to give out', is appropriate to the communication or transmission of motion.

562 **devoid of the soul:** *anima*, though like *animus* 561 covering the complete soul, is probably used with especial reference to physical sensation (*sensibus*), the province of the *anima* proper. The claim about the body goes back to 333-6, where neither body nor soul could experience sensation without the other.

563-5 The analogy of a severed sense-organ, which was the basis of proof 9 which concerned the mind, is here extended to the complete soul. It applies at the level of general probability, in that the analogy of one of the parts of the body suggests that the soul, the body's intimately related partner, is itself likely to cease to function, and to decay, at death. This general argument is then (566-79) supported by a physical explanation of the mutual indispensability of soul and body, in terms of their close structural union which has been traced in the first part of the book and in which the body houses and protects the soul.

It is clear that . . . plainly: the combination of *scilicet* with the Lucretian passive *uidetur* (cf. on 35) exemplifies both the poet's tendency to pleonasm (cf. on 108) and his confidence in the self-evident clarity of his logic.

by itself . . . independently: *ipse* (cf. 631) and *per se* each make the same point as *sola . . . per se* 561.

in isolation from the body: *sorsum* with the ablative here uniquely replaces the usual *sorsum a*: the phrase answers *sine corpore* 560.

566-72 **mingled throughout . . . the bones:** the description is more accurate for the atoms of the *anima*, which was established as *per totum dissita corpus* at 143, than of the *animus*, but is nevertheless valid for those of the complete soul, viewed as a single entity. *mixtim*, a very rare adverb with a favourite Lucretian termination (see on 526-7), is not found earlier and is doubtless coined by the poet.

are held in by the whole body: an echo of *tenetur corpore ab omni* 323; see notes there.

leap apart freely over great intervals: as they would do without the body to protect and enclose them. The intervals are the spaces traversed by the atoms between their collisions within the soul-compound, which would be greater outside the body than they are within it; these collisions would soon cease as the soul-compound dissolved and its atoms were dispersed and scattered. For the ablative *magnis interuallis*, see on 394.

they are confined: *conclusa* develops the idea of the body's protection conveyed in *tenentur* 567 and 572.

move with the motions conveying sensation: whether physical (the province of the *anima*) or mental (that of the *animus*); cf. *sensus animi* 578, and see on 240. These motions clearly involve shorter trajects between collisions than the soul-atoms would perform outside the body. *motus*, like *quos* with *moueri*, is a cognate or internal limiting accusative, used with certain intransitive verbs.

573-5 A characteristic *reductio ad absurdum*, reminiscent of the conclusion of the opening proof at 440-4, rounds off the argument and brings out its close links with that key passage.

and indeed an animate creature: *atque* here adds a still stronger point. For *animans* in the 'etymological' sense, 'containing a soul (*anima*)', cf. 97 and note.

if it is going to be able to enclose the soul within itself: as at 440-4, it is the idea of air acting as the soul's container that is the object of ridicule; Wakefield's emendation, which makes *aer* the subject of *poterit*, is thus far superior to the reading of O, *sese anima*, which Bailey retains.

to confine it to allow those motions: *concludere* picks up *conclusa* 569 just as *eos motus* refers back to *sensiferos motus* 570. *in* with the accusative here expresses the purpose or end in view.

in . . . the actual body: *in ipso corpore* is used, as at 483 and 506, to contrast the soul's unprotected state outside its container.

576-9 **Therefore again and again:** the formula, for which see on 228, acknowledges the recurrence of a fundamental point from proof 1.

once all the body's shelter has been dissolved: the phrase is a Lucretian version of τοῦ στεγάζοντος λυθέντος, Epicurus, *ad Herodotum* 65; cf. on 323.

the vital breaths: i.e. the soul; the phrase provides a poetic variant on *animus* and *anima*, scientifically appropriate in so far as they contained wind, and also suggests that they will quickly be merged and absorbed in the breezes (*auras* 570) into which they are constantly described as escaping at death.

the consciousness of mind and spirit: a periphrasis for the complete soul, in which *sensus*, though attached only to *animi*, is no less applicable to the *anima*.

the well-being of the partners is linked: again there is ring-composition, with *coniunctast causa* (where *causa* is equivalent to *causa salutis*: cf. 348), taking up *coniuncta ualent* in the opening sentence at 559. The context makes it clear that *duobus* refers to body and soul (*corporis atque animi uiuata potestas* 558), despite the allusion to the soul's two parts earlier in the sentence.

580-614 Proofs 11-13: further demonstrations of the division which the soul suffers at death, and approaches even in life

Like proofs 8 (526-47) and 16 (634-69), these three arguments turn on the soul's divisibility, from which its mortality automatically follows (see introductory note to 526-47).

580-91 *Proof 11: the body's decay at death must result from the soul's departure from deep within it by a process of permeation in which the soul is divided*

In atomic terms, the loss of the soul from deep within the body disrupts the previous pattern of harmonious atomic motions in the soul-body compound, resulting in the body's total collapse and decay. The emphasis falls on the soul's permeation of the body as it seeps (*emanare* 583 and 586) through all the bodily apertures (586-8) and on the division this involves (*diffusa* 583, *dispertitam* 589, *sibi distractam* 590): the inference, that division entails mortality, is not stated, but assumed on the basis of proof 8. The converse argument, that a pre-existing soul would be divided in *entering* the body at *birth*, appears at 698-712.

580-1 **the sundering of the soul:** primarily from the body, as at 342 (see note) and 347, but perhaps also suggesting the soul's atomic dissolution which it is the object of the proof to establish, since in Lucretius' mind the divorce of the two partners involved the atomic dissolution of them both.

without decomposing: *quin = ita ut non*.

an appalling stench: symptomatic of the body's total inner disintegration; in Epicurean theory, the atoms responsible for smells issued from deep within the compound from which they emanated (cf. IV 90-4 and 694-7).

582-3 **seeped out ... scattered:** key-words in the argument: see introductory note above.

from deep down in its depths: this idea, developed in the image of 584-6 (see note below), is equally crucial to the argument; the degree of the body's decomposition is attributed to the soul's escape from its very core.

like smoke: for the image, cf. 456 and note.

584-6 **crumbling . . . collapsed in such ruins . . . foundations . . . :** the image of the decaying body as a collapsing house, in which *penitus . . . mota loco sunt fundamenta* takes up the idea of *ex imo penitusque* 582, is not only poetically effective but scientifically apt; not only does the removal of the soul, and the foundations, result in the total disruption of the body, and the house, but neither soul nor foundations can be extricated in one piece, without their own disruption.

has been transformed: by the loss of the soul, corresponding to the shifting of the house's foundations. Change is a symptom of mortality (cf. 519-20), here that of the body.

587-8 **all the winding ways and apertures which the body contains:** *uiarum . . . flexus* and *foramina* (denoting the pores, but also applicable to exits from buildings) harmonise with the image of the body as a house. *omnis* and *qui* agree with *flexus*, the nearer noun, but are equally applicable to *foramina.*

589-91 **has undergone division . . . its parts have been disrupted:** *dispertitam* and *sibi distractam* (literally 'torn apart from itself') are the key-words; see introductory note above.

while actually in the body: again with the implication that it is still more vulnerable outside it; cf. 483 and 506-9.

before it could glide outside and swim: the subjunctive after *prius . . . quam* indicates that the soul's division is a precondition for its exit.

592-606 *Proof 12: the soul's disruption in fainting fits reflects its liability to complete dissolution*

Loss of consciousness in fainting or black-out is here attributed to temporary, partial disruption or division of the soul, most clearly indicated by *conquassatur* 600 (cf. *dissoluere* 602; see notes there); the physiological explanation may well have been similar to that of sleep, in which the *anima* was divided, some of it temporarily leaving the body and some of it being drawn deeper inside (see on 112-3). But while the main idea is that even in life the soul approaches division, thus providing the connection with proofs 11 and 13 which has escaped editors, and making transposition superfluous, this example is also reminiscent of earlier cases of the soul suffering while still in the body (proofs 3-6); the parallel with epilepsy is especially close, since there too the division of the *anima* was emphasised, while the repetition of two points from the earlier passage in 602 and 603-6 (see notes below) reflects the general parallel with proofs 3-6.

592 **What's more:** an even stronger point, in that the soul approaches division even in life.

remains: *uertitur* = *uersatur.*

within the boundaries of life: for the anastrophe of *finis . . . uitae . . . intra*, cf. 140-1 and note.

593-4 **it is . . . observed that:** the Lucretian passive (see on 35) again marks an appeal to common experience.

the soul: *anima* is again used inclusively, since both mind and spirit lose consciousness in a fainting fit, as *mens animaeque potestas* 600 confirms.

undermined: *labefacta*, literally 'made to slip (or 'totter')', like *collabefiunt* 601, is an appropriate term to suggest the loosening of the soul's fabric which is the first step in its disruption and division.

ready to depart and to be released completely from the body: probably with the implication that it does partially depart, as did the *anima* in sleep; see introductory note above.

595-6 **the expression grows glazed . . . bloodless body:** the physical evidence of the soul's *malaise*. With *corpore* supplied to complete the defective text of 596 (on the assumption that the corruption in 594, where the ending *omnia membra* has been mistakenly copied from 596, occurred when *corpore* had already been lost), the rhythm, with correspondence of ictus and stress throughout the last three feet, is appropriate to the lifelessness described.

597-9 **This sort of thing occurs when:** for *quod genus est cum*, cf. 221 and note.

had a black-out . . . suffered a turn: the Latin phrases are popular expressions for fainting; cf. (a) Plautus, *Miles Gloriosus* 1331, *animo male factumst huic repente miserae*; (b) *ibid.* 1347, *animus hanc modo hic reliquerat*, and Caesar, *De Bello Gallico* VI 38.4, *relinquit animus Sextium*. Though *animus* is usual in each phrase, Lucretius substitutes *anima* in the second, partly, no doubt, because both parts of the soul are affected (cf. on 594 above), but partly, perhaps, because so adapted the popular phrase supports the idea that the fainting fit involves the departure of part of the *anima* from the body (see introductory note above).

consternation reigns . . . last link with life: the alarm of the onlookers, graphically introduced by the impersonal passive and vivid *iam*, emphasises the soul's vulnerability by showing just how closely the state of the living victim resembles death.

600-1 **are . . . shattered:** as at 441, *conquassatur* suggests physical disruption, here of the soul's two parts, along with a consequent loss of their functions (*potestas*).

they are reduced to collapse: *haec* is neuter plural, with reference to *mens* and *anima*, even though both are feminine (see on 136). For *collabefiunt*, see on 593 above.

602 **a slightly severer shock could dissolve them:** the same point was made in the case of intoxication at 484-6 (see introductory note above). *dissoluere*, denoting the complete and permanent division which would result from a more serious *causa* than that of 593, reflects that the fainting fit itself involves an approach to such division.

603-6 The point that the soul's sufferings in the body will be vastly magnified without the body's protection, hinted at in connection with intoxication at 483 and developed (as here, in a rhetorical question) in the case of epilepsy at 506-9, provides a second link with earlier proofs; cf. also 434-44 and 566-79.

Why, I ask: *tandem* renders the rhetorical question indignant.

the soul: *anima* (in its inclusive sense) is to be supplied as subject.

out of doors . . . shelter taken away: the tricolon climax of adverbial expressions vividly conveys the soul's vulnerability. *tegmine dempto* serves as a reminder of the body's role as the soul's protection and shelter; cf. 576-7 and note.

the whole of time: *aeuum*, masculine rather than neuter, exhibits archaic fluctuation of gender, as also at II 561 and Plautus, *Poenulus* 1187.

briefest . . . you care to nominate: *minimum quoduis* (in which *quoduis* has its root sense 'that you like') = *quamuis breue.*

607-14 *Proof 13: the dying man does not feel his soul departing complete, but rather being fragmented as it fails in different areas*

The soul's division at death, argued for on more theoretical grounds in proof 11, is now supported from the introspective experience of the dying man; the argument, though presented from a different point of view, overlaps to some extent with that of 526-47 (proof 8).

607 **Indeed:** the explanatory *enim* introduces a justification either of the soul's divisibility (602) and general fragility (603-6), or, if proof 12 is regarded as parenthetical, of its division at death which proof 11 sought to establish.
it is clear that: the Lucretian passive suggests that the dying, and those who had come close to death but recovered, had reported on their experience.

608 **his soul:** *anima* (cf. *mens* 612) is again inclusive; both parts of the soul perish at death, even though the main emphasis is on the departure of the technical *anima* from different areas of the body which it pervades.
is going outside intact: cf. *sincera exsistit* in the partly similar argument at 532.

609 **throat and gullet above:** the account of the soul's steady progression from lower throat (*fauces*) to upper (*iugulum*) pours ironical scorn on the process which rival theories would require. For the form *supera* (here adverbial), cf. 385 and note.

610 **failing . . . where it is stationed:** implying its fragmentation; the allusion is presumably to parts of the body, and the *anima* within them, growing numb and losing the sensation of touch.

611 **each of his senses . . . in its own area:** e.g. sight in the eyes, hearing in the ears. The Latin is probably to be explained along the lines suggested by Kenney, as a conflation of *sensum alium in alia parte* and *sensum quemque in sua parte*, but *alios* also marks a distinction between touch, the subject of 610, and other senses. For the ablative form *parti*, cf. *Heliconi* 132 and note.

612 The line lacks a normal main caesura, though there is a quasi-caesura between the prefix and root of *im-mortalis*, as at 715; cf. also 174 (*ex-surgendi*) and 630 (*intro-duxerunt*).
is being dissolved: *dissolui* (probably quadrisyllabic; see on 330) again focuses on the central theme of division; not only is the soul as a whole fragmented, but so are the parts of it situated in the sense-organs.
our soul: *mens*, the seat of the emotions, is chosen to represent the whole soul here (cf. on 608 above) because of the allusion to its complaining in 613.

613-4 **it would not complain . . . but would rather sense:** the *quam* expected in 614 after *non tam* is replaced by *sed magis*, with a conflation of two idioms. There is probably also an element of zeugma, in that a neutral verb like *sentiret* is to be supplied out of *conquereretur* to govern the second accusative and infinitive, though it would not be impossible for Lucretius to suggest that the soul's escape intact from the body would also warrant complaint; certainly an antonym, like *gauderet*, should not (as some editors suggest) be supplied, since Lucretius would never concede to his rivals that the soul's survival would be a matter for rejoicing.

shedding its garb, like a snake: *uestem* is metaphorical for the slough *(exuuiae)* cast by the snake, as at IV 61 (cf. its application to the spider's moult at 386), and also for the body as the soul's protection (cf. Plato, *Phaedo* 87b-e and 91d). With *anguis*, *relinquit* is to be supplied.

615-23 Proof 14: the mind has its fixed place in the body and could not exist elsewhere

This is a new, inductive argument from experience and the uniformity of nature's patterns, which involves the distinct, but related, generalisations that everything in nature has its fixed place (618-9) and that every complex organism can have its different parts arranged in only one way (620-1); the corresponding inferences, which are not drawn explicitly, are that the mind can only exist in the human breast, and could not exist anywhere else in the body (much less outside it). The same argument is given a wider application at 784-99, where it is extended to cover not only the mind but also the spirit, and is directed not only at the soul's survival, but is the first of the more general arguments directed at its eternity (see introductory note to 417-829); 615-23 might accordingly have been omitted had the poem been revised.

615 **intellect . . . rational power of the mind:** the phrase (cf. 94-5 and note) concentrates on the intellectual aspects of the *animus*, even though the evidence adduced for its location in the breast (141-2) depended exclusively on its emotional aspects.

616-7 **clings in all men to a single abode:** *haeret* was similarly applied to the mind's fixed place at 140. *omnibus* is dative of reference or possession; *sedibus*, like *regionibus*, is poetic plural, hence the rare plural *unis*, for which cf. II 919 and V 897.

618-9 **are allotted to each type of thing:** *reddere* often has the sense 'to give duly' rather than 'to give back'. For the sense of *quidque*, see on 34.

where each can endure . . . : *quicquid* is archaic for *quidque* as in the parallel argument at 787; cf. also, e.g., V 264, 284 and 304. The *ubi* clause balances *ad nascendum*, approximating in sense to *ad uiuendum*.

620-1 The transition to the second generalisation (see introductory note above) is abrupt, in that *cuique* and *quicquid* in 618-9 are naturally taken as referring to parts of the body, whereas in 620-1 *quicquid* remains the subject (with *esse* governed, like *durare*, by *possit*) but now refers to a complex organism; Munro's suggestion of the loss of a line beginning a new sentence, with the general sense 'Our body too must conform with this law', thus has much to commend it.

comprise members made up in manifold ways: Lachmann's emendation of the corrupt manuscript text yields satisfactory sense, with *multimodis perfectis* approximating to *diuersis*. Bernays' *partitis*, despite its widespread acceptance, is open to the fatal objections (a) that it cannot denote arrangement, as is supposed, but implies physical division, as e.g. at 710 which is cited in support; (b) that *multimodis* then makes the opposite point to that required, since the claim is that the arrangement of parts in a given species is uniform, not various. The ablative *perfectis artubus* is descriptive.

but without . . . : *ita . . . ut* introduces a limiting consecutive clause, as did *ut* at 285.

a reversal in the order . . . : in which the diverse parts were assigned to the wrong places.

622-3 The concluding generalisation implies, without explicitly stating, that the mind goes closely with the human breast and could not exist or survive in an alien environment elsewhere.

one thing go closely with another: e.g. flame with fire, cold with, e.g., ice; the link is between a thing and its natural home, as the examples adduced make clear.

flame . . . in rivers or cold . . . in fire: Lucretius is fond of introducing such paradoxical physical impossibilities (ἀδύνατα), a recurrent motif in Greek and Latin literature, as the automatic consequence of rival theories; cf., e.g., 748-53, 784-6, and I 159-66 and 881-92. The irony is heightened by *solitast* (cf., e.g., *solere* 118), and perhaps, as Kenney suggests, by the assonances with *gn* and *g* in *igni gignier algor*. For the archaic passive infinitive *gignier*, see on 67; *algor* is a rare and archaic synonym for *frigus*.

624-33 Proof 15: a sentient spirit which survived the body would require a fresh set of sense-organs

This new argument, though reinforced by the premiss that the body, as well as the spirit in it, participates in physical sensation (350-69), could be advanced simply on the basis that the loss of sense-organs (e.g. the eyes) in life can be observed to result in failure of the corresponding sense (e.g. sight), in order to show that any sensation enjoyed by an immortal soul without the body would at least be totally different from what we know as sensation: it is thus one of the few Lucretian arguments that could be seriously advanced without adaptation today.

624-5 **spirit . . . sensation:** since the argument turns on consciouness through the five senses, not mental consciousness, it concerns the spirit alone in the first instance, even though the mortality of either part of the soul follows from that of the other (421-4).

626 **we must, I suggest, imagine it to be equipped:** for the construction, with the impersonal gerundive of obligation replacing the normal personal idiom, [*ea*] *faciunda est . . . aucta*, cf. 391 and note; for the form of the gerundive, cf. 409 and note. *ut opinor* is a favourite phrase of the poet's, often employed, as here and at 676, as an ironic understatement in rejecting a rival theory and its implications.

organs of the five senses: for this concrete use of *sensus*, repeated in 630 below, cf. 550 and note.

627 **This is the only way:** i.e. with bodily appendages or in bodily form.

we can picture to ourselves: the emphatic suffix of *nosmet* serves to emphasise the reflexive idea; cf. *ipsi se* 77 and note.

628 **underworld spirits . . . in Acheron:** here and in 630 below, the Lucretian technical term for the spirit is applied to the shades of the traditional underworld. For the reference to Acheron, cf. 25 and note.

629 **painters and writers of earlier generations:** the writers are exemplified most obviously by Homer, who in *Odyssey* XI describes the hero's encounter with the ghosts of the dead, who drink blood and then converse with him, the painters by Polygnotus, who depicted Odysseus' meeting with the shade of Teiresias in a fresco at Delphi in the fifth century. Cicero, *Tusculan Disputations* I 37, also alludes to the poets' misguided attribution of physical features to the souls of the dead; cf. also I 50, where he criticises those who deny the soul's immortality because they cannot conceive its nature without the body.

630 **have portrayed:** *introduxerunt* is a metaphor from bringing onto the stage. The line lacks a normal main caesura, though there is a quasi-caesura between the *intro-* prefix and the root: cf. 612 and note.

631-2 **by itself . . . a hand:** the representative organ of touch, as at 551. *ipsa* (cf. 564) has the same force as *per se* 633, reinforcing the emphatic idea of isolation from the body (*sorsum* 631 and 632).

for the benefit of the spirit: the use of the dative of possession or advantage is not without irony.

633 **are incapable of sensation or existence . . . :** once more there is ring-composition, with *esse* taking up *immortalis <e>st* 624 just as *possunt sentire* answers *sentire potest* 625. The inference that spirits cannot *exist* independently of the body, which the argument of the passage does not in itself warrant, reflects how closely Lucretius equates the spirit's life with sensation, just as he equates that of the soul with consciousness (physical and mental) in general; cf., e.g., the recurrent phrase *uitalem sensum* (215, 527, and, significantly, 635 immediately below). As subject of *possunt*, *animae* has to be supplied from 628 and 630.

634-69 Proof 16: the loss of parts of the body in battle and the vivisection of a snake entail the soul's division and mortality

The proofs concerned with the soul's non-survival now reach an unforgettable culmination with a gruesome pair of examples which serve the didactic purpose of imprinting graphic images of the soul's division indelibly on the reader's mind. As in proofs 8 (526-47) and 11-13 (580-614), the *animus* sometimes features in the argument, but the main emphasis falls on the division of the *anima* distributed throughout the whole body; the principle, on which those proofs equally depended, that division entails mortality, is now presented more axiomatically than hitherto, at 640-1. The evidence for the soul's division lies throughout in the temporary retention by all the severed parts of the signs of life, usually movement, revealing the presence of *anima* in them all; every detail in the two pieces of description thus reinforces the argument, and the passage contains no gratuitous violence.

634-5 **we feel . . . and can see:** the verbs mark yet another appeal to experience, partly, at least, introspective.

the sensation of life: for Lucretius' equation of the two, see on 633 above.

the whole body . . . the whole of it: the presence of *anima* everywhere in the body means that, wherever the body is severed, it must be severed too.

animate: *animale* is used in the root sense, 'containing *anima*'; cf. V 141, and *animans* at III 97, 417, 666, 720 and 749.

636 **with a lightning blow:** the four dactyls in the line fit the rapidity described. The spirit might survive a less instantaneous blow without being divided, either, if the victim died, by escaping gradually from the two parts at the point of impact, or, if he survived, by concentrating gradually in one of them (cf. the process envisaged at 533-5).

637 **to sever and isolate:** *sorsum* emphasises the key idea of separation conveyed by the *se-* prefix of *secernat*.

638-9 **the spirit:** after *uis aliqua* 637, the periphrasis *uis animai* involves a word-play, or verbal conceit, with one type of *uis* disrupting another; cf., e.g., 364, 378-80 and 387 and notes.

divided, sundered and forced apart: for the repetition of the *dis-* prefix to emphasise the key idea of division, cf., e.g., 435-8, 500-1 and 589-90; M.F. Smith suggests that Plato's repetition of the prefix δια- in *Phaedo* 80c4-5 and 84b6-7 may have influenced the poet here, a possibility supported by the fact that Lucretius is here contradicting the argument of *Phaedo* 78-80 that the soul is a single existence which cannot be dissolved. The arbitrarily doubled *s* of *dissicietur* marks the first syllable as long; in compounds of *iacio*, the spelling with *ii* was not used.

640-1 For the axiom that division implies mortality, on which proofs 8 and 11-13 equally depend, cf. the still broader principle established at 513-20, that any form of change implies mortality.

is split asunder and separates into any parts: *scinditur* echoes *discissa* 639, and *discedit* the *dis-* prefixes of the two previous lines. *ullas*, normally used in a negative, virtually negative or conditional context, is used as if *si quid*, rather than *quod*, had preceded.

obviously: because division is a form of destruction.

renounces any claim to eternal status: for this type of personification, cf. 208 and 517 and notes. *aeternam* is a variant on *immortalem*, and properly embraces pre-existence as well as future survival; even though at this point Lucretius is concerned to rule out the latter, the two are mutually complementary (see introductory note to 417-829).

642 **they record how scythed chariots . . . :** *memorant* shows that the ensuing account, for all its vividness, is not first-hand, but based on literary sources. Chariots fitted with scythes were an oriental invention never used by the Greeks or Romans, and are first mentioned by Xenophon, *Anabasis* I 8.10; Livy XXXVII 41.7 describes their use by Antiochus III at the battle of Magnesia in 189, while Quintus Curtius, writing in the first century A.D., provides a post-Lucretian account (*Historia Alexandri* IV 9.5 and IV 15.17). The compound *falciferos* (cf. 11 and note) is used instead of the standard prose term *falcatos*.

643 **in the heat of indiscriminate slaughter:** *calentis* appears to be both literal, denoting the body-heat imparted to the chariots by the carnage, and figurative, suggesting the blood-lust of the drivers; the phrase recurs at V 1313, where it is applied to lions frenzied as a result of their use in battle.

so suddenly: *de subito* answers, and is an archaic variation on, *subito* 636.

644-7 **the part which has been hewn off . . . :** the staccato effect of the two monosyllables *id quod* at the end of the line is not inappropriate to the context of sudden amputation.

is seen to quiver: providing visible evidence that it contains *anima* which has been cut off by the same blow.

while the warrior's mind is nevertheless unable to sense the pain: for the periphrasis *hominis uis*, cf. 8 and note; 'the mind and the warrior' is a hendiadys, denoting 'the warrior's mind'. The allusion to the mind reflects that the spirit in the severed limb has been divided not only from the rest of the spirit but from the other part of the soul too. Quintus Curtius, in the second of the passages cited on 642 above, also mentions the absence of pain, and the consequent continuation of fighting, while the wounds were still fresh. For *cum* with the indicative *quit* in a concessive context, cf. 107 and note.

because of the suddenness of the disaster: the dactylic rhythm of *mobilitate mali* fits the speed of the blow, the alliteration with *m*, continued from 645, the grimness of the macabre scene.

and at the same time because . . . : the *quod* clause adds a second reason to that expressed by the causal ablative phrase *mobilitate mali* 646.

preoccupied with lust for battle: for *deditus* with *in* + ablative, rather than with the usual dative, cf. IV 815.

648 **the remainder of:** Lucretius always uses the original, quadrisyllabic, form of the adjective; the trisyllabic *reliquus* is used only by post-Augustan poets. For the long *e* (as in *reliquias* 656), see on *religio* 54.

he keeps trying to: *petessit* (cf. V 810) fits best as an iterative, or perhaps intensive, form of *petit*, rather than as a desiderative ('wishes to seek'); cf. Festus 206.

649 **his left arm:** *laeuam* (sc. *manum*), like *dextram* 651, probably acquires in the context the extended sense generally assigned to it by editors and translators, even though *membra* 642 could include smaller members than complete limbs.

650 Dactyls and spondees alternate throughout the line, as if to express the contrast between the swift advance of the wheels and the bumpier progress of the severed limb which they whirl along.

carried away: *abstraxe* is a rare and striking contraction of *abstraxisse*; cf. *consumpse* I 233, *protraxe* V 1159, and *confluxet* (= *confluxisset*) I 987.

greedy scythes: Lucretius often uses *rapax* and *rapidus*, each derived from *rapere*, in contexts appropriate to their root sense of 'carrying off'; cf., e.g., *fluuiosque rapaces* I 17.

651-6 After the main illustration, a climactic sequence of briefer vignettes, to which one, two and three lines in turn are devoted, provides the no less memorable conclusion.

651 **as he climbs up and attacks:** i.e. as he mounts the chariot in an attempt to kill the driver. *instat* is appropriate both to setting foot on the chariot and to approaching with hostile intent.

652-3 Rhythm once more contributes to the graphic description; the unusual weak, or feminine, main caesura in 652 fits the stumbling alluded to, the dactyls at the beginning of 653 the convulsive twitching of the toes, while its concluding monosyllable (cf. 644 and note above) helps starkly to convey the isolation of the severed leg. The attempt to stand (like the attempts to continue fighting in 648-51) involves the victim's mind and the spirit he still retains, while the twitching of the toes shows that they contain spirit which has been severed with the leg.

nearby: *propter* is here a local adverb, as at II 417.

654-6 Editors compare Ennius' account of decapitation in *Annales* 483-4 (Skutsch), *oscitat in campis caput a cervice reuolsum / semianimesque micant oculi lucemque requirunt* (the head shorn from the neck gapes on the plain, and the half-live eyes blink and seek the light), adapted by Virgil at *Aeneid* X 394-6, but the resemblances to the Lucretian passage are minimal.

living: for *-que* appended to short *e*, cf. 163 and note.

expression of life . . . wide-open eyes: different evidence of the presence of spirit from the movement adduced earlier at 644 and 653.

surrendered: on the sense of *reddere* and its prefix, see on 618.

657-60 **What's more:** introducing a stronger example, in that whereas the previous illustrations, summed up in 636-7, involved bisection, the division of the snake and its *anima*, which is treated as parallel to the human *anima*, is multiple, and thus proves, and exemplifies, the spirit's destructibility still more fully.

imagine . . . and suppose . . . you will . . . observe: mixed future conditionals of this type are not uncommon in poetry; the perfect subjunctive *sit libitum* suggests that Memmius, and so the reader, is unlikely to opt for the grim experiment, while the future indicative *cernes* graphically portrays its results.

tongue . . . tail . . . body: the ablatives of description focus on the snake's extremities and the long body connecting them, the whole extent of which is pervaded by spirit (cf. 634-5), as the movement of the tongue illustrates in the case of the head. The tail is menacing, presumably, as it seems to the onlooker, rather than in fact, but there is much to be said for Lachmann's emendation of *minanti* to *micanti,* a virtual synonym for *uibrante*, which would provide a clearer indication that the tail too contains spirit.

cut it apart . . . at each end, into many segments: the manuscripts' *serpentis . . . utrumque* can scarcely mean 'both parts of a snake', alluding, as editors variously suggest, either to two segments into which it has been cut, or to its body and spirit, and Marullus' *serpentem . . . utrimque* yields satisfactory sense; *utrimque* is used with reference to the front and rear ends on which *lingua* and *cauda* have just focused, and goes closely with *in multas partis*, showing that the snake and its spirit are capable of multiple division throughout their whole length. *discidere*, which recurs at 669 below, is a compound of *caedere* probably coined by Lucretius to provide yet another verb prefixed with *dis-*; cf. 638-9 and note.

each portion which has been hewn: *ancisa* (= *ambicisa*, 'cut round') is another compound from *caedere* without literary parallel.

661 **writhing:** indicating the presence of *anima* in each of the severed parts. *tortari* is a rare, old variant on *torqueri.*

spattering . . . with gore: for the spelling of the compound of *spargere*, see on 539. The escape of the gore provides a model for the gradual escape of the *anima* from the various segments after the initial division.

662-3 **and . . . making for its own hind part:** literally 'making for itself behind', whether *retro* is taken closely with *petere*, or as quasi-adjectival with *ipsam se* (= *posteriorem sui ipsius partem*); the movement, and the reaction to pain, once more reveal the presence of *anima.* For the postponement of *-que* with two closely linked words, cf. *aequo animoque* 939 and 962.

in order to bite it: i.e. in an attempt to ease the pain. The word-order, with *ut morsu premat* separating *uulneris ardenti* from *icta dolore,* is not inappropriate to the convolutions described.

664-6 The *reductio ad absurdum* is an effective dialectical weapon, which reinforces the conclusion that the spirit has been divided (667) by showing that the implications of the only obvious alternative are nonsensical.

in all those tiny parts: the diminutive *particulis*, reserved elsewhere by Lucretius, as, e.g., at 708, for more microscopic particles, not only reflects that the division has been multiple, but also heightens the absurdity of each small segment containing its own spirit.

a single animate creature . . . many spirits: the word-order, with the contrasted *unam* and *multas* emphatically placed at the beginning and end of the line, and with the singular *animantem*, suggesting a creature endowed with an *anima* (cf. on 97), in juxtaposition with the plural *animas*, further heightens the absurdity.

667-9 **the single spirit it had:** the facts of the case are now contrasted with the preposterous alternative of 666.

each of the two: i.e. both spirit and body.

since each alike is cut apart . . . : the axiom that division implies mortality (640-1) is here applied to body as well as spirit, hinting once more at the general argument from the analogy between soul and body on which proofs 2-7 in part depend (see introductory notes to 445-58 and 459-525), and suggesting that division is no less symptomatic of mortality in the case of the spirit than in that of the more obviously mortal body.

670-783 ***(b) The soul is born with the body***

670-8 **Proof 17: the soul has no memory of a former existence**

This, the first of the arguments designed to show that the soul is *natiuus* (417: see introductory note to 417-829), raises a cardinal point for any theory which involves its pre-existence. Though Socrates, in Plato's *Phaedo*, denies the Lucretian premiss, claiming that the soul remembers the immaterial Platonic forms or ideas (e.g. 'the good', 'the just', or 'the true') or, roughly speaking, has an innate sense of morality, Lucretius would deny the very possibility of such metaphysical knowledge, and both Platonists and Pythagoreans conceded that the soul forgot the details of its previous existence, an idea reflected in the popular belief that the soul drank the waters of Lethe, the river of forgetfulness, in the underworld; cf. the myth of Er which closes Plato's *Republic*. It is to counter this Platonic and Pythagorean admission that Lucretius argues at 674-8 that such forgetfulness is tantamount to death, an assertion dependent on the axiom established at 513-20, that change implies mortality.

670-1 **the soul:** since the argument turns on memory, the sphere of the mind (cf. the technical *animi* in 674 below), *animai* clearly has its inclusive sense.

is immortal . . . winds its way into our body at birth: i.e. is neither *mortalis* nor *natiuus*, in the terminology of 417; the complementary ideas are coupled at this point of transition from the former to the latter. 670 exactly repeats 624, except that<*e*>*st* is replaced by the synonymous *constat* in 671. *insinuare* (on whose overtones and construction see on 485) is used eight times in this second category of proofs, and twice in book I, to denote the entry of a pre-existing soul into a ready-made body; so applied, the term is loaded and incredulous, suggesting a process which is both improper and so devious and difficult as to be impossible.

672-3 **why . . . why . . . :** the rhetorical questions once more add impact to the argument, and confidently present the premiss, which Plato had denied (see introductory note above) as self-evident.

remember our previous life: which the soul spent in, and between, various bodies. Verbs of remembering often take an accusative rather than a genitive in early Latin and in Cicero.

as well: i.e. in addition to the events of our present life; *super* is adverbial, = *insuper*.

674-6 For the appeal to the axiom that change implies death, see introductory note above. Epicurean memory seems to have depended on the presence in the *animus* of a store of material images (*simulacra* 433) from the objects of past experience; their removal would thus involve physical disruption of the *animus* which would be enough to prove its mortality.

the powers of the mind: *potestas* here has more of its full force than in some other instances of the periphrasis (for which see on 8).

recollection: *retinentia*, found only here, is coined, like *repetentia* 851, as a metrical alternative for the inadmissible *memoria*; cf. *tenemus* (= *memoria tenemus*) 673.

it seems to me: for the ironically understated *ut opinor*, cf. 626 and note.

677-8 **the soul which existed before:** i.e. the pre-existing soul of his rivals, which he claims has perished when it lost its memory of any former existence. With *quae fuit ante*, *anima* (cf. 670) is to be supplied in its inclusive sense.

has only now been created: i.e. when our present life began, when in the Epicurean view soul and body were created simultaneously.

679-712 Proof 18: the soul is too intimately connected with the body to have entered it ready-made

The intimate structural union of soul and body, for which the sentience of the whole body is adduced as evidence, is here used to show that the soul was born with the body rather than inserted from outside as the Pythagoreans supposed. The reply, that a pre-existing soul enters the body by permeation, is met (698ff.) with the now familiar argument that permeation implies division and so in turn death. The passage presents in essence the converse of two of the preceding arguments for the soul's mortality, proof 10 (558-79), which also depended on its close union with the body, and proof 11 (580-91, re-echoed at 695-7 here), where it could not leave the body undamaged, just as it could not here enter the body without being destroyed. The argument applies to both parts of the soul (*anima atque animus* 705, while *animus* 680 and 708 and *anima* 687, 699 and 712 are used inclusively: see on 708), but much more forcibly to the *anima*, which, unlike the *animus*, was interwoven with all the body-tissues and the limbs, and which is primarily in mind in much of the passage.

680 **the soul's lively power:** the same periphrasis was used at 558, in introducing the first of the converse passages mentioned above.

being imported into us: *inferri* is a variant on *insinuari* (see on 671), and is itself not devoid of sarcasm.

682-3 **it would not then be appropriate:** with *ita*, *eam inferri* is to be supplied to complete the construction (literally '<that it should be imported> in such a way that'), unless the impersonal *conueniebat* here governs the *uti* clause, a usage not paralleled in Lucretius, with *ita* = 'as actually happens'. The idiomatic imperfect indicative shows that the conditional has now become remote: indicative, rather than subjunctive, is used because the appropriateness is regarded as absolute (it is appropriate, whether or not it happens), but the imperfect is used by analogy with the corresponding tense of the remote subjunctive, producing a compromise between *conuenit* and *conueniret*; cf. the potential *conueniebat* I 881, *decebat* I 885 and *debebat* I 959. The idiom of the tense, however, is far from universal, as the parallel *conuenit* 685 reflects.

it should manifestly have grown: *uideatur*, again a true passive, as in 695 and 711 below, makes *haud conueniebat* a highly ironic understatement. *cresse* (= *creuisse*) makes good sense as a past tense (cf. 69), even though the perfect infinitive came to be used timelessly in poetry, like a Greek aorist.

in the very blood: reflecting, like *per uenas* 691, that the Lucretian *anima* was omnipresent in the body; contrast the popular view which identified the soul with blood (43).

684-5 **in its own cage, so to speak:** *cauea*, any hollow, covers a cage or prison, and is contemptuous, probably satirising the Pythagorean idea of the body as the soul's prison (σῶμα σῆμα); *uelut* apologises for the grotesque notion. The Lucretian *animus*, localised in the chest, came close to having its own *cauea*, but it is the idea that the whole soul could be so compartmentalised that is the object of scorn.

yet in such a way . . . sensation: a highly sarcastic addition, fatal to the *in cauea* idea, since in Lucretius' eyes the proviso demands the omnipresence of part of the soul (the *anima*) in the body.

690 **Plain fact teaches us:** another appeal to experience, with the same sort of personification as at 208 and 640-1.

the complete opposite of this is the case: literally 'the whole of this (*quod*, connective relative) takes place in the opposite way'; i.e. the soul, so far from living in a separate compartment, is intimately connected with the body. With this interpretation, Lachmann's transposition of 690-4 gives excellent sense, without the need to emend or delete 685, and produces a far superior sequence of thought, avoiding a cumbersome and unsatisfactory parenthesis between the *neque* and *nec* clauses in 688-9 and 695-7; the order of lines may have been 'corrected' in the manuscripts under the mistaken impression that 690 contradicted the *ut* clause of 685 rather than *uelut in cauea . . . uiuere solam* 684.

691 **it is so interlaced:** *animi uiuata potestas*, referring to the whole soul, is to be supplied from 680 as subject of *conexa est*, even though the description of 691-2 applies only to the *anima* section.

through the veins, the flesh, the sinews: for this formula, cf. 217.

693 **shock of cold water:** *stringor*, found only here, reflects Lucretius' fondness for rare or coined abstract nouns. The harsh sound of the archaic genitives is not inappropriate to the sense.

694 **encountered in the bread:** cf. Horace's complaint of gritty bread at Canusium, *Satires* I 5.91. The general sense, though not the precise text, is clear; of the conjectures closest to the reading of the manuscripts, Bernays' *subiit si e frugibus* (literally 'if one steals up from the bread') is preferable to Clark's *subsit si frugibus* ('should one be lurking in the bread'), on metrical grounds, as Lucretius would more probably have written *si subsit* to secure coincidence of ictus and stress in the fourth foot.

686 **Therefore again and again:** for the recurrent Lucretian formula, cf. 228 and note.

687 **or exempt from the law of death:** though the prime concern of this group of arguments is to show that the soul is *natiuus*, Lucretius naturally reverts at frequent intervals to the complementary idea of its mortality.

688-9 The lines reiterate that a soul inserted at birth would have to live *in cauea* 684.

laced so closely onto our bodies: *adnecti*, used only here by Lucretius, is a loaded term, contrasting with *conexa est* 691 and *contextae* 695, and suggesting that a pre-existing soul could only be loosely grafted onto the body, not intimately interwoven: *tanto opere adnecti* is deliberately paradoxical, a virtual contradiction in terms.

had they found their way in from outside: for the loaded use of *insinuatas*, see on 671; *extrinsecus* (cf. 698 and 722) heightens the incredulous tone. The participle here does the work of a conditional clause.

695-7 A reminder of the argument of 580-91, which justifies the claim *nec leti lege solutas* 687.

make their way out undamaged . . . safely extricate themselves: *saluas exsoluere sese* provides a characteristic variation, with chiasmus, on *exire . . . incolumes*. The repeated sibilants in 696, together with the assonance *saluas exsoluere*, contribute to the contemptuous, incredulous tone.

698-9 **the soul:** *animam* (see introductory note above) is inclusive, as *anima atque animus* 705 proves, even though only the *anima* 'proper' is present in the limbs (*membra* 699, *artus* 707 and 710).

in the habit of permeating our limbs: instead of dwelling *in cauea* 684, the 'appropriate' course if it entered at birth. However, even a soul entering a *cauea* would not be exempt from the permeation argument, unless it did so complete (e.g. through mouth and throat).

700 **perish . . . through fusion with the body:** at the time of the supposed permeation process. *fusa* is used causally and with present rather than perfect force, like *dispertitus* 702 and *partita* 710.

all the more: either 'than on the assumption that it is born with the body' or 'than if it dwelt *in cauea* and had only that to permeate'. *quique*, an old ablative, appears to intensify *tanto magis*, though how it comes to do so is unclear: the idiom, repeated at V 343, is confined to Lucretius.

701 **what permeates is . . . destroyed:** the point is made axiomatically; cf. 640-1 where division involves mortality, and 519-20 and 756 where change in turn implies death.

702-4 The analogy of food permeating the body in digestion is loaded, since it changes in the process, eventually turning into the various body-tissues which it goes to augment: it would have been fairer to choose a case where the permeating compound was itself recreated (e.g. water seeping through rock). The Lucretian rejoinder would be (a) that permeation alone proved mortality, since the division it involved might on some future occasion be permanent, and (b) that the reconstituted compound was merely a replica of the original, which had itself been destroyed.

by being dispersed: for the use of the participle see on 700 above. The manuscripts' *dispertitur* (sc. *anima*) requires a full stop at the end of the line and produces an abruptly lame sentence.

all the apertures: elsewhere, Lucretius refers to food being distributed only to the veins (II 1125 and 1136, IV 955 and VI 946) and to the limbs (703), but there is no difficulty in supposing that the *caulae*, or 'tiny hollows', represent the final stages of its journey to supplement the various body-tissues.

perishes in division: the prefix of *disperit* has point; cf. *dispertitus* 702 and *diditur* 703.

705-6 **however whole they enter:** *integra* is synonymous with *incolumes* and *saluas* 696; for the neuter agreeing with nouns of different gender see on 136, and for *quamuis* with indicative on 403.

are . . . dissolved: *dissoluuntur* is pentasyllabic; cf. 330 and note.

707 **there are distributed to the limbs:** answering *in . . . artus . . . diditur* 703.

through all the apertures: answering *per caulas . . . omnis* 702.

so to speak: *quasi* apologises for the eccentricity of the hypothesis that the soul gains access to the body in this way, adding a note of incredulity: cf. 729.

708-10 **this soul of ours . . . which now holds sway in our body:** *animi* is again inclusive, as at 680 above. The idea of the whole soul holding sway in the body is paralleled at 279-81 (see notes), where the fourth nature is the 'soul of the soul', and, like the soul, *dominatur corpore toto*. The same terminology is differently applied to the *animus* 'proper' at 138-9, from which editors usually mistakenly assume that *animi* 708 is technical; they thus create insoluble difficulties, not least that the *anima* of 705 is totally lost in transit during the permeation process.

is created . . . born from the one which previously perished: the argument (cf. 677-8) is that the rival hypothesis entails two souls; the one which entered would perish in permeation, and our present soul would be a separate entity, born from its remnants.

by dispersal: *partita* answers *dispertitus* which introduced the analogy in 702, and, like it, is used causally and timelessly.

711-2 **neither to lack a birthday:** as *creatur* 708 and *nata* 709 have shown.

nor to be immune from death: as demonstrated by *periit* 710.

713-40 Proof 19: the maggots exuded by corpses are animated by remnants of the human soul, not by pre-existing maggot-souls

Though this argument is initially concerned to show that the soul is divided and therefore mortal, the main point at issue is once more pre-existence, and the bulk of the passage comprises a *reductio ad absurdum* of the idea of pre-existing maggot-souls which find their way into the bodies of the maggots, or worms, which infest the decaying corpse. Like the dissected snake argument at 657-69, it presupposes that living creatures (*animantes*) automatically possess a soul (an *anima* and an at least rudimentary *animus*; see on 97). The Lucretian position, that particles of the human soul are reconstituted to form the maggots' souls, just as flesh from the corpse is rearranged to form their bodies, involves the admission that parts of the human soul participate in conscious life after death, but the poet turns what might have appeared a weak defensive position into a brilliant rhetorical offensive, posing two inescapable dilemmas at 713-4 and 725-9 and satirically demolishing all alternative explanations to his own.

713-6 The Lucretian answer to the opening dilemma, that some soul-particles remain in the corpse, entails the soul's division and hence (cf. 640-1) its mortality. The earlier claim that no part of the spirit could remain in the body after the departure of the *animus* (398-9) was clearly an overstatement.

713 **seeds of the soul:** the allusion is primarily, or exclusively, to spirit-particles, but as these were identical in nature to mind-particles and thus capable of supplying whatever mind the maggots possessed, *anima* is most conveniently here translated as an inclusive term. *semina* need not denote the ultimate constituents, or atoms, but can cover more complex components: see on 127.

or not: *necne* for *annon* in a direct question, a very rare idiom, is paralleled in Cicero, *Pro Flacco* 59 and *Tusculan Disputations* III 41.

714 **deceased:** *anima* 713 provides a reminder of the root sense of *exanimo*, 'devoid of soul' (cf. *exos* and *exsanguis* 721), which is however potentially misleading in that it might suggest a negative, rather than an affirmative, answer to Lucretius' question.

715 **it will be quite impossible . . . :** *haud erit ut . . . possit* is an emphatic version of *haud poterit*; cf. *est ut . . . uideatur* approximating to *uidetur* in 725-6.

immortal: for the quasi-caesura in *im-mortalis*, cf. 612 and note.

716 **depleted by the loss of parts:** thus exhibiting not only division but also change (cf. 514) as symptoms of its mortality. On the sense of *libata*, see on 11.

717-21 The alternative answer, whereby the soul escapes division, leaves the problem of explaining the origin of the maggots and their souls, and involves the rejection of what Lucretius sees as the overwhelming circumstantial evidence (cf. 724-5) that they are produced from remnants of the human body and soul.

717-8 **is carried off and flees headlong:** *ablata profugit* answers *recessit* 716.

with its members intact, without leaving any parts of itself: literally 'with its members so intact that it leaves no parts . . .'; the words are antithetical to *partibus amissis . . . libata* 716. The unparalleled attribution of *membra* to the soul is ironic, and Faber's emendation is accordingly unnecessary. For *sinceris* = *integris*, cf. 532 and note.

719-21 Alliteration and assonance (e.g. the repetition of *c*, consonantal *u* and *r* in 719, of *ant* in 720 and of *ex* and the vowel *u* in 721) contribute to the effect of these graphically gruesome lines, which also contain three words, *rancenti* (= *rancido*), *exos* and *perfluctuat*, that are unique to Lucretius and later imitators.

how is it that . . . how is it that: the literal sense 'from what source' focuses on the nub of the question here raised.

breathe out worms . . . animate creatures: the metaphor *exspirant uermis* suggests the phrase *exspirare animam* of the dying man 'breathing out his soul', and *animantum* reinforces the comparison, suggesting that the corpse breathes out creatures containing *anima*. *exspirant* and *animantum* are thus loaded terms, which reinforce Lucretius' own view that the corpse provides the matter not only for the bodies of the worms or maggots but also, as *exspirant* specifically suggests, for their *animae*. For the Epicurean belief, shared with some other ancient philosophers, in the spontaneous generation of worms from decaying matter and similar sources, cf. II 871-2, 898-901 and 928-9, and V 797-8.

boneless, bloodless: *exos* (see also earlier note) and *exsanguis* contribute to the graphic description, the former conveying the flexibility of the maggots, the latter their whiteness.

undulates over the swelling limbs: the wave-image, for which the compound *perfluctuat* (see earlier note) is apparently coined, provides an unforgettably graphic conclusion.

722-3 **souls can find their way . . . a separate body:** implying their pre-existence, which is treated as the only alternative to their formation from remnants of the human soul, and on which the rest of the passage proceeds to heap scorn; applied to the maggots, *animae* is inclusive, embracing both spirit and whatever mind they possess. For *priuas* (= *singulas*), cf. 372 and note.

724-6 **why many thousands . . . one has withdrawn:** to Lucretius, conclusive circumstantial evidence for his own view that parts of the human soul have been recycled; opponents have to dismiss this evidence as mere coincidence.

we must . . . obviously raise . . . : for the periphrasis with *est ut* (in which *uideatur* is again a 'Lucretian' passive), cf. 715 and note. *hoc*, the subject of the *ut* clause, is emphatically placed outside it, and is anticipatory of the indirect question of 727-9.

727-9 The second dilemma, addressed exclusively to believers in pre-existing maggot-souls, is now introduced.

727-8 **pray:** *tandem*, as in a direct question (cf. 603), adds a note of indignation or exasperation, revealing the poet's scepticism of either alternative.

hunt out . . . personally construct . . . : the first possibility is treated as ludicrous from the start, before its formal rejection in 730-7.

of the tiny worms: the diminutive *uermiculorum* not only solves the metrical problem posed by the inadmissible *uermium*, but is also appropriate to the size of the maggots and heightens the irony of the imaginary situation.

somewhere to dwell: the subjunctive *sint* in the *ubi* clause expresses purpose.

729 **find their way into ready-made bodies, so to speak:** *quasi* (cf. 707) apologises for the strange idea, adding to the note of incredulity conveyed by the loaded *insinuentur*.

730-7 The systematic demolition of the first alternative, an easy enough target, is dialectically effective in forcing opponents remorselessly to the second. The argument, that pre-existing maggot-souls have neither the motive nor the opportunity to fashion bodies for themselves, carries the ironical implication that they possess rational powers.

730-1 **why they should . . . it is impossible to explain:** *neque cur . . . quareue* = *neque cur neque quare*; the indirect questions are deliberative. *suppeditat* is here used impersonally, literally 'it is available to say'.

when they are without a body: as they would be during transmigration: to expose its absurdities more vividly, the rival hypothesis is treated as fact.

732 **cold and hunger:** *algu* is from a rare fourth declension variant on *algor* (cf. 623). The final syllable of third declension *fame* is arbitrarily lengthened, as in *contage* in 734 below; cf. also I 806 and VI 1271.

733 **is more prone to suffer from these afflictions:** literally 'being more in contact with these afflictions suffers <from them more>'.

734 **the soul:** *animus* is used inclusively, since bodily afflictions can disturb not only the mind (e.g. 463-73), but also the spirit (e.g. 476-86 and 487-509).

goes through many ills: for *fungi* in the sense of 'suffer', cf. 168 and note; its use with accusative rather than ablative is characteristic of early Latin.

because of its intimate contact with it: *contages*, like the neuter plural *contagia* (cf. 345 and note and 740 below), is apparently coined to replace the metrically inadmissible *contagio*. The *e* of the ablative, short at IV 336, is here arbitrarily lengthened (see on 732 above).

735-6 An effective capping point: even if they had a motive to fashion bodies, they have not the opportunity.

in which to take refuge: the relative clause is purposive; cf. *ubi sint* 728.

737 **Therefore souls . . . :** while the reference is primarily to maggot-souls, the argument of 730-6 is equally applicable to the souls of any living creatures.

738-40 The second possibility, set out at 729, is now dismissed with the same argument that was applied at length to the human soul in the previous proof (679-712).

738 **Nor . . . is it the case that:** *est utqui insinuentur* approximates to *insinuantur* (cf. 715 and note); *utqui* is an old, emphatic, form of *ut* ('that in any way': *qui* is the old ablative of the indefinite pronoun), used also at I 755 and II 17.

739-40 **to be subtly interlaced:** i.e. with their bodies; the same point was made about the human soul at 688-9, while 691-4 provided a vivid illustration of the latter's intimate interweaving with the body.

mutual contacts by which they share in sensation: for the participation of both body and soul in sensation, which was only possible because of their close structural union, cf. 333-6 and 350-69. *consensus* (here genitive) acquires from the context the specialised meaning 'joint sensation'; the repetition of the prefix in *conexae*, *consensus* and *contagia* highlights the close union of soul and body on which the argument turns.

741-75 Proof 20: difficulties besetting the theory of transmigration

The passage raises a series of objections to the Pythagorean theory of metempsychosis, according to which the soul was reincarnated in a succession of bodies, including those of animals (cf. I 116-7, where Ennius, who laid claim to the possession of the soul of Homer after its earlier embodiment in a peacock and Pythagoras, is presented as an adherent). Transmigration between species is first (741-53) ruled out on the evidence of the temperamental differences betwen different species, which in Epicurean theory are determined by the physical constitution of the mind (294-318) and are hereditary; the rival view would result in souls entering bodies to which they were temperamentally unsuited. The rejoinder that souls change according to the type of body is dismissed (754-9) with the familiar argument that change entails mortality (cf. 513-20 and most recently 674-8). The modified theory to which the Pythagoreans are now presented as reduced, of transmigration only within species, is next (760-8) demolished as involving the soul's loss of the maturity which it gained in its previous existence whenever it enters a new body; to explain this as change is again to admit mortality. The idea that the soul originates with the body rather than transmigrating ready-made is corroborated (769-71) from the parallel development of mind and body, which was used at 445-58 to prove mortality and is now conversely applied to refute pre-existence. In a characteristic concluding *reductio ad absurdum* of the rival position (772-5), the poet ironically enquires why an immortal soul quits the decaying body at death, implying that it has no need of a fresh series of bodies to which to transmigrate.

741-7 For the hereditary characteristics of different species, cf. I 597-8, II 665-6 and V 862-3, where the latter part of 742 is closely echoed.

breed . . . seed and breed: *seminium*, which appears from its use by Varro, *De Re Rustica* II 1.14 and 6.1, to be a technical term of cattle-breeders, focuses on the seed or *semen* by which Lucretius is claiming that the characteristics of the given species are transmitted; the assonance *semine seminioque* 746 adds further emphasis to the key idea.

passed on . . . by their sires . . . spurs on their limbs: the five dactyls and the *p* alliteration in 743 fit the swift, pounding flight described.

originate from the beginning of life: when in Lucretius' view the *animus* responsible for the characteristics under discussion itself originates. *generascunt* is apparently coined for *gignuntur*, almost as if to suggest *generatim gignuntur*, 'originate according to species'.

in the frame and the temperament: the pairing stresses the parallelism of mental and physical characteristics, both of which in Lucretius' view have a physical basis and are transmitted by the paternal seed. The rhyming assonance *ingenioque . . . seminioque* 745-6 seems to reinforce the link claimed between temperament and heredity or transmitted seed; on the assonance *semine seminioque*, see note above.

the capacities of the mind: *animus* is used technically, of the seat of the emotions and temperament (cf. *mens* 295 and 299), although the spirit must also have played its part to produce the connected physical symptoms: cf. on 288-9.

with each body: i.e. of each member of each species. O's *quoque* has more point than Q's *toto*; after the assonance *ingenioque . . . semine seminioque* in 745-6 (see notes above), the third rhyme provided by *quoque*, while without Lucretian parallel, is relatively inconspicuous.

748-53 Having presented his own explanation of the fixed temperaments of different species in terms of an *animus* which is *natiuus* and originates with the body, the poet now launches his attack on Pythagorean theory, tracing the absurd physical impossibilities (ἀδύνατα: cf. on 622-3) which he claims would follow from the transmigration of immortal minds or souls between species.

749 **animate creatures:** *animantes* is once more used (cf., e.g. 97, 417, 573, 666, 720) with reference to its root sense, here 'possessing an *animus*', picking up *uis animi* 747.

750-2 **a hound of Hyrcanian pedigree:** such hounds, from the vicinity of the Caspian Sea, were famed for their ferocity and believed to interbreed with tigers and other wild animals (cf. Grattius, *Cynegetica* 161-6 and Aristotle, *Historia Animalium* VIII 607a). The allusion in *semine* reminds the reader of the Lucretian account (cf. 746) in which the paternal seed determines temperamental as well as physical attributes; the choice of example is perhaps calculated to suggest that variations in the temperament of members of a species are limited to those produced by cross-breeding, like that of hounds and tigers which produces especially fierce hounds.

the charge of an antlered stag: the harsh *c* and *g* sounds in *cornigeri incursum cerui* (whereas *canis Hyrcano de semine* 750 has only two *c* sounds) vividly conveys the stag's unwonted ferocity, adding to the absurdity of the hypothetical situation. For compound adjectives like *corniger*, which is however used by Virgil and later poets, see on 11.

a hawk . . . a dove: a second reversal of the norm: for the usual pattern, cf., e.g., Ovid, *Metamorphoses* V 605-6.

753 **man . . . wild tribes of beasts . . . :** the antithesis, with asyndeton, provides a tersely effective climax for the tricolon of examples. *fera*, though pleonastic with *ferarum* (cf. on 108), gives a characteristic assonance and its juxtaposition with *saperent* brings out the paradox of the situation the more starkly. Lucretius frequently uses *saec(u)la* in the sense of *genera* (cf., e.g., IV 413 and 686); contrast the sense 'generations' at 629, 948 and 967.

754-9 A rebuttal of the counter-claim that the soul, while immortal, alters according to the type of body entered; see introductory note to 741-75 above.

755 **an immortal soul alters:** here and in 760-2 and 767 below, *anima* is used inclusively, covering the whole soul, even though the argument still turns primarily on the technical *animus*. As Kenney points out, the emphatic positioning of *immortalem* and *flecti* at each end of the line emphasises the paradoxical nature of the rival claim that an immortal entity can change, which to Lucretius is manifestly impossible,

when it switches bodies: as in 748 above, *mutare* is used of exchanging rather than changing, and *mutatur* 756 takes up *flecti*, not *mutato*, in 755. The terminology is perhaps designed to reflect that the rival view of the soul's exchange of bodies automatically entails its own change.

756 **because what changes . . . perishes:** the principle that change implies mortality, first established in the book at 513-20, is here presented axiomatically; the words exactly match those applied to permeation (a form of division and so in turn of change) at 701.

757 The transposition and rearrangement of parts serve to justify the claim of dissolution in 756. A fuller account was given at 513-8, where change could also involve the addition or subtraction of parts, of which the latter would also exemplify dissolution.

758-9 The admission that the soul changes when it transmigrates means that it is capable of future dissolution and death in its new body. Lucretius could equally have argued (cf. 519-20, 677-8, 705-10 and 766-8 below) that its change at transmigration would amount to the death of the previous soul and the birth of a new one.

they must . . . be dissolved: for *debere* applied to logical necessity, see on 187, and for the scansion of *dissolui* on 330.

throughout the frame: *per artus* is appropriate because the whole soul (see on 755) is now under discussion, not just the *animus* in the breast.

760-8 Transmigration within species is now ruled out as also involving change and so mortality: see introductory note to 741-75 above.

760-4 **it is always the souls of men that enter human bodies:** implying that a parallel principle applies to each animal species, as the equine allusion in 764 confirms.

mature . . . witless . . . discretion . . . well trained: the problem is that in its new body a transmigrating soul loses all the knowledge, wisdom and skills which have usually reached their maturity in its previous incarnation; cf. the argument from its loss of memory at 670-8.

a horse at the height of its powers: for the periphrasis *fortis equi uis*, cf. 8 and note.

765-6 **they will resort to the plea that:** *confugere* here governs an accusative and infinitive by analogy with verbs like *confiteri* to which it here approximates in sense; cf. Cicero, *Verrines* 2 III 191, where *illuc confugies* is followed by the same construction.

in a young body the mind becomes young: *mentem* reflects that, despite the inclusive *anima* in 760-2 and 767, the argument primarily concerns the technical *animus*. For the coined inceptive *tenerascere*, cf. *generascunt* 745; the juxtaposition with *tenero* makes the opponents' plea, however inadequate, appear the more obvious, while the word order of *in tenero tenerascere corpore* matches the pattern they envisage in nature, whereby the rejuvenation of the mind takes place within its new young body.

even if it does, you have to confess: for *si iam*, here used, as at 843, with indicative rather than the more usual subjunctive, cf. 540 and note; for the formula *fateare necessest*, see on 470.

767-8 **changed throughout the frame:** the picture seems to be that the transmigrating soul changes as soon as it has entered its new body. *per artus* is appropriate after the allusion to the whole soul (*animam* 767); cf. 758 and note above.

loses the life . . . it had before: i.e. the change it undergoes in transmigration amounts to its death and the birth of a new soul; cf. 519-20 and 677-8.

769-71 A closely related argument: the mind's parallel development with the body, like its immaturity at birth (761-4), also suggests that it originates simultaneously with the body rather than entering it ready-made: see introductory note to 741-75 above.

the capacities of the mind: the argument in the first instance again concerns the mind, as in the converse passage at 445-58.

reach the coveted flower of their span: this metaphor for attaining the peak or zenith of life is exactly repeated at V 847; cf. also *aeui contingere florem* I 564. Line 770 has elision at the main caesura (*cupitum aetatis*): cf. 83 and 773 below (*manere in*).

with each body: to which, as the Pythagorean opponents claim, it successively migrates.

its co-heir at the moment of origin: i.e. conceived with it; for the metaphor of *consors*, cf. 332 and note; 344-6, later in the same passage, stress the intimate union of soul and body from the moment of conception.

772-5 The concluding *reductio ad absurdum* (see introductory note to 741-75 above) implies that an immortal soul has no reason to abandon one mortal body for another.

772 **why does it wish:** literally 'wish for itself'; as at 1058, *sibi uelle* does not here have its usual idiomatic sense, 'to mean'.

from the aged limbs: *senectus* is an old adjective not found after Lucretius, apart from the use of the feminine (sc. *aetas*) as a noun for old age.

go outside: the first step in its supposed transmigration.

773-5 **Is it afraid to stay . . . in case . . . :** as *an* reflects, an ironic suggestion, which the final sentence (775) goes on to explode. *metuit* governs both the infinitive *manere* (a poetic construction, fostered by analogy with rough synonyms like *non uult*) and the *ne* clause.

crumbling body . . . its house: the image of the body as the soul's decaying dwelling has already been developed in detail at 584-8. The house-image (cf. the recurrent vessel-image: see on 434) is foreshadowed in Epicurus' term for the body as the soul's 'covering' (τὸ στεγάζον: see on 323), and is traditional in antiquity; Kenney cites Euripides, *Supplices* 534-5, Bion (the diatribe-satirist of Borysthenes) 15-16 (Hense), Cicero, *De Senectute* 84 and Seneca, *Moral Epistles* 120.14.

wearied by the protracted span of its years: the words closely echo II 1174, *spatio aetatis defessa uetusto.*

collapses on it in ruins: *obruat* is to be taken in its usual transitive sense, with *se* supplied as its object. The prospect of the soul being buried under the ruins may well suggest that the Pythagorean opponents are pressing their idea of the body as the soul's tomb (σῶμα σῆμα) illogically far.

But an immortal entity . . . : the predominance of spondees in the sentence, contrasting with the opening dactylic foot in the line, adds impact to this sobering reflection.

776-83 Proof 21: the idea of immortal souls fighting or queueing for mortal bodies is absurd

A further *reductio ad absurdum*, this time not just of transmigration but of all theories of the soul's pre-existence, now serves to conclude the whole series of arguments from 670. The presumed arrangements for the allocation of bodies to the pre-existing souls are here the main target of scorn, but the implication of 778, that immortal souls have no need of mortal bodies, provides a close link with the preceding *reductio* of 772-5; cf. also 730-4.

776-7 **it is manifestly:** *uidetur* again has its 'Lucretian' sense: see on 35.

unions inspired by Venus . . . births of the beasts: *conubia Veneris* (the *u*, despite the long *u* of *nubere*, is here to be scanned, with Munro, as short, rather than long with the *i* consonantal) = *concubitus*; the allusion to Venus is not to be taken literally, her name being used in the 'faded' sense to denote her traditional province, love or sexual attraction, a practice justified at II 655-60. The reference to conception as well as birth may suggest doubt as to when precisely the pre-existing soul makes its supposed entry (the phrase *nascentibus insinuari* 671 and I 113 suggests that the opposing schools favour the moment of birth, whereas the Epicurean view is that every soul originates at conception: cf. 344-6); alternatively, if entry is supposed to take place at birth, the allusion adds a further satirical dimension, and the souls are pictured as lying in wait or queueing for a body right from the moment of its potential conception. While the argument applies equally to human souls, wild beasts are no doubt specifically mentioned to make the competition for bodies the more ferocious and undignified.

778 **for all their immortality . . . mortal:** the juxtaposition *immortalis mortalia* underlines the paradoxical absurdity of the rival hypothesis. For the link with 730-4 and 772-5, see introductory note to 776-83 above.

779 **countless numbers:** for *innumero numero*, a second combination of paradox and assonance, cf. II 1054, and also *numero . . . innumerali* II 1086 and *innumerabilem. . . numerum* VI 485; for instances of similar oxymoron, cf. 472 and 869 and notes.

and should compete in precipitate haste: for *-que* appended to short *e*, cf. 163 and note. *praeproperanter*, found only here for *praepropere*, is a favourite type of Lucretian coining (cf. *praecipitanter* 1063, *moderanter* II 1096, and *praemetuenter* IV 824), which here contributes to a second successive four-word line.

780 **should receive preference and be first:** the collocation of *primus* with *potissimus* is frequent in Livy (e.g. V 12.12); see Munro's note.

to worm its way in: the potentially derogatory overtones of *insinuare* (see on 485 and 671) here heighten the absurdity of the picture of souls competing for a body.

781 **unless the souls happen . . . :** *si non forte* introduces the alternative, no less ironical suggestion of 'first come, first served'.

782 **gets in first:** though the context differs from that of 780, *insinuetur* remains, in part, contemptuous.

783 **no hint:** *hilum* (see on 220) is here adverbial accusative, as also at 813, 830 and 867.

trial of strength between them: perhaps a comparison with spectators crowding into a show. *inter se contendant* takes up *certare . . . inter se* 779-80.

784-829 ***(c) The soul is not eternal***

The central section of the book now concludes with some general arguments, based largely on Epicurean first principles, and applicable in equal measure to ideas of the soul's survival and of its pre-existence; see introductory note to 417-829.

784-99 Proof 22: the soul and each of its parts can exist only in their fixed place in the body, and must therefore be born and die with it

The argument which was applied to the mind at 615-23 (see introductory note there) is here given a wider application and extended to include the spirit; it depends on the fundamental principle of the uniformity of nature. 784-97 reappear, with adaptation of the first and last lines, at V 128-41, as part of an argument that our world and its parts are not animate or divine; the lines seem clearly to have been first written for their present context.

784-6 Similar impossibilities (ἀδύνατα) were traced in the parallel argument at 622-3 (see note there). The first three examples are strategically arranged, with tree, clouds and fish each exchanging their own environment for one another's; the heavens, ocean and fields represent the traditional triple division of the world into sky, sea and earth, which is often utilised by Lucretius (e.g. I 2-3) and roughly corresponds with the Epicurean view of earth, air, fire and water as the world's main elements, with the heavens comprising both air and fire. The denial of fish in fields may involve a conscious rejection of reports like that included in a list of alleged prodigies by Livy, XLII 2.5, while the allusion to blood in wood and sap in stones may proclaim similar scepticism in the case of statues reported to bleed and sweat. The assonance *aethere / aequore* and the alliteration with *a* and *s* helps to heighten the absurdity of the impossibilities described.

787 **each thing may reside and grow:** *quicquid* = *quidque*, and strictly denotes each type of thing, as in the statement of the same principle in the parallel argument at 618-9; see notes there. *crescat et insit* (contrast *esse et crescere* 795) exemplifies *hysteron proteron*; cf. 160 and note, and *durare genique* 797.

788-9 **the substance of the mind:** though the generalisation of 787 is applied to each of the soul's parts in 794-6, 790-3 concern the mind alone, and *animi* here is accordingly to be taken as technical, as it clearly is when the line is repeated in its different context at V 132, shortly after an allusion to *animi natura . . . consiliumque* at 127.

cannot . . . exist too far from: the idiomatic comparative *longius* forms part of a playful understatement of the mind's proximity to the body-tissues.

790-3 An *a fortiori* corroboration of 788-9: the mind is confined to the breast, and is never found in other parts of the body; how much less could it exist outside it?

790 **Indeed, if it could:** *enim* is to be taken in its archaic asseverative sense, as, e.g., in Virgil, *Aeneid* VI 28 (*sed enim*), VI 317 and VIII 84; 'But if it could indeed' approximates to 'But even if it could'. The combination of *quod* with inferential *enim* would produce a double connective paralleled only once, in Varro (*De Re Rustica* II 4.8).

the mind and its functions: the force of *ipsa*, attached to the periphrasis *animi uis*, seems to be to pin down *animi* quite unambiguously to its technical sense, and to exclude the *anima* which was present in all the parts of the body listed in 791.

793 The four elisions, including two of *-em* before a short vowel and resulting in the absence of a normal, strong, main caesura, are remarkable, and help to convey the poet's indignation at the idea of a disembodied mind; the difficulty of accommodating the words in the line matches his opponents' reluctance to accommodate the mind in the body.

but at least to remain . . . : the line adds a qualification of *innasci quauis in parte* 792, to which *manere* stands in asyndeton after *soleret*. *tandem* ('after all') approximates in this usage to *saltem*.

the same vessel: the image (see on 434) provides an incidental reminder of an important category of earlier proofs.

794-7 The argument of 789-93 is now applied, quite logically, to spirit as well as mind; spirit, like mind, has its fixed place in the body, the whole of which it pervades, and its location within the body, like the mind's, never varies: it is always distributed throughout the body, never localised in a specific part or parts.

But since: *quod*, adverbial accusative of the connective relative, is used adversatively, as often in *quod si*. Lucretius combines it with *quoniam* only in this passage.

there is a fixed arrangement . . . grow: the language of 787 is here echoed and expanded. The recurrent *q* and *c* sounds in 794 might be seen as appropriate to the constancy of the recurrent pattern concerned.

can each exist: *sorsum*, literally 'separately', serves as a reminder that mind and spirit each have a distinctive location in the body, without denying that they make up a single entity (136-7).

must it be denied that they can . . . : with *infitiandum*, *est* is to be supplied, and with *posse*, *ea* (= *animum atque animam*) as subject-accusative. The heavy rhythm of 797 lends weight to the Lucretian conclusion.

be born or . . . endure: for the word-order *durare genique*, see on 787 above. *geni* is the original, unreduplicated form of *gigni*, whose perfect *genui* and past participle *genitus* it supplies; in Lucretius, this form occurs in the manuscripts only here, but is a certain restoration at IV 143 and 159 (cf. on 433).

798-9 The idea that the soul can only be born within the body (*genique* 797) has ruled out its pre-existence; these lines draw the conclusion that it must perish with the body, developing the idea that it can only endure within it (*durare* 797).

has passed away . . . has perished: the juxtaposition of the synonymous compounds of *ire* underlines the inevitability of the link claimed between the two processes.

the soul . . . disrupted throughout the whole body: *anima* is used inclusively, to cover the two parts mentioned in 796; *in corpore toto*, though inapplicable to the mind, is perfectly appropriate to the sum of the two parts. The allusion to the soul's disruption at death is another reminder (cf. the vessel-image of 793) of crucial preceding arguments, in this case involving the soul's division (cf., e.g., 492, 501, 507 and 590).

800-5 Proof 23: a mortal body and an immortal soul are incompatible

This argument serves to corroborate that of the preceding passage, with which it is closely linked; it turns on a broader aspect of the uniformity of nature, which would preclude a combination of such incompatible opposites as mortal and immortal.

800-2 **Indeed:** the inferential sense of *quippe etenim* (literally 'For indeed'), a connective formula used some twenty times by the poet, reflects the corroborative nature of the argument and its connection with 784-99.

to couple . . . is totally irrational: the imposing edifice of 800-1 is abruptly collapsed like a house of cards by *desiperest* in 802; cf. V 1041-3, and, for the same effect on a much larger scale, V 156-65. *desipere*, like *iungere* and *putare* in the preceding lines, is used substantivally; *iungere*, as at I 713, probably involves a metaphor from the basic sense of yoking animals.

share their feelings . . . and mutually interact: *una consentire* (= Epicurus' συμπάσχειν) and *fungi* (in the sense 'to be acted upon') were also combined at 168-9 (see notes there), in the course of an account of the interaction of body and soul designed to prove the latter's physical nature. *mutua* is an adverbial or internal accusative with *fungi*.

802-5 **more incompatible . . . incongruous . . . inconsistent . . . :** two ideas are conflated in this sentence, which begins as if asking what is more distinct (*diuersius*) than mortal from immortal, but ends by asking what is more inconsistent (*discrepitans*) than their combination. The triple *dis-* prefix thus simultaneously emphasises the gulf between mortal and immortal and between the idea of their combination and common sense. After the singular subject *quid*, the use of *inter se* with *disiunctum* (literally 'disunited from one another') also defies strict logic. The iterative form *discrepitare* (cf. II 1018) is a Lucretian coining not found elsewhere in Latin.

be coupled in union: *iunctum* not only takes up *iungere* 800 (see note there), but is opposed to *disiunctum* 803; the contrast heightens the absurdity of attempting to combine the uncombinable. *concilium* is a Lucretian technical term applied either, as here, to an atomic compound (Epicurus' ἄθροισμα) or, as, e.g., at I 183, to its formation (Epicurus' σύγκρισις); these usages are metaphorical, in so far as the word normally denotes an assembly of people, just as *discidium*, the poet's term for atomic dissolution (see on 342), suggests a metaphor from divorce. *concilium* reflects the Lucretian view that the soul is material and with the body constitutes a single atomic compound, which automatically precludes its immortality.

the fury of the storms: on the one hand a general allusion to life's hazards, 'the thousand natural shocks Which flesh is heir to', on the other a technical reference to the constant battering of external atoms to which all atomic compounds (except the gods; cf. 819-23 and notes) were subject and which eventually proved fatal to them.

806-29 Proof 24: the soul satisfies none of the conditions of immortality

806-18, which appear also, with minor changes, at V 351-63, set out three conditions (absence of internal void, freedom from blows, and absence of external space), each of which would guarantee eternity, and each of which was satisfied in Epicurean theory by only a single category (atoms, void and the universe respectively). Whereas in V the conclusion, that our world satisfies none of these conditions and is therefore both *mortalis* and *natiuus*, is added at length (364-79), the implications for the soul in III are left unstated, a clear indication that the lines were first written for book V and added here without the composition of a passage applying them to the soul. 819-23 add a fourth set of conditions, which, after a lacuna, the soul is shown (824-9) not to meet; the probability is that the addition of the lines from V reminded the poet of the conspicuous omission in them of the fourth immortal category in Epicurean theory, the gods, and that, as suggested by Giussani, the fourth set of conditions is added here to account for their eternity (see also the notes on the relevant lines below).

807-10 **solid:** i.e. containing no void, the secret of the impenetrability and indivisibility referred to next: cf. I 510, *solida ac sine inani*, pairing these complementary ideas.

allow anything . . . to penetrate them: cf. the description of the atoms at I 528-9, *haec neque dissolui plagis extrinsecus icta / possunt nec porro penitus penetrata retexi*, where similarly expressive *p* alliteration is exploited.

disunite their close-set parts: the Epicurean atoms had theoretical parts which were not physically isolable because of the absence of void between them; cf. I 599-634. *dissociare*, used by Lucretius only in this passage, suggests the disruption of an alliance; the close cohesion of the atom's theoretical parts (cf. *artas partis* here) is expressed by the military metaphor of serried ranks (*agmine condenso*) at I 606.

the bodies of matter: i.e. the atoms, for which *corpora materiai* is one of the poet's technical terms.

I have disclosed earlier: i.e. at I 503-634, where the atomic nature of matter was established.

812-3 **like void which remains intangible:** cf. I 437-9, where intangibility is the criterion of void; *intactum* is synonymous with *intactile* there.

is not acted upon by impact in the tiniest degree: cf. I 440-3, where being acted upon is a criterion of matter, the reverse of void. For the passive sense of *fungi*, see on 168, for the redundant *ab* with the instrumental ablative on 323, and for the adverbial accusative *hilum* on 783.

814 **there was no . . . supply of space:** the subjunctive *sit* (contrast indicative *sunt* in the preceding *quia* clauses at 807 and 812) marks a condition far less likely to be met in a review of candidates for immortality; whereas there were infinite atoms and an infinity of void to satisfy the first two conditions, the universe, which alone met the third, was unique. Lachmann's emendation, both here and in V, to *fit* is accordingly unnecessary.

815 **could, so to speak, disperse and be dissolved:** *quasi* either apologises for the personification implicit in *discedere* or further indicates the remoteness of the whole possibility. For the scansion of *dissoluique*, see on 330.

816-8 **the all-embracing universe:** literally 'the sum of sums'; contrast *haec rerum summa* (e.g. I 235) denoting our own finite world, one of the infinite number of roughly similar worlds which the universe contained. *summa summarum* is used by the poet only in this passage; his other terms for the universe include *summa* (I 963), *rerum summa* (I 333), *tota summa* (I 984), *omnis summa* (I 620-1) and *omne quod est* (I 958); cf. Epicurus' τὸ πᾶν. The absence of space, and of matter, beyond the universe was a consequence of its definition as the sum total of matter and space, and also of its infinity, which was established at I 958-1051.

any space: *quis* (and at V 362 the corresponding adjective *qui*) replaces the more usual *ullus*.

into which things could scatter: *quo diffugiant* (and at V 362 the variant *quo dissiliant*) takes up the idea of 815, from which *res* is to be supplied as subject.

nor are there bodies . . . impact: the absence of external matter, though not specified in the original statement of the third condition in 814-5, is nevertheless automatically entailed by the absence of external space, which would be required in order to accommodate any external matter. For the destructive effect of the external atoms which constantly bombarded the surface of atomic compounds, cf. 805 and note above.

819-23 The absence, after 818, of lines showing that the soul satisfies none of the three conditions so far specified is much more probably attributed to the poem's lack of completion than to textual loss: the fourth condition, introduced here, was most probably satisfied by the Epicurean gods: see introductory note to 806-29 above.

820 **is shielded and protected by life-giving forces:** the eternity of the Epicurean gods was probably explained along these lines, even though no full account has been preserved and its ultimate physical basis remains a mystery; the scanty evidence (e.g. Cicero, *De Natura Deorum* I 49) suggests that the gods resembled a never-failing fountain, in that the atoms constantly discharged from their surface were constantly replaced by a supply of appropriate atoms streaming towards them, enabling them eternally to preserve the same form. In their case there was thus a constant balance between the forces of creation and destruction in nature referred to respectively at II 569-72 as *motus genitales auctificique* and *motus exitiales*, whereas in the case of other atomic compounds life-giving forces (*uitalia rerum*) sometimes (temporarily) prevailed, sometimes were overcome (II 575-6). For the redundant *ab* with the instrumental ablative, cf. 813 and note above; the rendering 'protected from lethal forces', which gives *munire ab* the sense usual in other authors, involves either emendation to the non-Lucretian *letalibus* or the assumption that *uitalibus* is an utterly uncharacteristic euphemism.

821-3 **either because . . . or because . . . :** though the first *aut* is ambiguous and could be translated 'or', the clauses are more probably mutually exclusive subdivisions of 820 (of which the first is likelier to apply to the gods) than independent alternatives to it. Certainly 824-9 seek to show that the soul meets neither of the conditions of 821-3; were these independent of 820, a separate demonstration that the soul fails to meet the condition of 820 would have to be presumed lost before 824.

influences alien to its well-being: like the *saeuas procellas* of 805 (see note there). For *alienus* with genitive rather than the usual ablative, cf. VI 69 and 1065; though found occasionally in Cicero, the idiom is no doubt influenced by Lucretius' partiality to the archaic genitive of separation, e.g. *auersa uiai* I 1041, *secreta teporis* II 843 and *orba pedum . . . manuum uiduata* V 840.

before we can sense what harm they do: sc. to our souls; the condition presented in 822-3 is related directly to the soul, unlike those of 807-18, which were each related to the one category which satisfied them.

<plain fact . . . the case>: a rendering of the line suggested (in his translation) by Munro to fill the gap in the text after 823.

824-9 This climactically arranged list of the soul's sufferings in life, designed to show that it enjoys no immunity from the destructive influences (*aliena salutis*) of 821 (and thus none of the special protection by life-giving forces envisaged in 820), provides an effective conclusion to this section of the book, to parts of which it looks back, and an appropriate transition to the next; see notes below.

824 **apart from the fact:** the separation of *praeterquam* into its two components occurs occasionally in prose (cf. *antequam* and *priusquam*), and is not a full-blown example of Lucretian tmesis (contrast 262, and see note there).

it falls ill during the body's diseases: a reminder, in a more general context, of the argument of 463-73. Though this concerned the mind, *anima*, in its inclusive sense, is again, as in 819, to be supplied as subject, as *eam* 825 confirms.

825-7 The soul's various emotional sufferings (the province of the mind) recall the argument of 459-62, and afford a telling contrast with the mental calm (ἀταραξία) of the immortal gods; they also look forward to the conclusion of the book, where the poet seeks to eliminate fear of death as a prime source of such mental distress.

thoughts about the future . . . sorry state of fear: fear of the future, including fear of death which in the context of book III is the obvious example, is characteristically used to prove the soul's mortality, which in turn makes fear of death groundless; cf. the paradox that cure proves its mortality (510-25) and the ironic evocation of the death of Socrates (see on 526-30). The tricolon of expressions in 826 paints a graphic picture of the anguish to which the soul is reduced by such fear.

after past misdeeds . . . remorse: *praeteritis* is opposed to *futuris* 825; *male admissis*, which serves as the noun in the ablative absolute construction, approximates in sense to *peccata*. In Epicurean moral theory, remorse for misdeeds and guilty conscience arose from fear of future retribution (cf. 1014-22 and notes), and were to be avoided by conformity with justice (see Introduction III).

828-9 **madness peculiar to the mind:** i.e. distinct from the impairment it can suffer during bodily disease, referred to in 824.

forgetfulness of things . . . oblivious waters of coma: *obliuia rerum* denotes amnesia in life (like *furorem animi proprium*, a new example of the soul's sufferings which has not featured in previous arguments) but also suggests the myth of the departed soul drinking the waters of Lethe, the river of forgetfulness, in the underworld; this in turn is the basis of the image of its being plunged into the black waters of coma, as the implicit echo of 'Lethe' in *lethargi* confirms. For terminal coma as an example of the soul's sufferings, cf. 465-9 and notes; here it serves to complete the climactic sequence of 824-9, and the whole sequence of proofs of the soul's mortality, by implying its actual death, and an oblivion parallel to the amnesia which can affect it in life.

830-1094 DEATH IS NOT TO BE FEARED

After the two technical sections preceding, the conclusion of the book provides both the poetic and the philosophical reward, rising to a generally higher poetic plane as it draws the consequences from the previous arguments. Its scope and purpose are twofold; it not only establishes the logical conclusion that since death is the end of consciousness there is no reason to fear it (830-69, which 870-930 go on to reinforce), but also seeks to reconcile the reader to the prospect of oblivion, aiming to overcome man's instinctive reluctance to die and his instinctive desire to prolong life (the central purpose of 931-1094); it thus has two distinct targets, fear of survival after death and fear of death as the end. The passage, especially the latter part of it where the poet comforts mankind in the face of man's own mortality, has much in common with the *consolatio*, the philosopher's words of comfort in some crisis, usually bereavement, but also in other circumstances such as exile, a literary form practised both in Greece and Rome; it also exploits some of the themes and techniques of the Hellenistic diatribe, or popular philosophical street-sermon: see Wallach (1976) 11-109, and cf. Kenney (1971) 17-20 (where the general influence of the diatribe on the poem is perhaps overstated).

830-69 *Death does not concern us, since in it we shall no more possess consciousness, or exist, than we did before our birth*

The passage elaborates the second of Epicurus' *Principal Sayings*: 'Death is nothing to us: for what is dissolved lacks consciousness, and what lacks consciousness is nothing to us (ὁ θάνατος οὐδὲν πρὸς ἡμᾶς· τὸ γὰρ διαλυθὲν ἀναισθητεῖ· τὸ δ' ἀναισθητοῦν οὐδὲν πρὸς ἡμᾶς).' Lucretius' comparison of our lack of prenatal consciousness, a characteristically

Epicurean appeal to analogy, is especially effective in the ancient context, where the soul's immortality implied its pre-existence, and fits in with, and reinforces, the arguments of 670-783. 843-61 constitute a parenthesis, corroborating the central contention of the passage by making two concessions and showing that neither would affect it: see notes below.

830 **Death therefore is nothing to us . . . :** *igitur* marks the passage, and the whole conclusion of the book, as the logical inference from the proofs of the soul's mortality. The line is a Lucretian version of the opening of the second of Epicurus' *Principal Sayings* (see introductory note above), and is echoed at various later points; cf. 845, 850, 852, 926 and 972. *hilum* (cf. also 867) is again adverbial accusative (see on 783), like the matching *quicquam* in 850.

831 **the soul's . . . nature is established:** *habetur* in the context is stronger than 'is considered' (cf. 532 and 819), having the sense 'is <firmly> held to be'. *animi*, like *animai* 838, is inclusive, denoting the whole soul; contrast 844 below.

832-3 **in time past:** i.e. before our birth, as is at once made clear by the allusion to the Punic Wars of the third century, to which the Romans looked back as amongst their greatest hazards.

when the Carthaginians . . . quarters: the spondees in the first two feet of the line fit the menacing purpose of the enemy armies, the dactyls in the third, fourth and fifth the rapidity of their advance.

834-5 **beneath the lofty shores of heaven:** a poetic periphrasis for 'on earth'; the collocation *aetheris orae* recurs at II 1000, IV 215, and V 143 and 683, confirming Gifanius' correction of the manuscripts' text.

shaken by . . . shuddered and trembled: an apparent echo of Ennius, *Annales* 309 (Skutsch), *Africa terribili tremit horrida terra tumultu*, though there is no reason to suppose, with Kenney, that Lucretius is parodying his model; any suggestion that Ennius exaggerated the importance of the event would weaken the Lucretian point that, despite its scale, his contemporaries were oblivious to it.

836-7 **under which nation's dominion . . . all mankind must fall:** cf. Livy XXIX 17.6, where a Locrian envoy addresses the Roman senate in similar terms: *in discrimine est nunc humanum omne genus, utrum uos an Carthaginienses principes orbis terrarum uideat* (The whole human race is now on edge, as to whether it is to see you or the Carthaginians as masters of the world). For *humani* = *homines*, cf. 80.

838-9 **when we do not exist:** Lucretius makes explicit a point implicit in the second of Epicurus' *Principal Sayings*, that loss of consciousness means the end of our very existence.

the divorce of body and soul: *discidium* is primarily a metaphor for the sundering of the two partners, and forms an antithesis with *coniugium* 845. Their divorce results in the atomic dissolution of each, for which *discidium* is also the appropriate technical term; see on 342.

whose union gives us our single identity: more literally 'from which we are fitted into one'; for the anastrophe *quibus e*, cf. 140-1 and note. *uniter* (= *in unum*) is a characteristically coined Lucretian adverb, combined with *aptus* also at 846 below and at V 537, 555 and 558. The poet has already (e.g. 323-69) sought to establish that neither soul nor body can be conscious or exist without the other.

840-1 **at that time we shall not exist:** the *qui* clause emphasises the new step in the argument, introduced in 838; once body and soul are separated, we shall not be there to have any conscious experience.

842 **earth is mingled . . . sea with the sky:** this proverbial expression presents an even more disastrous upheaval than the Punic Wars of 833-7, which were confined to land and sea (*omnia . . . sub altis aetheris oris . . . terraque marique*), but the contingency alluded to, as the open future conditional reflects, was in Epicurean eyes inevitable; cf. V 91-109, predicting that earth, sea and sky, the three traditional divisions of our mortal world, will eventually be destroyed and collapse in the space of a single day. The alliteration with *m* and *c* adds to the impact of the line.

843-6 The first of the two parenthetical concessions which the central contention can withstand (see introductory note to 830-69 above).

even if the mind and spirit do feel: for *si iam*, here as at 766 with indicative, see on 540; *animi natura animaeque potestas* has the same reference as *animai* and *animae* in 838 and 846, where the term is used inclusively.

after they have been sundered from our body: the hyperbaton, with *nostro* placed not only, like *de corpore*, outside the *postquam* clause but also before *sentit*, the verb of the preceding *si* clause, throws great emphasis onto the possessive, and suggests that the poet is conceding, simply for the sake of argument, the possibility of our soul transmigrating to *other* bodies. 713-40 suggested the related, but quite different idea that after death *parts* of our soul (and also of our body) actually do participate in consciousness (that of the maggots exuded by the corpse); cf. also 967, where our matter is required to make up future, conscious, human generations. In these two cases Lucretius would have insisted, just as he does in the purely hypothetical present case in 845-6, that the future consciousness involved was not ours.

it is still nothing to us: a reassertion of the central point, deliberately echoing 830.

single identity . . . union and marriage . . . : a reminder of the argument of 838-40, where our conscious existence is that of the soul-body compound, which gives us our identity; *uniter apti* is repeated from 839 and *comptu coniugioque* is opposed to *discidium* 839; see notes above. The repetition of the *con-* prefix in *comptu*, *coniugio* and *consistimus* emphasises the links between the twin partners in the *concilium* or compound.

847-61 The second concession, that our matter might be exactly reassembled after our death, goes further than the first but differs from it in introducing a real rather than a purely imaginary possibility, as 852-8 make clear. Though the doctrine of rebirth (παλιγγενεσία), associated with the cyclical recurrence of events after a periodic world-conflagration, was Stoic and attributed to Chrysippus, the Epicurean doctrines of the infinity of time and the eternity of atoms and space made the reconstitution envisaged here possible as a result of mere chance, as 854-8 suggest. Lucretius' claim (850-1 and 859-61) that the break in consciousness would mean that the consciousness of our replicas was not ours raises knotty philosophical problems of identity.

847-50 **even if time were to collect . . . :** *tamen* 850 shows that *si* is concessive (= *etsi*); though the possibility is shown later to be real, the conditional is of the remote future type, with perfect subjunctives (*collegerit*, *redegerit*, and *fuerint data*) in the protasis. *fuerint data* = *data sint*: this type of perfect (and pluperfect), one stage further back than usual, is an extension from cases where the participle becomes adjectival and timeless or where completion or 'pastness' is stressed; Lucretius, doubtless influenced by metrical convenience, has a number of examples, including *posta . . . fuisse* 857-8 and *fuerit . . . natus* 868.

our matter: i.e. all the atoms comprising our soul-body compound. For the fifth declension form, see on 59.

would even that eventuality at all concern us: like 845, reasserting the main point and echoing 830 in its turn. *id factum*, literally 'this having been done (= the doing of this)' is a construction of the *ab urbe condita* type.

851 **our self-remembrance had once been interrupted:** i.e. the break in consciousness would give our recycled 'selves' a different identity from our own; see on 847-61 above. *repetentia*, with which *nostri* is objective genitive, is another Lucretian coining.

852-3 This appeal to our present non-recollection of, and indifference to, former 'selves' or replicas corroborates the previous point, that future 'selves' would have no recollection of us but would have their own distinct identity. The allusion to our former selves, *nobis . . . ante qui fuimus*, with the indicative, shows that the replication introduced as a remote hypothesis in 847-9 is now accepted as fact.

854-8 The reconstitution just taken for granted is now shown to be feasible on Epicurean principles; see on 847-61 above.

you look back at . . . you could . . . come to believe that: *respicias* and *possis* are subjunctives of indefinite second person; *adcredere*, an extremely rare compound, is used by Lucretius only here. *hoc* anticipates the accusative and infinitive of 857-8; the *c* was pronounced as double (original *hocce*), lengthening the naturally short *o* of the nominative and accusative singular before a following vowel, as also at 912, 932, 974, 1000, 1008 and 1024 (cf. also 914 note).

all the past expanse of measureless time: the repeated *m* sounds add to the awesomeness of the phrase. The infinity of time in Epicurean theory was the natural corollary of the eternity of the universe and its two ultimate constituents, atoms and void.

manifold variety of the motions of matter: the indirect question, in which *quam* is postponed to fourth position, exhibits further impressive *m* alliteration. The adverb *multimodis* is used in place of an adjective; the adjectival *multimodi*, the reading of almost all of the manuscripts, is not certainly attested elsewhere. The Epicurean atoms remained in constant motion (*aeterno percita motu* 33); their eternity, and that of the void in which they moved, is equally vital to the argument, but was alluded to at 806-13 above and is here taken for granted.

seeds of which we are now composed: i.e. our component atoms; for *quibus e*, cf. 839 and note.

have often been placed: the suggestion of repeated reconstitution on the one hand brings home the awesome implications of the infinity of time, and on the other perhaps hints at the grain of truth in the Stoic theory of a recurrent cycle of world-history. *posta . . . fuisse* = *posita esse*; cf. *fuerint data* 849 and note.

859-61 Our non-recollection of our previous 'selves' is now explained in the same way as our obliviousness to future 'selves' in 851. The key step in the argument is thus reiterated, and, as in 852-3, the past provides a model of the future, so corroborating the claim of 847-51.

retain: *reprehendere*, as at 599 'to hold on to', takes up the idea of *repetentia* 851.

a severance of life has, you see, been interposed: an expansion of the idea of the interruption of recollection (*interrupta repetentia*) in 851. The tmesis *inter enim iectast* (= *interiectast enim*) is expressive, mirroring the interruption described; cf. *inter enim cursant* 262 and note.

all the motions have strayed . . . away from the senses: i.e. the atoms which previously performed the motions which produced sensation and consciousness, including presumably memory, have been separated and have fallen into other patterns of motion; the converse situation is expressed rather more precisely at 923-4, where in sleep the atoms (*primordia*) do *not* wander far from the motions that carry sensation (*sensiferi motus*). *deerrarunt* is scanned as three syllables, the *e* of the prefix coalescing with that of the stem by synizesis. The spondaic rhythm of 861 helps to suggest the suspension of consciousness.

862-9 After the parenthesis of 843-61, the main argument resumes at the point where it was interrupted, our non-existence after death, which rules out the possibility of our experiencing any subsequent suffering. This theme, however, also relates closely to the parenthesis, which has argued that, whatever the fate of our soul or of all our atoms, *we* (i.e. our present soul-body compound) will cease to exist at death.

862-3 **Why:** *enim* looks back over the parenthesis and introduces a justification of the claim of 840-2; the abrupt transition would probably have been made smoother in revision.

must himself exist: *debet* again denotes logical necessity: see on 187.

864 **and rules out the existence:** *prōbet* (cf. I 977) is a metrically convenient form of *prŏhĭbet*, perhaps used by conscious analogy with *debere* and *praebere*, which are also compounds of *habere*. For *-que* appended to short *e*, cf. 163 and note.

865 **misfortunes can be conferred:** a paradoxical expression, since *conciliare* is normally applied to the acquisition of desirable things, which perhaps ridicules the poet's opponents for their eagerness to confer the dubious blessing of an after-life on mankind.

866 **it is plain to see that:** for *scire licet* with accusative and infinitive, cf. 229 and note.

868 **whether or not he has ever been born:** *utrum aliquo* is to be supplied before *an*: for the ellipse, Heinze compares Livy XLIV 25.11 (*aiebat . . . pecuniam . . . Samothracae in templo depositurum . . . uidere Eumenes nihil interesse an Pellae pecunia esset*, where *utrum ibi* is to be supplied before *an*: 'he said he would deposit the money in the temple on Samothrace: Eumenes saw that it made no difference whether the money was there or at Pella') and XXXVI 17.11. For *fuerit . . . natus* = *natus sit*, cf. 849 and note.

869 **once his mortal life . . . immortal death:** the antithesis, the paradox of *mors immortalis*, the personification (prepared for in *mors eximit esseque probet* 864), and the sonority and solemnity of the line provide a memorable conclusion to the passage. For the immortality of death, cf. *mors aeterna* 1091; the idea appears earlier in the fourth century comic poet Amphis, cited by Athenaeus VIII 336c: ὁ θάνατος δ' ἀθάνατός ἐστιν, ἂν ἅπαξ τις ἀποθάνῃ (death is deathless, once one dies).

870-930 ***Apprehensions based on an unconscious assumption of survival***

This passage reinforces the last, and is designed to prove the Lucretian case to the hilt, by taking three common types of anxiety about death and attributing each of them to an intellectual mistake and a failure to accept the full implications of the argument so far.

870-93 (a) Concerns for the fate of the body after death

The man who, while professedly sceptical of an after-life, worries instinctively about his corpse's fate is accused of mistakenly projecting himself into the future and imagining himself there to witness its misadventures. The poet makes great play with the inconsistencies of his adversary's position, vividly depicting his confusion of his present self not only with his insensate corpse but also with a disembodied self standing by to witness its fate. The scornful paragraph is rounded off (888-93) with a side-swipe at the desirability of a proper funeral and of conventional forms of corpse-disposal, a further illustration of the irrelevance, to the deceased, of the fate of his body.

870-2 **you see:** the subjunctive *uideas* is of indefinite second person, as in 854 and 856.
complaining of his own future, how . . . : *se . . . ipsum . . . fore ut* approximates to *fore ut ipse*; the expression is of the biblical 'I know thee, who thou art' type, and focuses on what turns out to be the adversary's crucial logical mistake in confusing his true self (*se ipsum*) with the corpse. For *indignarier*, the archaic form of the deponent infinitive, cf. 67 and note.
once buried: *posto* does duty for the compound *composito*.
be destroyed: *interfiat* serves as a rare passive of *interficere*; the verb highlights the man's illogicality in complaining that after death he will again 'be killed'.
or the jaws of wild beasts: as a result of exposure after, e.g., death in battle. Following burial and cremation, this fate provides the climax of the imaginary horrors, and is taken up at 880 and 888-9; there is no reason to suppose any allusion to the strange practice of the Persian Magi, of exposing corpses to mangling by wild beasts prior to burial, recorded by Cicero, *Tusculan Disputations* I 108. The repeated *p*, *f* and *m* sounds in 871-2, like the more pronounced *m* alliteration in 888 below, help to convey both the violence of the imagined fates and, like the repeated *s* and *c* sounds of 873-4, the poet's scorn.

873 **it is plain to see that:** for *scire licet*, cf. 866 above and see on 229.
does not ring true: the metaphor, for which cf. Ennius, *Scenica* 108 (Jocelyn), is of a flawed pot. *sincerum* is an internal accusative; for the form *sonere*, cf. 156 and note.

874 **subconscious:** *caecum* makes the same point as *inscius* 878.
his heart: the seat of his emotions (cf. 140-2), in particular of his fear for his corpse's fate.

875 **any consciousness:** for *quemquam* replacing *ullum*, cf. 234 and note.

876 **as I see it:** for *ut opinor*, cf. 626 and note.
what he professes: that he will have no consciousness in death (cf. 874-5).
the basis for it: the soul's mortality; *unde* = *e quo* (sc. *promittit*).

877 **expel:** *eicit* scans as a disyllable; cf. 383 and note.

878 **some part of his own self survives:** *esse . . . super* = *superesse*, with tmesis (cf. 262 note) and inversion (cf. *facit are*, for *arefacit*, at VI 962); the present tense is prophetic (he imagines this actually happening after death). *ipse* emphasises the reflexive idea conveyed by *sui* (partitive genitive with *quiddam*), but the Lucretian case is that no part of the man's *true* self consciously survives; cf. 870 and note.

879-87 The point of 876-8 is now confirmed by a more detailed analysis of the false assumptions behind one of the fears under discussion.

879-80 **that birds and beasts will mangle his body:** taking up the climactic example of the fears listed in 871-2, with birds of prey now added.

881 **he feels sorry for himself:** *sui* is opposed to *corpus*, which was emphatically placed outside its *uti* clause in 880 (where *futurum . . . uti* = *fore ut*); the contrast indicates the error of confusing the corpse with the true self, while *ipse*, as in 878 (see note above) reinforces the point. The personal use of the active form *miseret* is archaic.

divorce himself from it: the contrast between the corpse and the real self continues; *illim* (literally 'thence') = *a corpore*, as 882 confirms.

882-3 **fancies that person to be himself:** *illum* refers once more to the dead body (*corpus*), but the use of masculine rather than neuter is a reflection of the adversary's error in giving the insensate corpse a personality.

infects him with his own consciousness: the metaphor of tainting or defiling contained in *contaminat* conveys both the scientific impropriety of transferring one's consciousness to one's corpse and the misery resulting from the delusion that one is conscious of its fate.

as he stands by: a new dimension of self-delusion is here laconically introduced; as well as identifying himself with his corpse, the adversary also imagines a disembodied future self on hand to witness its fate (see introductory note to 870-93); the idea is taken further in 887.

884 **This is why he complains:** *indignatur* answers *indignarier* 870; the reason for the complaints which opened the passage has now been revealed.

885 **in actual death:** as opposed to his own, deluded, picture of it.

886 **live to bewail its death:** the paradoxical expression, with a second self alive (*uiuus*) but bewailing (*sibi lugere*) its death (*se peremptum*, alluding to the death of the 'original' self) heaps maximum scorn on the adversary's delusions.

887 **stand by . . . the prostrate self:** the juxtaposition of *stans* and *iacentem se* matches the imagined juxtaposition of the two selves described, whilst simultaneously exposing the absurdity of supposing not one but two future selves; cf. 883 and note above.

or cremated: since 879 the discussion has concerned exposure to wild beasts; the reminder of cremation (cf. 872) provides a transition to the passage's closing theme.

888-93 A digressive attack on the desirability of conventional methods of treating the corpse; cremation, embalming and burial are no less (and no more) frightening than mangling by predatory beasts. Whereas in 870-2 adversaries feared burial and cremation as well as wild beasts, in 888-93 their anxieties seem confined to the latter, an anomaly which would no doubt have been resolved in revision.

888 **Indeed:** *nam* introduces an explanation of the mention of cremation (*uriue*) in 887.

gnawing jaws: *malis morsuque* ('jaws and bite' = 'biting jaws') is a hendiadys. On the effect of the marked *m* alliteration, and the assonance *mălumst mālis*, see on 872.

889 **how it is not a cruel fate:** *qui* is the old ablative of the interrrogative; cf. 443.

890 **scorched by burning flames:** as with the allusions to embalming and burial which follow, the subjective vocabulary suggests the sentient corpse assumed by the adversaries. The inceptive form *torrescere*, which in classical Latin is found only here, is another Lucretian coining.

891-2 **set in honey:** a frequent method of embalming.

and to be stiff . . . chill slab: an allusion to the placing of the embalmed body on a stone surface in a rock tomb. *rigere frigore* and *gelidi saxi* present the corpse as confronting the opposite extreme to the *calidis flammis* of 890.

893 **be crushed by a weight of earth . . . :** an inversion, as Kenney notes, of the hopes contained in the stock prayer *sit tibi terra leuis* ('May the earth rest lightly on you'). The crushed corpse of the burial victim contrasts with the embalmed corpse lying uncovered on its slab, just as the latter contrasted with that of the cremation victim (see previous note). The elision of *superne* before *obtritum* at the main caesura (cf. 83 and note) here imparts a touch of breathlessness to the line as if the corpse were being stifled (cf. *suffocari* applied to embalming in 891).

894-911 (b) Concerns of the mourners

The laments of the bereaved, that the deceased has lost all life's blessings, are now attributed to a parallel false assumption, that he will retain the desire for them in death (894-903). The mourners' complaint that whereas the deceased is at eternal rest their own grief will be everlasting is met with the suggestion not only that their outlook is too self-centred but that death at least will end their sorrow (904-11: see notes there). This, the only attempt in the poem to deal with the grief of the bereaved, is less concerned to offer soothing comfort than to criticise its exaggerated manifestations and to jolt the victim out of an obsessive reaction to his loss.

894-9 Here and at 904-8 below, the mourners' complaints are dramatised and put into the mouth of an imaginary adversary, a familiar rhetorical technique especially favoured by the Greek diatribe. 894-6 are imitated by Gray, *Elegy Written in a Country Churchyard*, 21-4 (For them no more the blazing heath shall burn, Or busy housewife ply her evening care: No children run to lisp their sire's return, Or climb his knees the envied kiss to share), and, in a different, positive, context, by Virgil, *Georgics* II 523-4 (*interea pendent dulces circum oscula nati, / casta pudicitiam seruat domus*: meanwhile his sweet children hang upon his kisses, and his chaste home preserves its innocence).

894 **No more now:** the repeated *iam*, normally applied to an event which is on the point of happening, serves in this context to emphasise the pathos of the new situation.

895-6 **your darling children . . . delight:** *dulces* (literally 'sweet') and *dulcedine* suggest the pleasure (the Epicurean *summum bonum*) whose loss is the burden of the mourners' first complaint.

run to snatch the first kiss: *praeripere* (to snatch in advance, sc. of the other children) is infinitive of purpose with the verb of motion *occurrent*, an old construction not uncommon in Plautus.

897-9 **to flourish in your achievements:** *factis florentibus* is ablative of description, and the first of two predicates of *esse*, balancing the noun *praesidium* 898.

to protect your family: another source of pleasure and pride now lost to the deceased; the mourners' opening complaint is presented exclusively from his point of view, not from their own.

Unhappy man . . . unhappily: like the repeated *iam* in 894, the echo conveys pathos; cf. Cicero, *Ad Atticum* III 23.5, where he has involved his brother Quintus in his own ruin: *quem ego miserum misere perdidi*. The elisions of *misere* before *aiunt* and of *omnia* before *ademit* add to the pathetic effect.

one cruel day . . . all the many prizes of life: the sentiment, and the antithesis between *una* and *omnia . . . tot*, are paralleled in epitaphs; cf. *Carmina Latina Epigraphica* 405, *abstulit una dies animam corpusque simitur* and 1307.7-8, *apstulit haec unus tot tantaque munera nobis / perfidus infelix horrificusque dies*. Though the poet disagrees with the speaker's outlook (as 900-3 are about to make clear) he is not to be seen as parodying his expression; cf. V 91-6, where he exploits a similar antithesis in his spectacular prediction of the destruction of our world and its three conventional divisions. As there and in 908 below, *dies* is feminine, a gender normally reserved in classical prose for an appointed day.

900-1 The mourners are accused, like the man concerned for the fate of his corpse in the preceding passage, of an unconscious assumption that the deceased will survive, in this case to miss life's pleasures.

at the same time: sc. as the blessings have been lost.

either: i.e. any more than you retain the blessings. For *super* = 'as well', cf. 672 and note; the combination with *una* produces an emphatic pleonasm characteristic of the poet.

903 **they would release:** *dissoluant* is to be taken as quadrisyllabic: see on 330.

mental anguish and fear: arising, in the first instance, from concern for the plight of the deceased, but extending also to anxiety and apprehension as to their own eventual state in death.

904-8 In this second dramatised complaint, the mourners accept the poet's reply to their first; acknowledging that the deceased is forever at peace, they now proclaim their own grief and sense of loss.

904-5 **For your part:** *tu quidem* (cf. Greek σὺ μέν) is opposed to *at nos* 906. The elision of *quidem* before *ut* fits the context of pathos; cf. 898 and note.

lulled in death's sleep: the speaker's words, taken up by the poet in 910, foreshadow the sustained comparison between sleep and death which follows at 919-30.

for the rest of time: *aeui* is partitive genitive with *quod*, with which *id*, accusative of duration, is to be supplied.

delivered: for the suppressed *s* in *priuatu'*, cf. 52 and note.

all pain and distress: including unsatisfied longing for life's pleasures; the point of 900-1 has now been conceded.

906 **pyre:** *bustum* (cf. Servius on Virgil, *Aeneid* XI 185) properly denotes the burnt-out pyre.

reduced . . . to ashes: *cinefacio*, not found elsewhere, is doubtless another Lucretian coining.

907-8 907 is a remarkable hexameter, comprising only three words and containing a fifth-foot spondee: the long words and the slow rhythm of the line-ending (cf. 191 and note) help to convey the protracted nature of the funeral lamentations and the supposed endlessness of the sorrow in the future. Though the poet regards these protestations as exaggerated, as 909-11 go on to show, there is nothing obviously grotesque or mocking about their expression, as West (1969) 29 and Kenney on 904-8 and 907 have claimed.

bewept: *deflere* is the appropriate technical word for the mourners' formal lament.

insatiably: *insatiabiliter*, a rare adverb of a type favoured by the poet, is here put into the speaker's mouth; it recurs (in a less elevated context) at VI 978.

no day . . . everlasting sorrow: *nulla dies . . . demet* immediately reinforces the idea expressively conveyed by the preceding *aeternumque*, which answers *aeui quod superest* 904-5: while the deceased will be at eternal rest, the bereaved will suffer 'eternal grief', an exaggeration commonly attested in epitaphs, which the poet proceeds to expose. The elision of *maerorem* before *e pectore* fits the context of pathos; cf. 904 and note. For the gender of *dies*, see on 899.

909-11 **this individual:** i.e. the spokesman for the mourners.

what is so . . . bitter: *amari* is partitive genitive with *quid.*

a return to sleep and rest: *somnum atque quietem* answers the spokesman's *sopitus* 904; *redit* denotes a reversion to the prenatal state (cf. 832-42).

as to enable anyone to waste away in everlasting sorrow: the indirect question ('so bitter <as to explain> why . . . ') acquires the force of a consecutive clause; *quisquam* is used in a virtually negative context, implying that no one could.

The point of the Lucretian rejoinder (in which *aeterno . . . luctu* takes up the mourner's *aeternum . . . maerorem* 907-8) is usually taken simply to be that the peace of the deceased is a reason for joy which should counteract the grief and sense of loss of the bereaved, but this overlooks the further implication, which *possit* clearly underlines, that the prediction of eternal grief is grossly exaggerated, since it will be healed, if not by time, at least by the peace which the bereaved themselves will find in death; the words thus hint at both the main commonplace consolations open to the poet, the peace of the deceased and time as the great healer. The reply to the mourners is sometimes criticised as heartless and cold-blooded, but the passage is not to be seen as a condemnation of the grief of the bereaved in general but rather of its exaggerated forms; Lucretius does not deny that the loss is bitter, but that it is so bitter as for eternal grief to be possible. There is no reason to suppose that he dissented from Epicurus, who approved of mourning and regarded the grief of the bereaved as natural and as one of life's inevitable pains (cf. Plutarch, *Moralia* 1101a).

912-30 (c) Concerns of the (non-Epicurean) hedonists

The philosophy of 'Let us eat, drink and be merry, for tomorrow we die' is now attributed to the same false assumption as that of the mourners, that the desire for life's pleasures will be retained in death. The passage well illustrates the gulf between orthodox Epicurean morality and the debased hedonism which made pleasure in the sense of continuous sensual gratification its goal (cf. Introduction III). At 919-30 the point is reinforced by the analogy of dreamless sleep, which like death is free of longings; this analogy is equally applicable to the argument advanced against the mourners in 894-903.

912-5 **garlands:** regularly worn at a festive symposium.

have the habit of saying: *ut dicant* is explanatory of *hoc* 912.

in all sincerity: as the wine reveals their true feelings.

'Shortlived . . . later': the thoughts of the hedonists, like those of the mourners, are vividly dramatised; see on 894-9. For their commonplace sentiment, cf., e.g., Amphis (see on 869), cited by Athenaeus 336c, πῖνε, παῖζε· θνητὸς ὁ βίος, ὀλίγος οὑπὶ γῆς χρόνος (Drink and sport; life is mortal, and little is our time on earth), Petronius 34, where Trimalchio sets a toy silver skeleton on the table, advising his guests *eheu nos miseros, quam totus homuncio nil est! / sic erimus cuncti, postquam nos auferet Orcus. / ergo uiuamus, dum licet esse bene* (Alas, wretches that we are, how utterly nothing is puny man; this is how we shall all be after Death carries us off. So let's live, while we can enjoy ourselves), and the pseudo-Virgilian *Copa* 37-8, *pone merum et talos; pereat qui crastina curat! / mors aurem uellens 'uiuite' ait 'uenio'* (Set out the wine and the dice; damnation to him who cares for the morrow. Death plucks us by the ear, crying 'Live! I'm coming.'). The philosophy of *carpe diem* (pluck the day) is also a familiar theme in Horace's symposiastic odes (cf., e.g., I 11 and II 14).

this enjoyment: *hic* is long before the vowel because of the double pronunciation of the *c*; cf. *hoc* 912, and see on 856.

for poor mortals: the diminutive *homullis*, like *homuncio* in the Petronian passage cited above, is used for pathetic effect.

it will be over: the future perfect *fuerit* idiomatically denotes its future end; cf. Virgil, *Aeneid* II 325, *fuimus Troes, fuit Ilium* (it's all up with us Trojans and with Troy).

916-8 **As if . . . :** the revellers are accused of the same delusion as the mourners at 900-1 (*desiderium insideat* 918 echoes *desiderium . . . insidet* 901), but rather more peremptorily; whereas the mourners omitted or overlooked the crucial logical step (*non addunt* 900), the *tamquam* clause presents the revellers as embracing an obviously preposterous assumption. In the context, the *m* alliteration imparts a scornful note.

this . . . amongst their . . . tribulations, that . . . : *mali* is partitive genitive with *hoc*, which the noun clause with *quod* goes on to define; its three verbs are subjunctive because, like *sit* after *tamquam*, they refer to purely imaginary situations.

parching thirst should . . . scorch the poor wretches: *arida* is used predicatively with *torrat*, subjunctive of a third conjugation by-form of the normally second conjugation verb (contrast 1019). For similar Lucretian fluctuation, cf. 156 and note; there is no need to emend to *torreat*, assuming it disyllabic by synizesis. *miseros* underlines the irony implicit in the whole *tamquam* clause.

for some other thing: *cuius* = prose *alicuius*. The feminine genitive singular *aliae* (for *alius*, or *alterius* which was normally preferred to *alius* in all genders) is found in classical Latin only here and in Cicero, *De Diuinatione* II 30 and Livy, XXIV 27.8. *rei* is monosyllabic by synizesis; cf. 383 and note.

919-22 On the corroborative analogy introduced here, see introductory note to 912-30 above.

when mind and body alike are lulled: i.e. in dreamless sleep, when the mind as well as the body is inactive. *sopita*, neuter plural referring to nouns of different gender (see on 136), takes up *sopitus* 904, where the mourner conceded the similarity between death and sleep.

misses himself and his waking life: *sibi . . . se uitamque requirit* (feels regret to himself for himself and his life) corresponds closely to *desiderium nostri* 922. *sibi*, as well as *se*, draws attention to the suspension of identity which follows from the suspension of consciousness.

in this state: i.e. when lulled into unconsciousness.

no longing for our waking selves: *desiderium* echoes the argument of 900-1 and 916-8. *nostri*, as the form shows, is objective genitive; contrast the partitive *nostrum* in 932 below.

923-30 If dreamless sleep is free of desires, how much more will this be true of death, which involves far greater atomic disruption.

923-5 **in that case, where a man . . . :** the emphatically placed *tunc* introduces a contrast with the situation in death, and is further defined by the *cum* clause of 925, which though purely temporal also contains the evidence for the claim of 923-4; the awakening shows that the relevant atoms have not strayed too far.

gathers himself together: *ipse* not only reinforces the reflexive idea, but also reflects that in sleep the suspension of identity (cf. on 919 above) is only temporary. The precise mechanics of Epicurean awakening are unknown; see on 163.

those primary particles: i.e. the atoms essential to consciousness. *per artus* suggests that Lucretius is thinking especially of the *anima*, which in Epicurean theory (cf. on 112-6 and 163), was physically disrupted in sleep; part of it temporarily withdrew from the body and part of it was drawn deeper within the body, as explained later at IV 916-8. However, the allusion to *mens* in 920 shows that *sensiferis motibus* here embraces the motions not only of physical sensation but also of mental consciousness: cf. 240 note.

are by no means straying far . . . sensation: the contrasting situation in death, summed up in 928-30 below, has already been described in similar terms at 860-1.

926-7 The idea that death is much less than the dreamless sleep which can be seen to be nothing is a rhetorically effective amplification of the opening claim of 830, strategically placed at the end of the passage directed at the first of the two main targets of the conclusion, fear of any form of survival after death.

928 **a greater disturbance and dispersal of matter:** than occurs in sleep, when the *anima* is temporarily disrupted (see on 924 above). The proofs of the soul's mortality have often stressed the speed with which it will disperse without the body to act as its container or *uas* (e.g. 425-44), while in death the body too is disrupted and decays.

929 **nor does anyone wake and rise:** antithetical to *correptus homo ex somno se colligit ipse* 925.

930 **severance of life:** *uitai pausa* was used in the same context (cf. on 924 above) at 860.

931-77 *Nature remonstrates with those reluctant to die*

The poet's attempt to rule out survival in any form of after-life is now complete: in the rest of the book, while he does not lose sight of this first conclusion and includes a number of reminders or reinforcements of it, his primary concern is the instinctive reluctance to die, the instinctive desire to prolong life, which can certainly coexist with, and be strengthened by, apprehensions about an after-life but can also exist quite independently of them. The passage on the mourners and hedonists preceding forms a bridge to the new theme and is essentially an anticipation of it, in that both groups regret death as the end of life's pleasures; apart from their mistaken assumption that the dead will somehow be there to miss earthly pleasures, neither seems to regard death as the beginning of some unpleasant form of survival. But even after accepting that life's pleasures will not be missed in death, their loss can still be regretted in anticipation, and it is this attitude which is Lucretius' primary target in what follows. This second aspect of the fear of death was recognised by Epicurus, *ad Menoeceum* 124-5, where he sums it up as the craving for immortality (τὸν τῆς ἀθανασίας πόθον) and suggests that it is automatically eradicated by a proper understanding that consciousness ends in death, dismissing as idle the idea that death can be painful in anticipation, on the grounds that what is painless when it comes can, in anticipation, cause only empty pain (προσδοκώμενον κενῶς λυπεῖ). Apparently realising the inadequacy of such rational reflections in the face of the instinctive human desire to prolong life, Lucretius in what follows devotes much more energy than Epicurus appears to have done to the attempt to deal with this second aspect of the fear of death, and from this point his argument is not only intellectual but also emotional and moral.

Here, he begins with an appeal to the highest authority he could possibly invoke, personifying Nature (*rerum natura* 931), the embodiment of all the physics and of all the scientific laws which he sets out in the poem, to berate mortals who recoil from their own mortality; the pattern is climactic, in that she first addresses a man still reasonably young (as 946-7 clearly imply), thus insisting that even a comparatively premature death is no cause for undue regret, and then (952-62) confronts an older man who has completed his allotted span, with whom she is correspondingly angrier and more impatient. In each case, the reluctance to die is put down to insatiability, a cardinal sin for the Epicurean (cf. 1003-10), and is thus represented as a betrayal of Epicurean moral values (for another idea based on Epicurean moral theory, see on 938-9 and 944-9). Nature's final *necessest* 962 introduces a new argument, from death's inevitability, which the poet, supported by Nature's own authority, himself develops with an appeal to the relentless cycle of creation and destruction in nature (963-71); he concludes with a memorable reminder of one of the key ideas of 830-69, that our state in death will mirror our state before birth, so corroborating Nature's assumptions (939 and 943) that death will bring carefree peace.

931-2 **suppose Nature were . . . to take voice:** the apodosis to the *si* clause follows the speech at 950. Lucretius frequently personifies Nature (e.g. *rerum natura creatrix* I 629, II 1117 and V 1362, *naturaque daedala rerum* V 234) but gives her direct speech only here; significantly, he refers to her as *rerum natura*, evoking the title of the poem. The *prosopopoeia*, and the aggressive tone of the speech, provides an obvious link with the Hellenistic diatribe, where Bion (Hense 7-8) had put a speech into the mouth of Poverty, but Lucretius' is a far more meaningful and authoritative personification (see introductory note above), and the device is well attested in other genres; cf., e.g., Plato, *Crito* 50a, where the Laws speak, and Cicero, *Catilinarians* I 18 and 27-9, where Rome remonstrates with Catiline and Cicero respectively.

direct this reproach: for the scansion of *hoc*, an internal accusative with *increpet*, cf. 856 and note.

933-4 **What ails you, mortal, so desperately:** for *quid tibi tanto operest*, cf. *quid tibi aegre est?* in Plautus, *Menaechmi* 626. *mortalis*, placed like *mortem* 934 immediately before the fifth foot, underlines the effrontery and futility of a mortal objecting to his mortal fate; cf. Nature's closing reminder of its inevitability in 962.

to excess: *nimis*, like *amplius aequo* 953, implies that some measure of regret for one's mortality is natural and legitimate.

935-49 Nature here justifies her criticism by posing a dilemma, the first horn of which is covered in 935-9, the second in 940-9.

935 **was pleasing to you:** implying gratitude for it, just as the antithetical *ingrata* 937 and *ingratum* 942 suggest ingratitude. Gratitude for past pleasures was important to Epicurus: thankful recollection of the past enabled the old to renew the blessings of their youth (*ad Menoeceum* 122).

936-7 **as if consigned to a punctured vessel**: this image of insatiability evokes the mythical punishment of the Danaids in the underworld, which Lucretius rationalises as a projection of insatiability in life at 1003-10, where *pertusum congerere in uas* 1009 exactly matches the language used here.

been ungratefully dissipated: on the sense of *ingrata*, see on 935 above.

938-9 **like a sated guest at life's banquet:** this memorable image, further exploited at 959-60, is not original to Lucretius but is found in Bion (Hense 16); it is imitated by Horace, *Satires* I 1.118-9 and *Epistles* II 2.214. The advice to withdraw is all the more appropriate in the light of the Epicurean idea (*Principal Sayings* 19) that infinite time cannot bring an infinite increase in pleasure; complete pleasure, in the form of freedom from bodily pain and from mental disturbance, could be attained in limited time and could not then be increased. *uitae* is genitive with *plenus*; cf. *plenus . . . rerum* 960.

carefree rest: which death has now been shown to entail; cf. the anticipatory use of *leti secura quies* at 211.

with equanimity: this mental calm, ideal Epicurean ἀταραξία, is the antithesis of the insatiability conveyed in 936-7.

940 **But if:** *sin* introduces the second horn of the dilemma which began at 935.

whatever things have been placed at your disposal: *fructus es*, which like *fungitur* 734, *perfunctus* 956 and *potitus* 1038 governs an accusative rather than the classical ablative, here, as in its legal usage, denotes 'having the use of' rather than positively 'enjoying', which would fit neither the antithesis with 935-7 nor the rest of the *sin* clause. For the tmesis of *quae . . . cumque*, cf. 550.

have been poured away and wasted: *periere profusa* sustains the image of 936-7, corresponding to *perfluxere atque . . . interiere*.

941 **life is objectionable to you:** antithetical to *grata fuit tibi uita* 935. The form *offensa* is used figuratively by Cicero, *Ad Atticum* IX 2a.2: for the literal clash of atoms, Lucretius uses *offensus* to replace the metrically inadmissible *offensio.*

seek to add: like *petentes* 86, *quaeris* governs the prolative infinitive by analogy with *conari* or *uelle.*

942 **for it . . . to be . . . wasted . . . pass unappreciated away:** the subjunctives in the relative clause express both purpose (after *quaeris*) and result. *ingratum occidat* echoes *ingrata interiere* 937.

943 **and not rather make an end of life and of tribulation:** Nature is not seriously recommending suicide, which in Epicurean theory became necessary only in the rare cases where a surplus of (genuine) pleasure over pain could not be attained. The point is rather that the ungrateful, insatiable non-Epicurean addressed has made his life such a misery that he would be better off dead: the real solution is for him to limit his desires and to embrace Epicurean values. As in 939, death is again seen as *secura quies*. The clause stands in asyndeton to *non amplius addere quaeris*.

944-9 Nature concludes her case with an admission of her inability to devise fresh pleasures to delight the plaintiff, which serves to heighten the picture of his ingratitude and insatiability. As in 938-9, there is a connection with the Epicurean principle that beyond a certain point pleasure cannot be increased with time; Kenney also compares Seneca, *Moral Epistles* 24.26, where monotony eventually makes life unbearable, and 77.6, where this idea is said to be a Stoic consolation in face of death.

944-5 **that I can devise or invent to please you:** *machiner inueniamque* are prospective subjunctives; *placeat* expresses purpose.

945 **all things are always the same:** a consequence, in Epicurean theory, of the finite number of atomic types, which limited the number of their possible combinations in compounds and so of the types of atomic compound.

946-7 **If your body . . . in exhaustion:** clearly indicating that Nature is here addressing a reasonably young man (see introductory note to 931-77 above); *si* approximates to *etsi*, 'even though', as *tamen* in the apodosis shows.

all things . . . remain the same: the repetition of the identically placed *eadem sunt omnia semper* in *eadem tamen omnia restant* two lines later itself mirrors the monotony described.

948 **surpass all generations in survival:** though Lucretius usually uses *saecla* in the sense of species, *uiuendo condere saecla* 1090 and *multaque uiuendo uitalia uincere saecla* I 202 suggest that it here denotes (human) generations, as also in 629 and 967; cf. also Virgil's imitation (*Georgics* II 295), where men are specified (*multa uirum uoluens durando saecula uincit*).

949 **if you were never going to die:** Nature ironically imagines a suspension of her own laws. The switch from open future conditional (*perges* 948) to remote future (*sis*) underlines the impossibility of the second contingency.

950-1 **What do we reply:** the indicative *respondemus* is unexpected, not because of the remote future protasis, which came 18 lines earlier at 931-2, but because the question is deliberative; the idiom is probably to be explained as colloquial.
bringing a just action . . . presenting a valid case: the legal imagery (cf. also on *fructus es* 940) is especially apposite in that Nature is herself the embodiment of *scientific* law.

952 **But now:** *hic* is the local adverb, 'at this point'.
of maturer, more advanced years: *grandior seniorque* is a characteristic pleonasm.

953 **beyond reason:** cf. *nimis* 933 and note. The second plaintiff has less justification for his lamentations because he has completed his allotted span.

954 **more sternly . . . more aggressive:** *magis* goes closely with both *inclamet* and *acri*.

955 **Away with your tears:** *abhinc*, usually temporal ('ago'), is here local (= *hinc*), a perhaps colloquial idiom, without parallel before Apuleius.
insatiable glutton: Bailey's tentative suggestion of *baratro*, said in a scholium on Horace, *Satires* I 2.2, to denote those who devour their substance as if consigning it to a pit (*barathrum*), fits the context better than *balatro* (buffoon) or *blatero* (babbler); the manuscripts' *baratre* can scarcely be explained as 'deserving to be cast into a pit' on the strength of the late use of the Greek βάραθρος in this sense.

956 **You've had your full share of life's prizes:** *perfungor* here takes the accusative rather than the classical ablative (contrast 968 below); cf. 734 and 940 and notes. The *per-* prefix denotes completeness.
are withering away: *marces* echoes *marcet* 946, pointing the contrast with the younger plaintiff addressed there.

957 **you . . . long for what is not to hand and despise what is:** a virtually proverbial analysis of the roots of human dissatisfaction, paralleled at 1082-4; the thought goes back to Epicurus and Democritus, his atomist predecessor, without being confined to their schools. *aues* and *temnis* stand in asyndeton.

958 **incomplete:** because the opportunities for full enjoyment of available pleasures have been wasted.
unenjoyed: as in 937 and 942, *ingrata* also implies ingratitude; see on 935.

959-60 **unexpectedly:** *nec opinans* is a set expression in which *nec* has the sense of *non*.
found death standing at your head: i.e. as you recline at life's banquet, where death has stolen up on you unawares; there is a return to the image introduced in 938, as 960 goes on to make clear.
depart filled and sated with good things: echoing *plenus uitae . . . recedis* 938; *satur ac plenus . . . rerum* also contrasts with the *imperfecta uita* of 958.

961 **Still:** i.e. despite having wasted life's opportunities.
behaviour inappropriate to your years: i.e. refusal to accept death gracefully.

962 **come on:** *-dum* colloquially sharpens the imperative *age*.
now make way for others: though Lucretius does not elsewhere elide *iam* before a short vowel, Marullus' *iam aliis* is as satisfactory as any of the many conjectures for the corrupt text of the manuscripts.
with equanimity: like a good Epicurean, as the first plaintiff was instructed to behave at 939 (see note).

it is inevitable: Nature finally delivers her trump-card, foreshadowed at 933-4 (see note).

963 **Justifiably . . . would she plead her case:** the apposite legal imagery is continued from 950-1 (see note).

rail and scold: *increpet* echoes 932, where Nature was first introduced. The spondaic fifth foot provided by *inciletque*, an archaic synonym of *increpet*, adds weight and solemnity to this concluding allusion to her strictures; cf. 191 and note.

964-71 The poet now himself develops Nature's final point, death's inevitability (see introductory note to 931-77 above).

964-5 For the idea of the constant cycle of creation and destruction in nature, in which constituent atomic matter is never annihilated but constantly transferred, cf. I 250-64 and II 67-79. This emotive theme has inspired some of the poet's most memorable lines, including I 263-4 where nature recreates one thing from another and allows nothing to be created unless assisted by the death of something else, II 79 where successive generations pass on the torch of life like a team of relay runners, and 971 with its legal imagery below.

the old order . . . the new: *rerum* goes with *uetustas* (= *res uetustae*) as well as with *nouitate* (= *rebus nouis*).

one thing is inevitably made up afresh from others: *necessest* takes up Nature's concluding *necessest* 962. The subject of *reparare* is left unexpressed, but it is Nature who is responsible for the renewal. *ex aliis* is a metrically convenient plural for the normal singular (cf. *alid ex alio* in 970 below and in the parallel passage at I 263).

966-7 The scientific idea preceding is now exploited to score an incidental hit at the primitive religious idea that the dead are consigned to Tartarus, the pit where sinners were punished in the underworld. Such ideas have already been ruled out by the demonstration that there can be no form of after-life; the appeal to the principle of the conservation of matter provides passing, satirical, corroboration, and the reference to Tartarus looks forward to the passage at 978-1023 which seeks to account for the ideas of such punishment.

Tartarus and its pit: the two are identical; the assonance of *barathrum . . . Tartara . . . atra* helps to link them together, and has a horrific or at least a satirical, mock-horrific effect.

matter is required: the nominative with *opus est* (instead of the ablative used, e.g., at I 206) is an old construction, of which Lucretus has six or seven examples. For the form *materies*, see on 59.

968-9 The appeal to future and past shows the principle just invoked to be an inexorable law of nature.

accordingly: the reasoning is inductive; inferences about the past and the more distant future are drawn from the two generations already specified.

they have perished . . . will continue to perish: the subject is still *postera saecla*, but *postera* now = 'subsequent to their respective predecessors', changing its reference with *cecidere* and again with *cadentque*; however, the combination with *ante haec* (before the subsequent generations of 967) is awkward, and the expression would no doubt have been polished in revision.

970 **one thing will never cease to arise from another:** a reassertion of the point of 965. *alid* is a metrically convenient archaism for *aliud*, used by Lucretius only in combination with *ex alio*, as in the parallel passage at I 263.

971 **life is given . . . freehold . . . on lease:** *mancipio* and *usu* (= *usui*) are predicative datives, respectively denoting absolute ownership and the right of use. This famous image (cf. on 964-5 above) has precedents in Euripides, *Supplices* 534 (cf. on 774), where our tenure of the body is no more than a life-tenancy, and, in the diatribe, in Bion (Stobaeus, *Florilegium* IV 41.56, where Fortune has loaned, not given, the rich their possessions). Since in Lucretius the donor is Nature, the embodiment of *scientific* law, the legal imagery is all the more appropriate, as at 950-1 and 963 (see notes there).

972-7 The inevitable to which we must bow holds no terrors, since our state in death is exactly mirrored in our state before birth. This encapsulation of the point established earlier at 832-42 is not only striking and effective but also entirely appropriate to its context; it also assists the transition to 978-1023 (see introductory note below).

972-3 **Look back . . . and see:** the poet turns once more to Memmius (Introduction I), and through him to the general reader.

the eternity of time . . . was absolutely nothing to us: the Epicurean idea that time was infinite assists the rhetoric of the argument, making it all the more remarkable that to us the infinite time past was nothing, and in turn reflecting the nothingness of the infinite time to come after our death. *nil ad nos* echoes the crucial opening claim of the book's conclusion at 830; see note there.

before our birth: *quam nascimur ante* = *ante quam nascimur*; the perfect *nati sumus* would be more usual, even if the first person were generalising and denoted successive generations.

974-5 **this . . . is a mirror-image revealed to us by Nature:** a striking and novel metaphor, in which the personified Nature is strategically re-introduced to conclude the passage. *hoc*, referring to *anteacta uetustas temporis aeterni* 972-3, is attracted to the gender of *speculum*, which as Kenney rightly insists here denotes a reflection rather than a mirror, to which *exponit* would be inappropriate. Since the time before birth was nothing to us (972-3), the reflection of the future amounts to a complete blank, making the metaphor all the more arresting. For the scansion of *hoc*, cf. 856 and note.

of the time to come once we finally die: *futuri temporis* answers *anteacta uetustas temporis aeterni* just as *post mortem denique nostram* answers *quam nascimur ante*; the matching phrases are similarly placed in their respective lines, as if to emphasise the exactness with which the one situation literally reflects the other.

976-7 The tricolon of rhetorical questions provides a resounding conclusion to the passage.

Is there . . . in the prospect: as *apparet* shows, *uidetur* is a true passive (see on 35), literally 'is seen'.

Is it not more carefree than any slumber: *futurum tempus* is to be supplied as subject from 974-5. The comparison looks back to 919-30.

978-1023 *The fabled punishments of Hades exist not in death but in life*

The passage serves two purposes, the second of which, usually overlooked or underemphasised by editors, accounts for its position in the book. One purpose is obviously to explain away the myths of punishment, and so to reinforce the original point of the conclusion that death is eternal peace; the reassertion of this point in 972-7 provides a natural transition to the denial that the mythical torments exist in death. The key to the rationalisation is supplied in the course of the fifth and final example at 1011-22: because of guilty conscience, men take the worst torments of life, symbolise them, and imagine them as lying in store after death. All five examples of mythical punishment are explained as mental projections of earthly sufferings, Tantalus with his overhanging rock symbolising fear of the gods and the future, Tityos with his liver eternally gnawed by vultures sexual infatuation and other extravagant desires, Sisyphus vainly rolling his stone uphill unsatisfied ambition, the Danaids collecting water in perforated vessels insatiability, and Tartarus and its horrors the pangs of guilty conscience. The purpose of the rationalisation is not so much to disprove the myths of Tartarus, which have already been ruled out by the demonstration that there can be no form of after-life (cf. the summary dismissal of the idea of consignment to Tartarus at 966-7; see note there), and which the poet's audience would in any case have been unlikely to take seriously in any literal sense; except at 985-91, where he cannot resist pointing out the sheer physical impossibility of Tityos, however giant-sized, providing the birds with *eternal* fodder, the non-existence of the sinners and their punishments is taken for granted and merely asserted. The object is rather to reinforce the general case against an after-life by suggesting a plausible explanation of the origin and prevalence of such myths and analysing whatever truth may lie behind them, as he seeks to do with the myth of Cybele at II 589-660. The passage thus provides no evidence of a Lucretian preoccupation with fears of mythical punishment or of a superfluous attempt to convince his educated readers that such myths were not literally true. But if rationalisation were the sole or the primary object of the passage, it would be strangely placed, and would have been expected earlier, either as an appendix to the proofs of the soul's mortality or at least in the first part of the conclusion which concerned fear of survival; its second purpose, however, is entirely relevant to its context. It constitutes a further argument for any reader not already an Epicurean to accept death: the point emphasised at both the beginning (978-9) and the end (1023) is that the fabled torments, while not existing in death, do, at least as far as non-Epicureans (*stulti* 1023) are concerned, exist in life, while 1020-1 refer explicitly to the release from earthly sufferings which death can provide. Consolations based on the miseries of life, while commonplace enough, were not in a general form open to an Epicurean, for whom a surplus of pleasure over pain in life was normally possible (indeed the master had specifically repudiated the pessimistic Greek idea that the shortest life is the best, and better still not to have been born at all); but it is entirely legitimate for Lucretius to base such an argument on self-inflicted miseries in life, and he proceeds on the ironic assumption that the non-Epicureans will find release only in death and are certainly not going to adopt the more immediate and less drastic remedy of ceasing to torment themselves (cf. Nature's ironic suggestion at 940-3 that the dissatisfied man has more reason to end his life than to cling to it, and 1045-52, where the mortal reluctant to follow the great men of history to the grave lives a life so wretched as to make his reluctance to leave it appear nonsensical). The passage is thus complementary to the complaints of Nature which preceded it: Nature argued against clinging to life's pleasures, while Lucretius here takes the worst of life's sufferings and advances them, in a spirit of irony, as a reason for welcoming death. Just as Nature addressed mortals who fell far short, in their dissatisfaction and insatiability, of Epicurean standards, so the present argument is relevant only to non-Epicureans (*stulti*), since the symbolic torments exemplify five of the cardinal sins from an Epicurean point of view; indeed, the passage contains an indirect moral lesson in its series of vivid images of the moral evils to be most studiously avoided in order to escape a life of Hell on earth.

978 **in the depths of Acheron:** denoting the underworld as a whole; see on 25.

980-1 **No wretched Tantalus . . . :** Seneca may have the passage which begins here especially in mind in *Moral Epistles* 24.18, where he disdains such denials of underworld torments, alluding to them as an 'Epicurean refrain' (*Epicuream cantilenam*). Tantalus, son of Zeus and king of Lydia, stole the gods' nectar and ambrosia; the derivation of the English 'tantalise' from his name reflects the nature of his punishment. In Homer, *Odyssey* XI 582-92, he was surrounded by ever-receding food and drink (cf., e.g., Horace, *Satires* I 1.68-9, where he is a symbol of greed or *auaritia*), but Lucretius follows the version more widespread in antiquity, in which his torment was fear of an overhanging rock (cf., e.g., Pindar, *Olympians* 1.55-64, Euripides, *Orestes* 5-7, Cicero, *Tusculan Disputations* IV 35 and Virgil, *Aeneid* VI 602-3); this afforded Lucretius an especially apt image for fear of the gods (see on 982 below). *nec* is answered by *nec* 984 (literally 'neither . . . nor').

empty dread: corresponding exactly with *metus . . . inanis* 982; the dread is empty because the rock will not fall, any more than the gods will interfere in human life.

982 **fear of the gods:** one of the poem's two great targets; cf. 14-24, where Epicurean philosophy removes it. The image of fear of the gods as an overhanging rock harmonises with the memorable image of I 62-5, where religion, which is equated with superstition (*superstitio*) by its description as standing over mortals (*super instans*), is portrayed as a monster which lours over mankind from the heavens, causing them to grovel on the face of the earth: cf. West (1969) 98.

oppresses . . . in life: *urget* matches *impendens* applied to the rock in 980; *in uita* takes up the opening *in uita* 979, which is echoed also at 995 and 1014.

983 **the fate which may fall**: *casum* not only denotes (ill) fortune, but suggests also the root sense of 'fall' appropriate to the image of the rock. An Epicurean would not fear the future unduly any more than he would fear the gods; his philosophy, which, like Stoicism, sought to provide self-sufficiency in face of fortune's vicissitudes, would allow him to obtain a surplus of pleasure over pain in most eventualities.

984 **No winged birds penetrate . . . Tityos:** for the attempted rape of Leto (Roman Latona, mother of Apollo and Diana), the giant Tityos was stretched on the ground to have his liver constantly devoured by vultures, as described by Homer, *Odyssey* XI 576-81. In this case the punishment, while symbolising dangerous desires in general (994), primarily represents the same sexual passion (992-3) which is exemplified in the crime. The accusative *Tityon*, like the nominative *Tityos* in 992, is the Greek form.

985-91 The scientist in Lucretius cannot resist this scornful gibe at the physical impossibility contained in the myth, even though the non-existence of underworld torments is simply taken for granted in the rest of the passage; see introductory note to 978-1023 above.

985-6 **deep in his giant breast:** *magno* looks forward to the ironical allusions to the giant's vast size in 987-9. For *sub* = 'deep in', rather than 'below', cf. I 474 and II 639. The *p* alliteration initiated by *pectore* adds impact to the poet's denial, also helping to convey his scorn.

to pry into: *scrutentur*, 'scrutinise' or 'explore', fits the scornful, sceptical tone. The subjunctive in the relative clause expresses purpose.

987 **however vast you suppose . . . :** literally 'let him extend with a spread-eagling of his body as vast as you please'; the use of *quamlibet* with a jussive subjunctive, common with its synonym *quamuis* which thus acquires the force of a concessive conjunction, is extremely rare.

988-9 **so that:** the subjunctives in the *qui* clauses are consecutive.

sprawling: *dispessis* is from the rare compound *dispando*, to spread out; cf. II 1126.

nine acres: an approximation, like *nouem iugera*, to the Homeric ἐννέα πέλεθρα (*Odyssey* XI 577).

the circle of the whole earth: pictured in Epicurean theory as a flat dish situated at the centre of our own finite world (Introduction III).

990-1 The alliteration, primarily with *p*, has a similar effect to that in 985-6; see note above. The common sense denial that (even in an after-life) Tityos can suffer eternal torment recalls the rejoinder to the mourners, that (given their mortality) their grief can scarcely last for ever (909-11).

992-4 **prostrated by love:** *in amore iacentem* answers *Acherunte iacentem* 984; Tityos, shackled to the ground, corresponds to the lover rendered prostrate and inactive by his passion; such infatuation, in Epicurean eyes one of the greatest sources of mental disturbance and unhappiness (Introduction III), is famously denounced by the poet at IV 1058-1287.

winged Cupids: *uolucres*, if the text is sound, answers *uolucres* 984, and is best explained, with Kenney and with Pius before him, as an allusion to the Cupids, themselves a symbol of sexual desire, whose metaphorical arrows rend the heart just as the vultures rend Tityos' liver: this interpretation is supported by *cuppedine* (= *cupidine*) applied to other forms of desire in 994 below. Editors often assume that *uolucres* still denotes birds, with *atque exest anxius angor* added to explain the metaphor and *atque* = 'that is', but the poet can hardly have referred to birds at the very point where he is rationalising the Tityos story.

devoured by gnawing anguish: *exest* is from *exedo*; the assonance of *anxius angor* helps to convey the insistence of the emotion.

torn by cares: like *lacerant* 993, *scindunt* is appropriate both to birds and to arrows.

any other form of Desire: the symbolism is now extended to cover obsessive desires in general. Lucretius occasionally uses *cuppedo*, a form not found in other writers but which is sometimes metrically convenient, as an alternative to *cupido*: the word supports the idea of an allusion to Cupids in 993 (see note above).

995-1010 The pattern of presentation is now carefully varied; with the two preceding examples of individualised sinners, the mythical punishment came first, the earthly torment it symbolised second, but with the two remaining examples this order is reversed. For similar structuring, cf., e.g., the triple ABBA sequence at I 159-214.

995 **Sisyphus:** a king of Corinth, renowned for his cunning, who was punished for variously reported crimes by being forced constantly to roll a stone uphill, only for it to roll constantly back again, as described by Homer, *Odyssey* XI 593-600. His torment provides the poet with an apt symbol for political ambition, another cardinal sin for the Epicurean, as already reflected at 59-64 where it is combined with, and seen as stemming from, avarice: see on 60-3.
exists in life: cf. 982 and note.

996-7 **thirsts to seek:** for *imbibere*, a rare but colourful term for deep longing, cf. VI 72.
the rods and cruel axes: carried for the consuls and praetors by the lictors, these symbolised the magistrates' right to inflict beating and execution respectively.
withdraws, beaten and dismayed: Sisyphus here symbolises frustrated political ambition, of which Catiline provided a conspicuous recent example; prevented from standing in the consular elections of 66 and 65, he was an unsuccessful candidate in 64 and 63 before resorting to less constitutional means to achieve power.

998 **to seek power:** *imperium*, which entitled the holder to the rods and axes of 996, is the appropriate technical term to denote the higher Roman magistracies.
which is empty and never conferred: i.e. power, even when achieved, is futile (because it does not achieve the desired objective and guarantee one's security in society: cf. V 1120-35) and illusory (because it does not confer the expected control and in any case is merely transitory). This new point, of which the power-struggles of contemporary Roman history provide abundant illustration, makes Sisyphus a more general symbol of political ambition, whether or not it is rewarded with office.

1000-2 Both metre and language are expressive: the five spondees of 1000, followed by the spondaic word *saxum* at the beginning of 1001, match the laborious effort of rolling the rock uphill, whereas the increasingly dactylic rhythm beginning with *quod tamen* 1001 fits the gathering speed of its descent and the repeated *p*, *t*, and *c* sounds of 1002 convey its thudding progress to the plain. The Homeric original, αὖτις ἔπειτα πέδονδε κυλίνδετο λᾶας ἀναιδής (*Odyssey* XI 598), combines still more marked metrical and alliterative effects.
is to labour to thrust a rock up a mountain: the image recalls the combined picture of ambition and avarice painted at 62-3 (see note), where II 12-13 are slightly abridged; note especially *ad summas emergere opes*, suggesting upward progress, and *niti praestante labore*, which matches *durum sufferre laborem* 999 and *nixantem*, a frequentative form of *niti* probably coined by Lucretius, in 1000. For the scansion of *hoc*, as also in 1008 below, see on 856.
revert to . . . the plain: as West (1969) 102 points out, *petit aequora campi* suggests also the descent of the candidate (*petitor*) to the *Campus Martius* to stand for election once more, either, as West suggests, after demitting office, or alternatively after electoral defeat.

1003-10 The Danaids, the fifty daughters of Danaus who with one exception followed their father's instructions to slay their husbands on their wedding night and were punished by being forced to collect water in a perforated vessel, are now introduced as a projection of another self-inflicted earthly torment, insatiability, a failing at which Nature has already directed her ire (see introductory note to 931-77), herself invoking the image of the Danaids' leaky vessel (936-7 and note). Though not included in Homer's underworld, they were depicted in the fresco of Polygnotus described by Pausanias X 31.9 and are alluded to by Plato, *Gorgias* 493a-d, and in the pseudo-Platonic *Axiochus* 371e.

1003 **an ungrateful disposition:** for the link between insatiability and ingratitude, see on 935. *animi . . . naturam* is again periphrastic for *animum*; see on 130-1.

1005-7 This illustration, from the bounty of the seasons, which for all its variety cannot satisfy man, forcefully conveys the depth of his dissatisfaction.

1008-9 **this . . . is the story of the girls . . . gathering:** literally 'this is that which they recount, <namely> that girls . . . gather', a rather loose way of expressing the relationship between the rationalisation and the myth, but there can be no doubt that the Danaids and their punishment correspond to man and his ungrateful insatiability (*animi ingratam naturam* 1003, *nec tamen explemur* 1007); to equate them, as do many editors, with the seasons (*annorum tempora* 1005, = Greek ῾Ωραι) is mistaken, since, whereas the seasons are blameless, the Danaids are being punished.

in the bloom of their years: an appropriate description of the brides which the Danaids were at the time of their crime.

a leaky vessel: cf. not only 936-7 and note, but also VI 17-23, where Epicurus realised that man's mind was a flawed vessel, partly because it was leaky and could never be filled, partly because it contaminated everything it took in.

1010 **can in no way be filled:** *expleri* answers *explemur* 1007, indicating that man, or his mind, is here equated with the flawed vessel itself (cf. previous note). *potestur* is an archaic use of the passive, employed because the dependent infinitive is passive, an idiom preserved in classical Latin with *coepi* (e.g. Cicero, *Brutus* 236: *minor haberi est coeptus*): cf. *suppleri queatur* I 1045.

Servius on Virgil, *Aeneid* VI 596, after alluding to Lucretius' rationalisation of the stories of Tityos, Tantalus and Sisyphus, claims that 'by the wheel he symbolises traders, who are for ever sent spinning by storms and gales', so suggesting that the passage included mention of the punishment of Ixion, who, for his attempt to violate Hera, was bound to an ever rotating wheel; Seneca, *Moral Epistles* 24.18, where the Lucretian passage is probably in mind (see on 980-1), also refers to Ixion along with Sisyphus and Tityos, going on to mention Cerberus and the darkness of Hades (cf. *Cerberus . . . et lucis egestas* 1011). If Servius is right, there are two possibilities; a passage on Ixion may have been lost before 1011, where the poet moves from specific mythical sinners to the general horrors of Hades (though this would disturb the structural pattern noted on 995-1010); the traders (*negotiatores*) symbolised by the wheel would then be examples of *auaritia*, which the poet sees also as the root cause of the ambition symbolised in Sisyphus (see on 60-3). Alternatively, Lucretius may simply have made passing mention of the wheel as one of the horrors of Hades in a line or lines lost from the list of 1011-2; the interpretation of the wheel as symbolising traders would then be Servius' own (like his interpretation of the constant regrowth of Tityos' liver as a symbol of the insatiability of passion). On the other hand, the whole claim could be the result of error or confusion on the part of Servius or his source.

1011-3 The poet now (cf. preceding note) moves on from the famous mythical sinners to the underworld's general horrors.

Cerberus: the three-headed hound guarding the entrance to Hades.

the Furies: the three snaky-locked goddesses of vengeance, Allecto, Megaera and Tisiphone, an appropriate symbol of the punishments which are the main theme of 1014-22.

denial of light: a traditional horror of the underworld; cf. *Tartara . . . atra* 966, and also the recurrent Lucretian image of children afraid in the dark (87-93 and note).

and Tartarus belching . . . from its jaws: the imagery suggests a primeval concept of Tartarus as a fire-breathing monster; the allusion is to the poisonous vapours supposed to arise from its openings, like the emanations from Lake Avernus. For the asyndeton, after *et . . . et* earlier in the list, cf., e.g., I 455-6. A line or lines, including mention if not of Ixion at least of his wheel, may have been lost after 1011; see on 1010 above.

these things: Marullus' *haec*, for the manuscripts' *qui*, removes the problem of the absence of a main verb; the neuter, referring to things of different gender, is also the usual Lucretian construction (see on 136, and cf. neuter *quae* in 1018 below).

1014-5 The twin earthly torments specified here, fear of, and actual, punishment for misdeeds, are again self-inflicted; the Epicurean would guard against them by conformity with conventional justice, in order to achieve the twin goals of clear conscience and security in society (Introduction III).

there does exist in life: *est* gains emphasis from its initial position in 1015; *in uita* (cf. 982 and note) again echoes the central theme.

signal fear of retribution for signal misdeeds: the juxtaposition *insignibus insignis* suggests that the fear is proportionate to the misdeeds. *poenarum* takes up *Furiae* 1011; since *Poenae* was another name for the Furies, the term partly sustains the personification which it serves simultaneously to rationalise.

atonement for crime: *luella*, a Lucretian coining to denote expiation, is found only here.

1016-7 The list of earthly punishments, which are characteristically Roman, stands in apposition to *luella* 1015.

incarceration: perhaps as a prelude to execution: the allusion may be to the State prison, the Mamertine, near the Forum.

precipitation from the rock: i.e. the Tarpeian rock on the Capitoline, from which traitors and other criminals were sometimes hurled to their death. For the suppressed *s* of *iactu'*, cf. 52 and note; *deorsum* is trisyllabic, like *seorsum* 500 (see note).

the dungeon: *robur* probably denotes the lowest dungeon of the Mamertine prison, known, from its attribution to King Servius Tullius, as the *Tullianum*, where Jugurtha and the Catilinarian conspirators were put to death. The usage is well-attested and fits the juxtaposition with *carnifices*, but some editors prefer to assume an unparalleled application of the word to a wooden instrument of torture like the *eculeus*, a sort of horse-shaped rack, while Jocelyn (1986) 46-7, reading *carnificis* and so interrupting the stark list of nominatives, would take *carnificis robur* as a wooden apparatus for execution by burning.

pitch . . . metal plate . . . torch: used in burning at the stake, a punishment of Roman incendiaries (cf. Juvenal 1.155-6), and perhaps also in torture by burning or branding which may have preceded it: cf. Jocelyn (1986) 45.

1018-9 The idea that guilty conscience leads men to imagine retribution awaiting them in death, even if they manage to escape it in life, is the key to the rationalisation not only of the general horrors of Tartarus introduced in 1011-2, but also of the torments of the specific great sinners detailed earlier (see introductory note to 978-1023); the idea goes back not only to Epicurus but to his atomist predecessor Democritus (Diels B.297).

even in their absence . . . still: two ideas lie behind the clause, 'even if you escape them in life' and 'even though they do not exist after death'. *tamen* and *at* both point the contrast between the concessive and the main clause.

the conscience-stricken mind: *factis* is perhaps to be taken as a poetic local ablative 'sharing knowledge with itself in its (mis)deeds' (cf. VI 393, *nulla sibi turpi conscius in re*); a double dative would be an unnatural construction with no certain parallel, nor can *sibi* or *factis* be taken solely with words in the next line. The emendation *facti* provides the objective genitive that would be expected, but after *factis* 1014 a singular is implausible.

applies the goad and the searing scourge: i.e. applies *metaphorical* torture to itself; *flagellis* takes up the literal *uerbera* of 1017, while the image of *torret* recalls the literal scorching inflicted by *pix lammina taedae* 1017. With *adhibet* and *torret*, *sibi* and *se* are to be supplied respectively from *sibi* 1018.

1020-2 Instead of welcoming death as the end of their afflictions and punishment, as these non-Epicureans ought to do, they dread it, imagining greater torments in store. The second purpose of the passage, as an ironic argument for non-Epicureans at least to welcome death, is clearly brought out at its climax (see introductory note to 978-1023).

its ills: in general, but including the punishment, both actual and imagined, (*poenarum* 1021) on which the passage concentrates; *poenarum . . . finis* 1021 contrasts with *metus . . . poenarum* 1014.

what end: Lucretius always gives *finis* its older, feminine, gender.

these very evils: *eadem . . . haec*, neuter plural referring back to *malorum* and *poenarum*, belong, like *magis*, in the *ne* clause.

1023 **In short:** for this sense of *denique*, cf. 50; contrast 1021, and the enumerative use noted on 59.

here on earth . . . a Hell: the contrasted sites are effectively juxtaposed in *hic Acherusia*; the resounding conclusion echoes the opening at 978-9, putting its point still more concisely.

fools: i.e. non-Epicureans; the poet appropriates from the Stoics the claim that *sapientia* is to be found only within his own school, whereas all outside it are *stulti*; cf., e.g., V 10, where Epicurus' philosophy is hailed as *sapientia*. *stultorum* makes clear that all the earthly torments alluded to in the passage are self-inflicted, and can be avoided by embracing the Epicurean moral code: see introductory note to 978-1023.

1024-52 *Far greater men have died*

The argument, which has been partly foreshadowed in the appeal to death's inevitability and the demise of earlier generations at 962-71, is commonplace and goes back to Homer, *Iliad* XXI 107, where, before killing Lycaon, Achilles advances the death of the vastly superior Patroclus by way of consolation (κάτθανε καὶ Πάτροκλος ὅ περ σέο πολλὸν ἀμείνων).

The Lucretian list of great men is climactic and reflects his scale of values; starting with conventionally great men of action, represented by rulers and military commanders, he moves on firstly to poets and then to philosophers, culminating in Epicurus himself. The presentation of the argument as one which the reader might address to himself gives Lucretius the freedom, at its conclusion, to put his message in the most forceful and aggressive terms, and to denounce those reluctant to die in the same stern, uncompromising tones that were allotted earlier to Nature.

1024 **This is a further argument:** for the scansion of *hoc*, see on 856.
you . . . yourself: *tute* (formed from *tu* and the emphatic suffix *-te*) reinforces the reflexive idea (cf. *ipse*). The severity of the self-criticism in which the second person is invited to engage at the climax of the passage, in 1045-52, suggests that Memmius has temporarily been lost sight of, and that the second person here represents the satirist's conventional butt: cf. Townend (1978) 276-7.

1025 A slight adaptation of Ennius' *postquam lumina sis oculis bonus Ancu' reliquit* (*Annales*, 137 Skutsch); both *sis* (= *suis*; cf. monosyllabic *suo* I 1022) and the suppressed *s* (see on 52) are characteristically Ennian.
Ancus: Rome's proverbially upright fourth king, from 642 to 614 B.C.
closed his eyes on the light of day: to Lucretius (cf. 364 and note), the Ennian line would suggest a contrast between two sorts of *lumina*, eyes and light.

1026 **in many ways better than you:** the tribute to Homer in 1037-8 below makes it all the more likely that this is a deliberate reminiscence of Achilles' words to Lycaon (see introductory note to 1024-52 above).
shameless creature that you are: in expecting a better fate for a nonentity like yourself; the vocative *improbe* forms an effective contrast with *bonus* 1025.

1027-8 **potentates:** *rerum* is objective genitive with *potentes*, 'having control of things'; for a similar description of political power (a conventional but strictly un-Epicurean goal), cf. *rerumque potiri* II 13.
held sway over: the iterative form of the verb, like *nominitamus* 352, is metrically convenient, and in this context yields an impressively weighty line-ending.
have passed away: for the short *e* of *occiderunt*, cf. 86 and note.

1029-30 **Even the very king:** i.e. Xerxes, who in leading the fruitless Persian invasion of Greece in 480 constructed a bridge of boats across the Hellespont; as later in Juvenal's tenth satire, where (173-87) he serves as the culminating example of the vanity of aspirations to military glory, he is identified by achievement rather than by name.
who once paved a path over the mighty ocean: the description of the bridging operation fully exploits the paradox of a roadway on the sea; here, *strauit* (literally 'levelled') is appropriate not only to paving a path but also to calming the sea. The alliteration with *q* and *m* helps to magnify the achievement, ironically so in view of the ultimate failure of the expedition.
enabled his armies to tread their route over the high seas: a second paradoxical expression. *dedit ire* approximates to prose *permisit ut irent*, and *iter* is internal accusative with *ire*.

1031-2 **to overcome the salty pools on foot:** a third paradox. *pedibus* confines the allusion to the infantry, as opposed to the cavalry (indicated by *equis*) of 1032. L's *superare* avoids the repetition of *ire* in successive lines; the conquest of one of the elements makes an ironic contrast with the defeat by the Greeks which followed. Like *mare magnum* 1029, the epic-style *salsas lacunas* is also not without irony.

despising the murmurs of the deep . . . pranced over it: *contempsit* and *insultans* both suggest the picture of Xerxes painted by the Greeks, and later by Juvenal, as an example of overweening pride (ὕβρις) visited by subsequent retribution, and indicate that Lucretius' appeal to this example of a conventionally great man is somewhat tongue-in-cheek. The juxtaposition of *insultans* with *murmura ponti* provides the crowning paradox in the description of the bridging of the ocean.

1033 **forfeited the light . . . breathed out the soul:** *lumine adempto* takes up the Ennian *lumina reliquit* 1025, while *animam fudit* (literally 'poured out his soul') recalls the broken vessel image of 434-44. The two elisions at the beginning of the line are not inappropriate to echo the gasps of the dying man.

1034-5 **The sturdy scion of the Scipios, that thunderbolt in war:** i.e. Publius Cornelius Scipio Africanus the elder, whose victory over Hannibal at Zama in 202 concluded the Second Punic War, rather than the younger Africanus, who was adopted into the family and whose success in the Third War was not quite so momentous. For the Greek-style patronymic based on a Roman name, which adds heroic dignity and is also metrically convenient, cf. *Memmiadae* (dative singular) I 26 and *Romulidarum* (genitive plural) IV 683. Both the patronymic and the thunderbolt image are applied to the two Africani in Virgil, *Aeneid* VI 842-3 and Silius Italicus VII 106-7 (for the latter applied to other members of the family, cf. also Cicero, *Pro Balbo* 34), and both may be taken from Ennius. As Munro suggested, a word-play may well lie behind *fulmen*, and indicate a connection of the name Scipio with Greek σκηπτὸς, a thunderbolt, as well as with Greek σκῆπτρον (= Latin *scipio*), a staff or support.

as if he were the most abject menial: an echo of Ennius, *Annales* 312-3 (Skutsch), despite the partly corrupt text of the fragment: with the emendation of the unmetrical *famul ut optimus esset* to *ut famul infimus esset*, Fortune there suddenly reduces the most exalted of mortals to the same status. *famul*, a form of *famulus* found only in these two passages, is explained by Ernout as based on the Oscan word *famel*.

1036 **founders of the sciences and the arts:** exemplified, in reverse order, by poets (1037-8) and philosophers (1039-44). *lepor* denotes the charm or attractiveness of the work of art for its public; it is this which Lucretius symbolically requested Venus, as the embodiment of creativity in nature, to confer on his poem at I 28, and with which he seeks to touch the whole of it, as he honeys the edge of the cup of bitter-tasting philosophical medicine, at I 934.

1037-8 **attendants of Helicon's maidens:** i.e. the poets, the servants of the Muses on Mount Helicon (see on 132); the expression recalls Hesiod, *Theogony* 1 (Μουσάων Ἑλικωνιάδων) and 100 (Μουσάων θεράπων). Despite the sceptical note at 132, the conventional imagery of the Muses figured prominently in Lucretius' famous account of his own poetic mission at I 921-50.

gaining the sceptre: for *potior* with accusative instead of ablative (or genitive), see on 940. *sceptra* is poetic plural.

lulled in the same rest as the others: for the suppressed *s* of *sopitu'*, cf. 1025 and 52, and notes. *eadem aliis = eadem atque ceteri (sopiti sunt)*: *aliis* is dative with *eadem* in this compressed comparison; for *aliis* = 'the others', cf. 530 and note.

1039-41 **Democritus:** the inclusion of the founder of atomic theory to pave the way for Epicurus himself is a mark of great honour (cf. the lofty tribute paid him at 371 prior to the criticism of one of his theories), and an indirect acknowledgment of the debt which Epicurus, for all his originality (cf. *primus* 2) and surpassing genius (1043-4), owed him.

motions of memory in his mind: technical atomic terminology appropriate to this atomic pioneer; the allusion is to one category of *sensiferi motus* (cf. 240 and note). The pronounced *m* alliteration in 1039-40 is to be found also in passages where it is exploited to illustrate Lucretius' favourite analogy between the atoms in compounds and the letters in words (see on 244), where the various types of atom are common to many different types of compound just as the various letters of the alphabet are common to many different words.

confronted death and himself sacrificed his life to it: by self-starvation, according to Athenaeus II 46e; cf. Diogenes Laertius IX 43. Lucretius implicitly approves of the suicide as satisfying the correct Epicurean criteria (see on 943), on the grounds that Democritus' declining mental powers made his life intolerable, and also as contrasting with the addressee's shameful reluctance to accept his eventual fate. *ipse* reinforces the idea of *sua sponte*; *leto caput obtulit* is a variation on the stock expression *morti se obtulit*, with death perhaps portrayed as an executioner.

1042-4 **Epicurus:** mentioned by name here for the only time in the poem (see on 1-3). Hailed for his originality in the introductory eulogy (*primus* 2, *rerum inuentor* 9), he now appears as the greatest of the *repertores doctrinarum* of 1036.

departed: for the contracted perfect form *obit*, cf. *redit* 502 and note.

when the daylight of his life had run its course: the fusion of light and race-track imagery arises naturally, as M.F.Smith points out, from the association of the sun with the mythical chariot which drew it. *lumine* introduces the light imagery which is to dominate the whole sentence.

outshone all the stars: i.e. eclipsed (literally 'extinguished') all other luminary intellects; the metaphor is immediately explained by the comparison with the risen sun. Lucretius here presents a striking variation on his recurrent image of the light of Epicurean philosophy, which dispels the darkness of ignorance and superstition (cf. 1-2 and note): Epicurus himself is now the fountainhead of light, which in this case is primarily a symbol of his pre-eminence. The idea may well have been inspired by the Hellenistic epigrammatist Leonidas, who praises Homer in very similar terms (*Palatine Anthology* IX 24); Lucretius, while choosing Homer as his sole representative of the poets and acknowledging his unique sceptre (1037-8), reserves Leonidas' lavish image for the greatest of philosophers, so implicitly rejecting Leonidas' scale of values.

1045-52 The rhetorical question forcibly indicates the unworthiness of the insignificant addressee (see on 1024 above) to escape the fate of the great men who have died before him. As the echo of *obit* 1042 in *obire* 1045 reflects, the primary contrast is with Epicurus, whose golden words permanently merit immortality (12-13), whereas the addressee wastes the life he is so reluctant to leave, and makes it a misery, by the un-Epicurean life-style sketched in 1046-52.

1046 **whose life is . . . defunct . . . live and breathe:** the paradox, explained in the long *qui* clause which follows, is paralleled in Sallust, *Catiline* 2.8 and Seneca, *Moral Epistles* 60.4 and 77.18. The alliterative *uiuo atque uidenti* (literally 'alive and seeing') is a stock phrase; cf. Cicero, *Pro Sestio* 59.

1047-9 **waste . . . in slumber:** there is not only a contrast with Epicurus' devotion to philosophical study, and the benefits this brought to all mankind, but also, as at 1066, irony in that the man reluctant to accept death devotes so much of his life to sleep which in Epicurean eyes so closely resembles it. The slumber may well be thought of as resulting, as at 1066, from restless dissatisfaction.

snore whilst awake: the oxymoron, differently applied to feigned sleep by Juvenal 1.57, suggests a state of semi-somnolence.

never rest from daydreaming: in view of *cassa formidine* 1049, *somnia* may well have the same reference as in I 105, where it was applied to the idle fancies which the prophets of religion can devise, with particular reference to fancies about punishment after death. The phrase completes the transition from slumber (*somno* 1047) to waking life. The use of *cessas*, properly applied to ceasing culpably, is ironic.

you are saddled with: *geris*, 'you carry', implies that the mind is a burden, foreshadowing the *pondus* of 1054.

baseless dread: in the context, primarily the fear of death, including both fear of an after-life and fear of ceasing to exist.

1050-2 **unable to discover what is the matter with you:** foreshadowing 1055-6 and 1070, where men cannot diagnose the cause of the burden on their minds and of their disease, just as the mental confusion in 1051-2 looks forward to the restless malaise described in 1057-69.

reduces you to a . . . stupor: inebriation (*ebrius*) here serves as a strong metaphor for mental confusion and disturbance.

drift erratically . . . unsteady fluctuation: the last four words in the line combine to convey the idea of lack of direction with great emphasis.

1053-75 *Man's restless dissatisfaction can be cured by Epicurean philosophy and its conclusions about death*

Whereas 931-1052 have sought primarily to reconcile man to his own mortality, this passage, which was almost certainly designed to conclude the book (cf. introductory note to 1076-94 below), takes a new turn, clearly implying that man's restlessness and *ennui* are to be attributed to his fear of death and recommending Epicurean philosophy as the remedy. Like 59-86, where avarice, ambition and even suicide were attributed at least in part (*non minimam partem* 64) to the same cause, the passage has been found puzzling and taken as evidence of gross Lucretian exaggeration of the fear of death and its importance, but, again like 59-86 (see on 65-7), is most easily explained if the poet has in mind fear of death as the end of life's pleasures; man's restlessness then arises from a subconscious attempt to escape his own mortality by constantly seeking to cram his life with new pleasures and diversions (cf. the misguided hedonists of 912-8), a quest doomed in Epicurean eyes to be self-defeating and to result in constant dissatisfaction and unhappiness. While the obvious Epicurean antidote lay in the ethical theory, with its insistence on the limitation of the desires and the pursuit of the correct brand of pleasure (freedom from bodily pain and from mental disturbance), 1071-5 imply that such restlessness can be cured by Epicurus' factual conclusions about death: the idea is no doubt that contemplation of the inevitability of death and of the eternity of our oblivion after it will reveal the folly of trying, as the restless man subconsciously does, to cheat or escape it, and will induce philosophical resignation to the prospect - the Epicurean ethical lesson can to this extent be deduced from the factual lesson. For Epicurus' own contention that a full realisation that death ended consciousness automatically removed 'the craving for immortality', see introductory note to 931-77.

1053 **obviously feel:** *uidentur* is again passive: cf. 35 and note.

1054 **a weight on their minds . . . heavy . . . wears them out:** the image dominates 1053-9; cf. *tanta mali tamquam moles* 1056, *onus* 1059.

1055-6 **the causes . . . the source:** i.e. their own mortality, as the sequel at 1071-5 goes on clearly to suggest. The second indirect question develops the first in terms of the weight image.

this huge mass of woe: the repeated *t* and *m* sounds in *tanta mali tamquam moles* unify, and add impact to, the figurative phrase.

1057-9 **in the way . . . we . . . see them, with no one knowing:** in the *ut* clause, *eos uitam agere, id est* can be supplied to complete the sense; *nescire* and *quaerere* define *how* they spend their lives. *nunc* contrasts the actual with the hypothetical situation.

what he really wants: literally 'wants for himself'; cf. 772 and note. In the soldiers' chorus in Ennius, *Scenica* 199 (Jocelyn), such a quandary is the product of leisure (*otioso in otio animus nescit quid uelit*, where *in otio* is Lipsius' emendation of the corrupt *initio* of the manuscripts).

seeking a change of scene: the restlessness introduced here and illustrated in 1060-7, like the avarice and ambition of 59-78, was characteristic of the age, and is often criticised later by Horace (e.g. *Satires* II 7.28-9, where in town the country is longed for and vice versa, and *Epistles* I 11.27, *caelum non animum mutant qui trans mare currunt*, where a change of scene does not change mental attitude) and by Seneca. For *quaerere* governing an infinitive, cf. 941 and note.

1060-7 The rich Roman leaves his spacious town house first (1060-1) for the city, then (1062-4) for his country villa, but in each case fails to find satisfaction.

1062 **because he finds it:** *sentiat* is causal subjunctive with *quippe . . . qui*.

1063-4 The emphasis on precipitate haste, conveyed by *currit, mannos* (imports from Gaul renowned for their speed), *praecipitanter* (whose sound echoes the pounding hooves), *instans* and the whole comparison with a fire emergency, makes the anticlimax of 1065 all the more telling and ironic. For the coined *praecipitanter*, found only here, cf. on 779.

1065 **he suddenly yawns:** after the dactyl *oscitat*, the three long syllables of *extemplo* before the main caesura apply a sudden brake, a rhythmic effect appropriate to the anticlimax described.

threshold: *limina* is poetic plural, like *sceptra* 1038.

1066 **escapes drowsily into slumber, seeking oblivion:** in terms of the analysis which follows at 1068-9, a third attempt to escape himself. As at 1047 (see note), the situation is in Epicurean eyes ironical: death, which turns out at 1071-5 to be the source of the man's anxieties and restlessness, will permanently provide the same escape and oblivion that he here seeks in sleep.

1067 **makes . . . back to revisit the city:** an effective final touch, returning us to the starting-point of the whole sorry cycle.

1068-9 **each man flees from himself:** in a subconscious attempt to escape his own mortality; see introductory note to 1053-75 above. The general motif of flight from oneself, and its impossibility, recurs in Horace (e.g. *Odes* II 16.18-20) and in Seneca (e.g. *Moral Epistles* 2.1, 69.1 and 104.8), who quotes the Lucretian passage, with comments, in *De Tranquillitate Animi* 2.14.

is bound . . . to the self . . . and loathes it: with *haeret* and *odit*, *ei* and *eum* are to be supplied respectively as grammatical antecedents to the preceding *quem* clause.

cannot . . . escape: for *potis est* = *potest*, cf. 468 and note; for the contrasted *fugit* ('flees') and *effugere* ('escape'), cf. the contrasted nouns *fuga* and *effugium* at I 983.

1070 **for this reason, that:** the causal clause explains *se fugit* and *odit* rather than *haeret*.

ill . . . knows not the cause of his disease: the opening image of a weight on his mind now gives way to that of a malady; as in 1055-6 the source, which he cannot diagnose, is subconscious fear of death, as 1071-5 now go on unmistakably to imply.

1071-2 **forget everything else:** *rebus relictis*, 'abandoning <other> matters', is a colloquial phrase: cf., e.g., Plautus, *Epidicus* 605 and Terence, *Andria* 412.

the nature of the universe: the allusion to *natura rerum*, which is also the title of the poem, at once elevates the tone; there is a contrast with the more trivial concerns referred to in *rebus relictis*.

1073-5 The implication, that the cure for the malady of 1070 lies in the Epicurean answer to the question of man's state in death, shows that the restlessness depicted in the passage is attributed to subconscious anxieties on this very score; these will be eradicated by Epicurean philosophy, which, as well as removing fears of any form of after-life, will convince the student of the lesson of 894-903 and 912-8, that life's pleasures will not be missed in death, and so expose the folly of his attempt to compensate for his mortality by a restless quest for new pleasures and diversions (cf. introductory note to 1053-75 above).

the question at issue is his state: *ambigitur*, which can be applied technically to a point at issue in a legal case, introduces another forensic metaphor (cf. 950-1, 963 and 971); this may also involve a play on *status*, which not only denotes 'state' but can be applied technically to the central issue in a case.

not for a single hour: like those which the restless vainly try to fill with new diversions.

the state in which . . . : the relative clause develops the idea of *temporis aeterni* 1073, adding to the awesomeness of the prospect.

mortals must await: as a non-Epicurean might see it: in Epicurean eyes, mortals would not strictly exist after death to await the future (cf., e.g., 840, 864-5 and 885-7). *mortalibus* is dative of the agent with the gerundive *manenda*; *sit* is sub-oblique subjunctive after *ambigitur*, which introduces an implied indirect question (of which the *quaecumque* clause in 1075 is treated as independent).

every morsel of the time remaining: like *omnis*, the indefinite relative helps to convey the immensity of infinite time; for the tmesis of *quae . . . cumque*, cf. 550 and 940.

1076-94 ***Miscellaneous reasons to accept death***

The attempt to reconcile the reader to his mortality, which the change of direction in 1053-75 had suggested was complete, is now resumed with a series of eloquently expressed but random and unconnected points, nearly all of which have been used or foreshadowed earlier and of which only the last, at 1087-94, is at all developed. The overwhelming probability is that, as suggested by Giussani, the lines are a collection of Lucretian afterthoughts, which the poet did not live to develop for incorporation earlier in the text, and that 1053-75, culminating in the recommendation of Epicurean philosophy, were intended as the book's conclusion.

1076-7 This argument, from life's uncertainties and hazards, closely resembles that of 1085-6 below, from its unpredictability: both have been anticipated in the argument that Hell is here on earth (978-1023), specifically so at 983 where the rock threatening Tantalus represented not only fear of the gods, but fear of what chance has in store. As there, the argument is primarily applicable to the non-Epicurean; Epicureans would enjoy a peace of mind which would free them from undue anxiety about the future and the vicissitudes of fortune.
amidst uncertainties and perils: for *in dubiis periclis*, cf. 55 and note.

1078-9 The theme of death's inevitability, introduced by Nature at 962, has already been elaborated at 964-71.
appointed: i.e. by nature, which has made us mortal and so made our end inevitable. The juxtaposition of *finis uitae* (= *mors*) with *mortalibus* reflects the inescapable logic of the contention that mortals must die. For the gender of *finis*, cf. 1021 and note.
cannot possibly be avoided: for *pote* (sc. *est*), a weakened form of *potis*, see on 319; it here provides another archaic variation on *potest* (cf. 468 and 1069). *quin* = *ita ut non*. The seven long syllables which begin the line add weighty solemnity to the sobering reflection.

1080-1 The argument that there are no new pleasures in life has already been developed in Nature's speech at 944-9 (see note); as there, it reflects the Epicurean idea that beyond a certain point pleasure could not be increased with time.
in the same place: i.e. in our own world, which in any case was roughly similar to the infinite number of other worlds in the universe.
is forged: a characteristic metaphor, applied also to the generation of fire from fire at II 1115 and to animal procreation at V 850 and 856.

1082-4 The idea that dissatisfied yearning for the unavailable makes men cling to life has also already been set out by Nature, at 957-60 in the course of her second tirade.
while what we crave is not to hand: the converse of *semper aues quod abest* 957. For the hiatus between *dum* and *abest*, a comparatively rare licence in the hexameter, see note on 374, and cf. *cum odore* II 681 and *cum eo* VI 276.
once it has come our way: *contingere*, used especially of good fortune, reflects the recipient's point of view.

we crave something different: comparable not only with 957, but with the account of the arbitrary fluctuation of man's values at V 1273-80.

thirst for life . . . open-mouthed: *hiantis* ('agape') not only sustains the thirst metaphor, but is also applicable to the yearning symbolised in it (cf. *inhians* of Mars' passion for Venus at I 36). The thirst recalls the image of the unsatisfied guest at life's feast: cf. 938 and 959-60.

1085-6 For the connection of these lines with the passage's opening couplet, and their anticipation at 983, see on 1076-7 above.

what fortune future time may bring: the expression may well have a proverbial flavour: cf. the use of *uehat* in the title of one of Varro's *Satires*, *Nescis quid uesper serus uehat*, echoed by Virgil at *Georgics* I 461.

what chance may send our way: strongly echoing 983, *casumque timent quem cuique ferat fors*.

lies in store: *instet*, 'is pressing', denotes the imminence of the impending event.

1087-94 The concluding point, that we are powerless to reduce the eternity of our death, provides an awesome indication of the transience and insignificance of the individual in the Epicurean scheme of things. It has been foreshadowed in the allusion to death's immortality at 869, and relates also to the theme of its inevitability (962-71 and 1078-9), but these ideas are here combined and developed in a new way; the thought is reminiscent of I 1002-5, where the infinity of space is brought home in a similar, equally powerful manner.

1087-9 **a single instant:** *prorsum* intensifies *hilum* (for which see on 220); cf. I 748 where it reinforces *quicquam*.

from the time-span of our death: for *de* placed after its case (but before a genitive dependent on the noun), cf. 140 and note.

to whittle anything away: on the usage of *delibare*, see on 24: *quicquam* (or *hilum* from 1087) is here to be supplied as its object.

so as somehow to reduce the period: *forte*, literally 'perchance', is ironic, given the impossibility of the objective. Final *ut* is replaced by *quo* because of the comparative *minus*, which, as in 1092 below, goes closely with *diu*.

1090 **live to lay to rest . . . generations:** reminiscent of *uiuendo uincere saecla* 948. *condere*, of witnessing the burial of the generations outlived, is applied metaphorically by other poets to witnessing the sunset, i.e. living through a day or days, as in Virgil's *longos cantando . . . condere soles*, *Eclogues* 9.51-2.

1091-4 **that eternity of death:** *mors aeterna* recalls the paradox *mors immortalis* 869 (see note).

none the less . . . for no shorter a time: the immediate echo of *nilo minus* in *nec minus* makes the logic of the argument appear all the more remorseless.

departing today's light . . . passed away: after the allusion to sunlight (cf., e.g., 1025, 1033 and 1042), *occidit* may well, as Merrill suggested, involve a metaphor from sunset; see on 414, where there is a more complicated word-play on the same theme.

now: i.e. from the moment of his death.

than the man: *et* replaces comparative *quam*, a very rare usage by analogy with *ac* and *atque* after *alius* and so in turn after a comparative (cf. *nilo minus ac* 96).

Select Bibliography

I. Editions and Translations (* indicates editions with commentary or notes)

(a) Editions of the poem
Editio Brixiensis (*editio princeps*): Brescia, *c.* 1473
Editio Aldina (Avancius, H.): Venice, 1500
*Pius, J.B.: Bologna, 1511
Editio Juntina (Candidus, P.): Florence, 1512
Naugerius, A. (*editio Aldina* 2): Venice, 1515
*Lambinus, D.: Paris, 1563–4
Gifanius, O.: Antwerp, 1565–6
*Faber, T.: Saumur, 1662
*Creech, T.: Oxford, 1695
*Havercamp, S.: Leiden, 1725
*Wakefield, G.: London, 1796–7
*Lachmann, K.: Berlin, 1850
Bernays, J.: Leipzig, 1852
*Munro, H.A.J.: Cambridge, 1864, 1886[4]
Bockemüller, F.: Stade, 1873
Brieger, A.: Leipzig, 1894
*Giussani, C.: Turin, 1896–8
Bailey, C. (Oxford Classical Text): 1900, 1922[2]
*Merrill, W.A.: New York/Cincinnati/Chicago, 1907
Ernout, A.: Paris, 1920
Diels, H.: Berlin, 1923
*Ernout, A. and Robin, L. (introduction and commentary only): Paris, 1925–8, 1962[2]
Martin, J. (Teubner): Leipzig 1934, 1969[6]
*Leonard, W.E. and Smith, S.B.: Madison, 1942
*Bailey, C.: Oxford, 1947
Büchner, K.: Wiesbaden, 1966
Müller, K.: Zürich, 1975
Smith, M.F. (a revision of Rouse's 1924 Loeb edition): Cambridge, Mass./London, 1975, 1992[3]
*Giancotti, F.: Milan, 1994

(b) Editions of Book III
*Lee, J.W.H. (Books I–III): London, 1884
*Heinze, R.: Leipzig, 1897

*Duff, J.D.: Cambridge, 1903
*Kenney, E.J.: Cambridge, 1971

(c) Editions of other single books

Book I: *Brown, P.M. (Bristol, 1984)
Book IV: *Godwin, J. (Warminster, 1987)
Book V: *Costa, C.D.N. (Oxford, 1984)
Book VI: *Godwin, J. (Warminster, 1991)

(d) Selections

*Sinker, A.P.: Cambridge, 1937
*Paratore, H. and Pizzani, U.: Rome, 1960
*Benfield, G.E. and Reeves, R.C.: Oxford, 1967
*Barigazzi, A.: Turin, 1974

(e) Prose translations

Munro, H.A.J.: Cambridge, 1864
Bailey, C.: Oxford, 1910
Latham, R.E.: Harmondsworth, 1951
Smith, M.F.: London, 1969

II. Other works

Amory, A.: '*Obscura de re lucida carmina*: Science and poetry in *De Rerum Natura*', *Yale Classical Studies* 21 (1969) 143–68

Boyancé, P.: *Lucrèce et l' épicurisme* (Paris, 1963)

Classen, C.J.: 'Poetry and rhetoric in Lucretius', *Transactions of the American Philological Association* 99 (1968) 77–118

Clay, D.: *Lucretius and Epicurus* (Ithaca/London 1983)

Cox, A.: 'Didactic poetry' in *Greek and Latin Literature*, ed. J. Higginbotham (London, 1969)

Dalzell, A.: 'A bibliography of work on Lucretius, 1945–1972', *The Classical World* 66 (1972–3) 385–427 and 67 (1973–4) 65–112

Deutsch, R.E.: *The pattern of sound in Lucretius* (Bryn Mawr, 1939: New York/London 1978)

DeWitt, N.W.: *Epicurus and his philosophy* (Minneapolis, 1954)

Dudley, D.R. (ed.): *Lucretius* (London, 1965)

Festugière, A.J.: *Epicurus and his Gods* (translated by C.W. Chilton) (Oxford, 1955: New York, 1977)

Friedländer, P.: 'Pattern of sound and atomistic theory in Lucretius', *American Journal of Philology* 62 (1941) 16–34

Galloway, A.: 'Lucretius' materialistic poetics: Epicurus and the "flawed" *consolatio* of book 3', *Ramus* 15 (1986) 52–73

Giancotti, F.: *Il preludio di Lucrezio* (Messina/Florence, 1959)

--------------- *L' ottimismo relatiuo nel 'De Rerum Natura' di Lucrezio* (Turin, 1960)

--------------- *Religio, natura, uoluptas: studi su Lucrezio* (Bologna/Pàtron, 1989)

Gigon, O. (ed.): *Lucrèce* (Vandoeuvres/Geneva, 1977)

Gordon, C.A.: *A Bibliography of Lucretius* (London, 1962, 1985[2])

Guthrie, W.K.C.: *A History of Greek Philosophy*, vols. I–III (Cambridge, 1962–9)

Hadzsits, G.D.: *Lucretius and his influence* (New York, 1935)

Jocelyn, H.D.: 'Lucretius, his copyists and the horrors of the underworld', *Acta Classica* 29 (1986) 43–56

Kenney, E.J.: *Lucretius (Greece and Rome – New Surveys in the Classics No. 11)* (Oxford, 1977)

Long, A.A.: *Hellenistic Philosophy* (London, 1974)

Martha, C.: *Le poème de Lucrèce* (Paris, 1867)

Masson, J.: *Lucretius: Epicurean and Poet* (London, 1907–9)

Rist, J.M.: *Epicurus: An Introduction* (Cambridge, 1972)

Santayana, G.: *Three philosophical poets: Lucretius, Dante and Goethe* (Cambridge, Mass., 1910)

Schrijvers, P.H.: *Horror ac divina voluptas: études sur la poétique et la poésie de Lucrèce* (Amsterdam, 1970)

Segal, C.: *Lucretius on Death and Anxiety* (Princeton, 1990)

Sellar, W.Y.: *The Roman Poets of the Republic*, chapters 10–14 (Oxford, 1889[3])

Sikes, E.E.: *Lucretius: Poet and Philosopher* (Cambridge 1936)

Smith, M.F.: 'Notes on Lucretius', *Sileno* 11 (1985) 219–25

Snyder, J.M.: *Puns and poetry in Lucretius' 'De Rerum Natura'* (Amsterdam, 1980)

Sykes Davies, H.: 'Notes on Lucretius', *The Criterion* 11 (1931–2) 25–42

Townend, G.B.: 'The fading of Memmius', *Classical Quarterly* 28 (1978) 267–83

Wacht, M.: *Concordantia in Lucretium* (Hildesheim/Zürich/New York, 1991)

Wallach, B.P.: *Lucretius and the diatribe against the fear of death* (*Mnemosyne*, supplement 40) (Leiden, 1976)

Waszink, J.H.: 'Lucretius and poetry', *Mededelingen der Koninklijke Nederlandse Akademie van Wetenschapen*, Afd. Letterkunde n.s. 17 (1954) 243–57

Watt, W.S.: '*Lucretiana*', *Hermes* 117 (1989) 233–6

Wellesley, K.: 'Reflections upon the third book of Lucretius', *Acta Classica Uniuersitatis Scientiarum Debreceniensis* 10–11 (1974–5) 31–40

West, D.: *The Imagery and Poetry of Lucretius* (Edinburgh, 1969)

----------- 'Lucretius' methods of argument (3.417–614)', *Classical Quarterly* 69 (1975) 94–116

Index

References in bold type are to pages of the Introduction, the others to lines of the text discussed in the Commentary

I. Latin words

II. Greek words

III. General

Printed and bound by CPI Group (UK) Ltd, Croydon, CR0 4YY

09/06/2025

14685803-0001